Seeking the Court's Advice

Law and Society Series

W. Wesley Pue, General Editor

The Law and Society Series explores law as a socially embedded phenomenon. It is premised on the understanding that the conventional division of law from society creates false dichotomies in thinking, scholarship, educational practice, and social life. Books in the series treat law and society as mutually constitutive and seek to bridge scholarship emerging from interdisciplinary engagement of law with disciplines such as politics, social theory, history, political economy, and gender studies.

Recent books in the series:

L. Jane McMillan, *Truth and Conviction: Donald Marshall Jr. and the Mi'kmaw Quest for Justice* (2018)

Sarah Grace Marsden, *Enforcing Exclusion: Precarious Migrants and the Law in Canada* (2018)

Jasminka Kalajdzic, *Class Actions in Canada: The Promise and Reality of Access to Justice* (2018)

David Moffette, *Governing Irregular Migration: Bordering Culture, Labour, and Security in Spain* (2018)

Constance Backhouse, *Claire L'Heureux-Dubé: A Life* (2017)

Christopher P. Manfredi and Antonia Maioni, *Health Care and the Charter: Legal Mobilization and Policy Change in Canada* (2017)

Julie Macfarlane, *The New Lawyer: How Clients Are Transforming the Practice of Law*, 2nd ed. (2017)

Annie Bunting and Joel Quirk, eds., *Contemporary Slavery: Popular Rhetoric and Political Practice* (2017)

Larry Savage and Charles W. Smith, *Unions in Court: Organized Labour and the Charter of Rights and Freedoms* (2017)

Allyson M. Lunny, *Debating Hate Crime: Language, Legislatures, and the Law in Canada* (2017)

For a complete list of the titles in the series, see the UBC Press website, www.ubcpress.ca.

Seeking the Court's Advice

The Politics of the Canadian Reference Power

KATE PUDDISTER

UBCPress · Vancouver · Toronto

27 26 25 24 23 22 21 20 19   5 4 3 2 1

Printed in Canada on FSC-certified ancient-forest-free paper (100% post-consumer recycled) that is processed chlorine- and acid-free.

Library and Archives Canada Cataloguing in Publication

Title: Seeking the court's advice : the politics of the Canadian reference power / Kate Puddister.
Names: Puddister, Kate, author.
Series: Law and society series (Vancouver, B.C.)
Description: Series statement: Law and society | Includes bibliographical references and index.
Identifiers: Canadiana (print) 20189069155 | Canadiana (ebook) 20189069163 | ISBN 9780774861106 (hardcover) | ISBN 9780774861120 (PDF) | ISBN 9780774861137 (EPUB) | ISBN 9780774861144 (Kindle)
Subjects: LCSH: Advisory opinions – Canada. | LCSH: Judicial review – Canada. | LCSH: Political questions and judicial power – Canada.
Classification: LCC KE4775 .P85 2019 | LCC KF4483.J8 P85 2019 kfmod | DDC 347.71/012—dc23

Canadä

UBC Press gratefully acknowledges the financial support for our publishing program of the Government of Canada (through the Canada Book Fund), the Canada Council for the Arts, and the British Columbia Arts Council.

This book has been published with the help of a grant from the Canadian Federation for the Humanities and Social Sciences, through the Awards to Scholarly Publications Program, using funds provided by the Social Sciences and Humanities Research Council of Canada.

Printed and bound in Canada by Friesens
Set in Myriad and Sabon by Apex CoVantage, LLC
Copy editor: Robert Lewis
Proofreader: Lauren Cross

UBC Press
The University of British Columbia
2029 West Mall
Vancouver, BC V6T 1Z2
www.ubcpress.ca

For my grandparents

Contents

Illustrations

Figures

Tables

Acknowledgments

I am incredibly lucky to be surrounded by excellent colleagues, mentors, and supporters; the completion of this book would not have been possible without their encouragement and guidance.

This project began under the skilful guidance of Christopher Manfredi, at McGill University. Chris has been instrumental to my success first as a graduate student and now as a scholar. His thoughtful and critical analysis of Canadian law and politics was an inspiration for much of this work. I thank him for his mentorship and support. I also thank Christa Scholtz and Maria Popova for providing important advice and insight, which have considerably strengthened my work and abilities as a researcher. Rainer Knopff, Hoi Kong, and Robert Leckey also provided generous feedback that helped to improve this project.

I am indebted to James Kelly for his guidance over the past several years. Jim has always provided valuable advice and has opened many doors for me as a junior scholar. I am forever grateful for his mentorship. Troy Riddell, Dennis Baker, and Byron Sheldrick have been unwavering in their support, which started when I was a master's student and has continued through to the present day. I hope to live up to the very high standards they have set as scholars and teachers.

This project benefited from the wisdom of many colleagues. Countless thanks go to Matt Hennigar, Emmett Macfarlane, Dave Snow, Chris

Chhim, Edward Koning (a magician with SPSS Statistics software), Tamara Small, and Emma Richez. Special appreciation goes to Erin Crandall, my McGill law and politics buddy. Thanks also go to my University of Guelph colleagues for supporting me and to my students for inspiring me.

I thank the attentive and skilful anonymous reviewers who provided invaluable feedback that undoubtedly improved this book. A large portion of this study would not have been possible without the participation of several individuals – former attorneys general, government counsel, and a first minister – who kindly agreed to be interviewed. I thank them for their time and insight. Thank you to my editor at UBC Press, Randy Schmidt, who showed a keen interest in this project early on and provided expert guidance throughout the publication process.

Completing this book would not have been possible without my family. In particular, I would like to thank my parents, Mike and Marie Puddister, for their unfaltering support and love. I am sorry there are no maps in this book.

Above all, I must thank my husband, Graham. Graham is truly a partner in every sense, and the completion of this book would not have been possible without his love and encouragement. Not only did Graham provide unwavering support, but he also reviewed and discussed various aspects of this project with me over the years. I benefited from his thoughtful advice in endless ways. I am so lucky to have Graham in my life.

Seeking the Court's Advice

Introduction: Reference Cases as a Mix of Law and Politics

Political and constitutional crises can arise in unexpected or unusual places. The so-called "chicken and egg war" between the provinces of Ontario, Quebec, and Manitoba is perhaps one of the most curious places in which a battle over Canadian federalism has originated. The chicken and egg war began in the mid-1960s when Ontario producers of broiler chickens gained control over production of their product through the creation of the Ontario Broiler Chicken Production Marketing Board. Once in place, the board established quotas for the production of broiler chickens within the province. Although the purpose of the board was to protect producers from competition within Ontario, it did not shield them from the competitive threat of producers outside the province, specifically neighbouring Quebec, a chicken-producing powerhouse without a marketing board (Moore 1971). As a result, without the imposition of quotas, Quebec had an excess of less expensive chickens. On the egg side of the conflict, Ontario was a powerful hub of egg production, and although there was an egg marketing board in place, unlike the chicken board, it was relatively powerless. With no strict limits on production, Ontario egg producers flooded the egg market in Quebec, with over 40 percent of the eggs sold in Quebec originating in Ontario or Manitoba (Moore 1971). In response, egg producers in Quebec sought to gain greater control over their market, much like the chicken producers in Ontario.

With marketing boards in place in both Ontario (for chickens) and Quebec (for eggs), not only did the prices of each product become controlled in each province, but the marketing boards also introduced additional measures that excessively favoured the marketing of internal products, resulting in discrimination against products from other provinces. Although Ontario may have been the target of Quebec's marketing scheme and Quebec may likewise have been the target of Ontario's, the restrictions introduced into the chicken and egg markets within Ontario and Quebec had a negative effect on agricultural producers in other provinces. Such was the case for farmers in Manitoba, who were now unable to sell their surplus chickens and eggs to the larger markets in Ontario and Quebec. Thus Manitoba "was the classic innocent and injured bystander in the 'chicken and egg war'" (Weiler 1974, 156).

From this account, it may be puzzling what the war over chickens and eggs, a political-economic dispute, has to do with courts and the reference power. Indeed, in response to the restrictive marketing schemes enacted by Ontario and Quebec, Manitoba could have responded by seeking an interprovincial agreement on agricultural policy through negotiation with the other governments. Perhaps, as Weiler (1974) suggests, the federal government could have been included to help broker an arrangement. However, instead of selecting what might have been the traditional political route, the Manitoba government decided to seek judicial review and ask for an advisory opinion from the courts through the reference power. But instead of simply asking the Manitoba Court of Appeal to review the constitutionality of the agricultural-marketing policies of Ontario or Quebec, Manitoba took the unusual step of passing legislation that mirrored the Quebec policy. After enacting the replica policy, Manitoba promptly submitted it to the Manitoba Court of Appeal for review, requesting an advisory opinion on the constitutionality of the agricultural regulation. In response to the Manitoba reference, the Court of Appeal rendered an advisory opinion that found the legislation to be unconstitutional. The Court of Appeal held that the Manitoba government's plan was ultra vires (outside) provincial jurisdiction and infringed on the Parliament of Canada's constitutional authority over trade and commerce provided in section 91(2) of the *British North America Act, 1867*.[1] This decision was promptly appealed to the Supreme Court of Canada in *Reference re Manitoba (AG) v Manitoba Egg and Poultry Association* [*Egg Reference*],[2] and the Supreme Court agreed with the Court of Appeal, finding the restrictive agricultural policy constitutionally invalid.

It is important to explicitly address the strategic actions of the Manitoba government during the chicken and egg war. In short, Manitoba passed legislation that copied a regulatory scheme with the sole purpose of asking the courts to weigh in through a reference case. This means that the Government of Manitoba passed a law that it did not want for the sole purpose of sending it to the courts for review in the hope that the courts would find it unconstitutional. For this plan to work, Manitoba needed to "lose" its case at the Court of Appeal and the Supreme Court of Canada in order to obtain a national ruling that would equally apply across the provinces. This national ruling would have the additional effect of invalidating the policies of Ontario and Quebec, Manitoba's intended targets. As Weiler (1974, 157) aptly explains, "Manitoba purported to argue for, and then appeal on behalf of, laws which it was proposing to enact with the sole purpose of having the Supreme Court declare them unconstitutional." The strategic use of the reference power by the Manitoba government resulted in a positive outcome for the province, as following the Supreme Court's decision in the *Egg Reference*, all ten provinces and the federal government reached an agreement on a national agriculture policy that instituted quotas in each province.[3]

Ordinarily, judicial review is relied upon to obtain a decisive outcome in an ongoing conflict – that is, when one party sues another, when an individual is charged with a criminal offence, or when a government alleges that another government has overstepped its legislative jurisdiction. Importantly, as regards the political role of the courts, it is the third grounds for judicial review that has played an important role in Canadian governance, doing so even before the adoption of the *Canadian Charter of Rights and Freedoms* in 1982. The judicial review of the constitutional division of powers requires courts to arbitrate conflicts between governments through the application of the legislative jurisdiction outlined in the Constitution. This judicial function has had a profound effect on many facets of Canadian federalism and governance (Monahan 1984, 1987; Lederman 1985; Bzdera 1993; Schertzer 2016). The judicial review of federalism-based disputes has meant that courts can play an instrumental role in the arbitration of debates regarding public policy, which sometimes results in a determinative effect on policy content – thus allowing for some form of judicial policy making. This activity provides a role for the courts that is fundamentally distinct from that of simply adjudicating a criminal law case or a private legal dispute. Reflecting on the role of the courts in arbitrating federalism, Lederman (1985, 2) notes that because of this responsibility, Canadians were acquainted with this form of judicial review, or what he refers to as judicial supremacy, prior to the adoption of the Charter.

Importantly, when judicial review is relied upon to sort out an existing conflict, whether it be between two private individuals or two orders of government, courts are asked to apply the law to a set of accepted facts with the goal of reaching a just outcome. Yet, in the *Egg Reference*, the courts were not asked to review the arguably discriminatory effects of the Quebec legislation on Manitoba farmers. Nor was one province suing another. Instead, in this case, through the reference power, the Manitoba government was able to successfully enlist the courts to resolve an ongoing conflict, in the abstract, by issuing an advisory opinion.

Yet Manitoba's use of the reference power in such a manner is not unique. Time and again, political actors have done so to ask questions aimed at sorting out highly divisive issues such as the constitutionality of same-sex marriage, the reform of the Senate, the requirements for appointment to the Supreme Court, the ability of the Parliament of Canada to amend the Constitution without the participation of the provinces, the legal authority of Quebec to unilaterally separate from the federation, and the role of Quebec in endorsing constitutional amendment.[4] As Russell (2011) argues, one would be hard-pressed to find another constitutional democracy that has relied on its courts as frequently as Canada to answer controversial issues related to the core of its survival. Many of the cases that have considered controversial and fundamental issues of Canadian politics and governance have been reference cases.

The Canadian Reference Power

The reference question procedure allows the executive branch of both the provincial and federal governments to obtain an advisory judicial opinion from a provincial appellate court or the Supreme Court of Canada on the constitutionality of legislation, either proposed or enacted, in the absence of a live legal dispute. When reference cases focus on an abstract question, which the majority do, they stray from the traditional adversarial nature of Canadian courts, as there is no concrete legal problem for the court to resolve. Instead, through the reference power, courts can be referred questions that must be considered in terms of a largely hypothetical or speculative context. Section 53 of the *Supreme Court Act* provides the federal government the power to pose questions directly to the Supreme Court of Canada.[5] Provincial governments rely on comparable provisions in provincial judicature Acts to submit questions directly to provincial appellate courts.[6] Whereas the federal government can seek a reference directly at the Supreme Court, provincial governments must first submit reference questions to a provincial court of appeal before they may appeal "by right" to the Supreme Court of Canada.[7] In the federal case, this power was created by Parliament through a provision of the *Supreme Court Act* in 1875.

The reference power provides governments the ability to sidestep the normal litigation route to the Supreme Court or provincial appellate courts, giving the executive privileged and timely access to judicial review, which is denied to citizens, interest groups, or opposing political parties. Political actors involved in these contentious episodes abide by the decisions made by the courts, making reference decisions more binding than advisory (Rubin 1960; Hogg 2012). The reference procedure allows governments to insert the courts and the judiciary into often highly controversial and normative partisan debates, with the goal of obtaining an authoritative judicial decision.

The Canadian reference power provides evidence of judicialized politics and a political role for the judiciary that is independent of Charter politics. In essence, politics is judicialized when decisions made about public policy and governance are, to a large extent, transferred to the courts and the judiciary at the expense of the bureaucracy, legislature, and executive (Vallinder 1995, 13). In the Canadian context, many scholars point to the entrenchment of the *Constitution Act, 1982,* which includes the *Canadian Charter of Rights and Freedoms,* as the demarcation point for the judiciary's enhanced role in Canadian politics and government.[8] As explained by Chief Justice Beverley McLachlin (1990, 49) of the Supreme Court of Canada, the adoption of the Charter has resulted in an "increasing tendency to transmute political and social questions to legal questions, thus placing the task of their resolution on the shoulders of the courts." This emphasis on the Charter has generated a dizzying array of political science, law, and sociological literature that assesses the impact of the Charter on the Canadian public, rights discourse, governance, and politics (see Mandel 1994; Morton and Knopff 2000; Hiebert 2002; and Kelly and Manfredi 2009).

However, many of these scholars overlook a striking example of courts engaging in a political role that predates the Charter: the Canadian reference power. Yet there is relatively little known about reference cases. Previous scholarship, although important, either focuses extensively on single reference cases or engages in analysis that relies on an examination of a limited number of leading, or high-profile, reference cases rather than conducting a more comprehensive analysis.[9] As a result, in addition to not knowing the total number of references, we have little understanding of how the reference process works, the implications of reference cases for the role of courts in Canadian politics, and why political actors would give up decision-making power to the courts by asking reference questions. This book fills this void by providing novel insight and original analysis of many of the unknown aspects of the Canadian reference power. In taking a comprehensive focus, I find that political actors increase judicial power for strategic purposes and that seeking judicial review through a reference case can help elected officials to achieve political ends, beyond the legal or constitutional clarification provided by a reference decision.

The Canadian Case

The Canadian practice of seeking advisory opinions through the reference power is quite distinctive when compared to many common law countries. Although the Parliament of Canada adopted a reference power to mirror a similar practice in the United Kingdom, advisory opinions there have essentially fallen into disuse (see Jay 1997). In comparison to most former British colonies, Canada is unique.[10] Advisory opinions and abstract review are prohibited in all American federal courts, New Zealand, and Australia. It is useful to briefly consider why each of these countries has eschewed advisory opinions – as these considerations can have important lessons for Canada.

In the American context, the United States Supreme Court also inherited the United Kingdom's practice of advisory opinions and initially provided advice to Congress ("Advisory Opinions" 2011). However, in 1793 the Supreme Court, led by Chief Justice John Jay, refused to issue an advisory opinion in response to twenty-nine questions submitted by the Cabinet of George Washington. The Washington government sought advice about American obligations to international law and treaties in the context of an ongoing war between the British and the French. The Jay Court responded by explaining that answering such questions would require the court to participate in an extrajudicial activity that would be improper in light of the separation of powers between the judicial, legislative, and executive branches (Jay 1997).

As a consequence, the United States Supreme Court has refused to provide advisory opinions since 1793. There are several reasons for this refusal. First, the ban on advisory opinions has been defended by interpreting the clause on cases and controversies in Article 3 of the American Constitution.[11] For example, in *Ashwander v Tennessee Valley Authority*, the Supreme Court explained that Article 3 prevents the court from considering "the constitutionality of legislation in a friendly, non-adversary proceeding," as with abstract review.[12] In short, if there is no controversy, there is no case. Second, the court has explained that, in the spirit of judicial independence and the separation of powers, the judiciary must operate as a coequal branch of government and, as such, that it cannot be compelled to advise the executive or legislature ("Advisory Opinions" 2011). Third, the court has objected to the abstract nature of the advisory process, finding that hypothetical questions can prevent the dynamic representation of all sides of an argument and thereby undermine the adversarial nature of courts ("Advisory Opinions" 2011).[13]

Although advisory opinions have been prohibited in American federal courts since the late eighteenth century, several state supreme courts do accept requests for advisory opinions from state legislatures and/or the governor. The state Constitutions of Colorado, Florida, Maine, Massachusetts, Michigan, New Hampshire, Rhode Island, and South Dakota authorize advisory opinions, whereas Alabama and Delaware provide the advisory power through statutes. Finally, North Carolina allows for advisory opinions based on judicial initiative (see Rogers and Vanberg 2002).

Like the United States Supreme Court, the High Court of Australia refuses to provide advisory opinions. During the Australian Constitutional Convention of 1897–98, delegates reviewed and considered the process provided in the United Kingdom's *Judicial Committee Act* of 1833 and in the Canadian practice of reference opinions.[14] Many convention participants found that the determination of abstract questions was not within the proper scope of the judiciary and thus rejected the practice of the United Kingdom and Canada, ultimately preferring to follow the American model (Zines 2010). The restriction on Australian advisory opinions was confirmed by the High Court in *Re Judiciary and Navigation Act*, where it found that Parliament does not have the ability to "confer power or jurisdiction upon the High Court to determine abstract questions of law without the right or duty of any body or person being involved."[15] Although the formal practice of advisory opinions is prohibited in Australia, Zines (2010) notes that the High Court has, on occasion, provided advice to governments through obiter dicta.[16]

When New Zealand engaged in institutional reform in the early 2000s, it too considered the practice of reference opinions. In creating the New Zealand Supreme Court in 2004, the government explicitly rejected a proposal to create a reference jurisdiction, citing the Canadian model (Office of the Attorney General 2002). The New Zealand Advisory Group for the Office of the Attorney General reviewed the Canadian reference power and found that "it has been a common complaint that some of the opinions rendered in references have propounded doctrine that was too general and abstract to provide a satisfactory rule" (48). After its brief review of the Canadian experience with a reference power, the Advisory Group recommended against adopting such a power for the New Zealand Supreme Court, shutting the door to a New Zealand reference-like power.

The United States, Australia, and New Zealand either explicitly rejected the creation of an advisory power for their high appellate courts or, if one had been provided in the past, abandoned it before the turn of the nineteenth century. New Zealand's rejection of the advisory function was a reaction to the Canadian experience with the reference power. Australia found that providing the judiciary the power to issue advisory opinions would require the courts to engage in a process that was ostensibly unjudicial. The American rejection of an advisory function for the Supreme Court was born out of concerns over judicial independence and the limited institutional capacity of the court to consider abstract and hypothetical questions. The American unease with advisory review is not unwarranted, and the present study demonstrates that many of the American concerns have arisen with the Canadian reference power. The implications of these concerns animate the critical analysis that follows.

When juxtaposed with its more common comparators, the Canadian reference power is unique. However, if the scope is expanded beyond the routine comparative cases, we find that abstract review, similar in principle to the Canadian reference power, is a routine feature in the constitutional courts of several European civil law countries. As discussed in Chapters 1 and 6, the high courts of many European civil law jurisdictions regularly engage in abstract review and issue advisory opinions to governments. The process of some European countries, such as Germany, France, and Italy, is considered in greater detail in the chapters that follow.

It is important to note here that institutional features, such as the executive-centred nature of the Canadian political system and reference process, distinguish the Canadian case from many of the constitutional courts of Europe. For example, abstract review in European constitutional courts is more accessible and often available to the legislature and groups outside the governing party. In Canada the power to initiate abstract review is the sole prerogative of Cabinet through the governor in council (or lieutenant governor in council). Moreover, there are few restrictions on the timing and nature of questions that a government can ask in a reference case, which creates a concentration of power not found in civil law countries, like France and Germany. Yet, even with a different institutional arrangement and a decentralization of the power to request abstract review, many European constitutional courts often find themselves at the centre of political and normative disputes, which has been well documented by scholars (see Stone 1992; Kommers 1994; Shapiro and Stone 1994; and Stone Sweet 2000). Comparatively little is known about the Canadian case and its parallels with European constitutional courts, despite some of the similarities.

This brief discussion of the comparative context of advisory opinions helps to establish that the Canadian reference power is a compelling case for analysis. Reference cases combine the abstract judicial review typically found in civil law jurisdictions with the executive-centred Westminster parliamentary system. This combination creates institutional and actor variables that provide interesting and unique circumstances for analysis, as well as fruitful opportunities for comparison with the constitutional courts of Europe. It is the intention of this study to encourage scholars of comparative law and judicial politics to take up this task, which requires eschewing the barriers imposed by the differences between common law and civil law legal systems.

Puzzle and Central Argument in Brief

The Canadian reference power raises several questions. Why would political actors effectively cede a portion of their decision-making power to the courts in reference cases? How does the reference power encourage or permit political tactics and strategic litigation?[17] Why would governments request, and choose to be bound by, an advisory opinion from the courts that could run counter to their policy or political goals? Why would elected officials value a definitive judicial decision over a flexible approach that could be conducted via interinstitutional or intergovernmental bargaining? Finally, what are the implications of the Canadian reference power for the relationship between courts and elected political actors? Each of these questions is considered in this book.

This study is driven by two central inquiries. First, how have Canadian governments used the reference power? Understanding how the reference power has been used over time and the nature of reference cases provides the necessary foundation for addressing the second question. Specifically, what are some of the reasons why a government would use the reference power? These questions raise several theoretical concerns regarding the relationship between the reference power and democratic governance. Chief among these considerations is the effect of the reference power on judicial independence and the separation of the judiciary from the partisan branches of government, with a particular focus on the executive.

I argue that Canadian governments ask reference questions to benefit strategically from the unique characteristics of the reference power and to draw on some of the advantages inherent in judicial review. There are five explanations that help to establish why governments rely on the reference power. Before reviewing some of the reasons, it is essential to note that these explanations should not be understood as mutually exclusive. Instead, my analysis makes it clear that a single reference case can be the product of several different strategic considerations on behalf of a government and that a reference case can satisfy multiple goals. Although governments may rely on the reference power more often to satisfy one strategy over another, it is unfortunately not possible to definitively state which type of strategy has been employed in each and every case. This finding highlights a key implication of this research: the Canadian reference power uniquely provides governments with many strategic opportunities that may not be achieved through routine ligation or the regular political process.

A government's decision to use the reference power can be the product of several considerations. First, governments will ask reference questions for strategic reasons and to avoid political controversy. Instead of dealing with a highly salient issue, governments will avoid their decision-making responsibilities by asking the courts to decide for them. Second, references help governments to understand the limits of constitutional jurisdiction and other matters related to federalism, such as negotiating with other governments, and to clarify their own constitutional or legal powers. In a related sense, throughout Canadian history, governments have used the reference power to protect constitutional jurisdiction from the intrusions of other governments. Third, a reference case can allow a government to benefit from the institutional authority and protection of the courts. A reference can protect government policy from future legal challenges or, at the very least, make it difficult to mount a challenge similar to that addressed in a reference. Fourth, because the reference process is relatively quick compared to routine review, governments can rely on the reference power to address pressing issues in a timely manner. Finally, governments will use the reference power to benefit from the structural advantages made possible through abstract review. Rather than waiting for routine litigation to materialize, governments have used reference cases because they allow for an amount of control, and even manipulation, in the framing of questions and issues considered by a court that is not possible in routine litigation.

In addressing these reasons for using the reference power, this book makes several important contributions. First, it provides a comprehensive political analysis of Canadian reference cases and the reference power since its creation in 1875. This book examines all reference cases adjudicated by provincial appellate courts and the Supreme Court of Canada from 1875 to 2017, a total of 209 cases.[18] Second, this project analyzes litigation strategy in reference cases and assesses why delegating decision making to a court can be a viable political option for a government, providing insight into this most common, yet generally understudied, litigant.

This study provides an examination of the central features of all Canadian reference cases, documenting important descriptive characteristics and trends over time. Addressing the use of references since 1875 shows that the use of the reference power has mirrored periods of great political and social contestation. This book also makes important contributions to understanding how reference cases compare to routine litigation across several dimensions, such as type of review (abstract or concrete), intervener participation, unanimity rates, authorship styles, and case disposition. This analysis engages with important theoretical questions that concern the ability of courts to refuse to answer reference questions and the implications of question refusal for the separation of powers and judicial independence.

Finally, building on the analytical description of reference cases, this study examines why reference cases are a viable political strategy. It addresses the benefits and potential pitfalls for governments that flow from the unique nature of the reference power. This dimension of the research is evaluated through in-depth interviews with individuals involved in past reference cases, such as former attorneys general, constitutional experts, government counsel, and a former first minister. These interview data are grounded in secondary scholarship and analysis of historical and archival documents. While demonstrating the benefits of the reference power, this study also analyzes potential drawbacks to references through an analysis of two cases in which governments considered a reference but ultimately abandoned this option. This analysis is conducted through the lens of delegation theory – a perspective that seeks to explain why principal decision makers will empower independent agents, such as the courts, by allowing them to control and manage some issues (Graber 1993; Salzberger 1993; Ginsburg 2003; Hirschl 2004; Finkel 2008; Hilbink 2009). Employing delegation theory helps to link the Canadian case to a larger literature that has been underexplored in previous Canadian scholarship.[19] In pursuing this delegation-based explanation, the study applies this theoretical framework in a novel manner to understand the relationship between courts and the executive as it relates to the reference power. This study demonstrates that the actual outcome of a reference case – win or lose – is *almost* secondary to the political benefits that can be attained from simply involving the courts through the reference power.

Scope of the Book

The intention of this book is not to engage in doctrinal analysis and detailed review of reference jurisprudence and related law. I leave much of this important work in the capable hands of legal scholars. Instead, the goal is to consider the political aspects of the Canadian reference cases, to address how political actors have used the reference power in the past, and to illustrate how references can influence and animate political debates, institutional contexts, and Canadian politics, shifting attention away from an exclusive focus on the courts. Although this book employs an original dataset of reference cases adjudicated by Canadian appellate courts, the focus here is less on the legal answers provided by the courts in these cases and more on the nature and use of the reference power. Specifically, the approach is to address the types of questions that are asked, the individuals and groups that participate, and how the courts respond to reference questions. Focusing on *how* and *why* the reference power is used by political actors, this book provides insight into its institutional implications, its effect on the centralization of power within the executive, and its consequences for judicial independence. This line of inquiry also helps to explain why governments will limit their own decision-making power by turning to the courts to resolve political disputes, and it considers the normative implications when litigation becomes a political strategy. Finally, this book is concerned with providing a greater understanding of the nature of judicial power and behaviour in Canadian politics within the context of reference cases.

This book approaches the study of the reference power and Canadian appellate courts with an understanding that courts are political institutions, a focus shared by many political scientists who study the judiciary and courts (Russell 1987; Knopff and Morton 1992; Macfarlane 2013; Hausegger, Hennigar, and Riddell 2015). Canadian courts have an important role to play in policy debates because other political actors recognize and appreciate the role that reference decisions can play in shaping both political debates and outcomes. To be sure, this is not to suggest that the decisions rendered by courts in reference cases are fully politicized and thus devoid of legal principle and analysis. Instead, the intention of this book is to appreciate and explain the highly political context in which courts can operate when governments seek judicial advice through reference cases.

Overview and Summary of Findings

This book consists of six substantive chapters. Chapter 1 details the origins of the Canadian reference power by looking at the parliamentary debates concerning its use in the late nineteenth and early twentieth centuries. This discussion also addresses the adoption of a reference power by the provinces. In addition to examining the statutory foundations of the reference power in Canada, this chapter considers the legal rationale used by the Supreme Court of Canada to defend its advisory jurisdiction in the two instances when the court was asked to review the legality of the power: *Reference re References* (1912) and *Reference re Secession of Quebec* [*Secession Reference*] (1998).[20] Chapter 1 also provides insight into the government process for seeking a reference opinion, with special consideration of the actors involved. The remainder of this chapter sets out the theoretical issues related to judicial independence, the separation of powers, and abstract review that are implicated by the analysis that follows.

Chapter 2 provides an overview of the important trends associated with the Canadian reference power by drawing on an original dataset of over two hundred reference cases adjudicated by provincial courts of appeal, the Supreme Court of Canada, and the Judicial Committee of the Privy Council.[21] This chapter demonstrates that increases in the use of the reference power are intimately related to periods of political contestation. More specifically, Chapter 2 engages in a detailed analysis of two periods – the 1930s and the 1980s – when the reference power was used with greater frequency than during all other periods in Canadian political history. Employing a political and historical account of these periods, this chapter advances the argument that use of the reference power corresponds to periods when governments undertake wide-ranging policy projects, engage in debates over the fundamental nature of the Canadian state, or are forced to respond to external pressures brought on by economic or social crises.

A closer look at these two decades shows that the 1930s were characterized by the federal government's attempt to deal with the financial disaster of the Great Depression within the confines of Canadian federalism and the constitutional division of powers. This period demonstrates the difficulty of applying the division of powers to contemporaneous problems of governance such as the expansion of social reform and the making of international treaties. The second period examined, the 1980s, represents a time in Canadian politics when governments were concerned with large-scale constitutional projects such as responding to Quebec nationalism (and separatism), the adoption of a new constitutional amending formula, and the role of the provinces in seeking a new Constitution and a charter of rights. This era is often referred to as one of "mega constitutional" politics – a time in Canadian politics when the fundamental nature of the political community was challenged in a manner that was fraught with intense emotion (Russell 2004, 74). This period was also characterized by several disputes between the provinces and federal government and by the expansion of executive federalism, of which the reference power was an extension. The reference cases of this period mirrored many of the events of mega constitutional politics, such as the patriation of the Constitution and the jurisdictional disputes between governments over various issues, such as natural resources.

The analysis of data in Chapter 2 demonstrates that although the federal government first created the reference power, provincial governments have made greater use of it over time. This chapter finds that although governments can use the reference power to challenge the legislation of other governments, this has become a less common practice, especially by federal governments, which have not referred provincial legislation since 1994. Chapter 2 concludes with the finding that the reference power has become a valuable tool for provincial governments, regardless of its origins as a federal power aimed at constraining their powers.

Chapter 3 examines the use of the reference power in the post-1949 era, as this year marks when the Supreme Court became the final court of appeal for Canada, fundamentally changing its role within Canadian politics and governance. This chapter analyzes the trends related to the types of reference questions asked, how courts have responded to reference cases, and the relationship between governments and interest groups when the reference power is used compared to routine litigation. Chapter 3 engages with existing scholarship on Canadian courts to highlight the fundamentally distinct nature of reference cases, while also detailing the relatively similar manner in which litigants and courts approach these cases.

The analysis in Chapter 3 demonstrates that the reference power has been used to deal both with issues that are concrete (i.e., live disputes) and with issues that are abstract. Furthermore, it finds that reference cases attract a much higher rate of participation by third-party interveners compared to routine litigation. As the chapter demonstrates, the high rate of intervener participation is linked to the abstract nature of many reference cases and to the unique opportunity that references can provide groups to influence the policy-making process. Additionally, this analysis finds that courts do not view their power to invalidate government legislation or policy as being any different in reference cases compared to routine litigation, regardless of the fact that most references do not arise out of a live dispute. Chapter 3 documents that the unanimity rate in reference cases is actually lower than the unanimity rate of the

Supreme Court in general, with a high number of concurring opinions issued in reference cases. Finally, in terms of government behaviour in reference cases, this chapter demonstrates that governments from all sides of the political spectrum are willing to use the reference power and that governments are most likely to initiate a reference when they have a majority in the legislature.

Along with providing context and explanation for the trends related to the use of the reference power, Chapters 2 and 3 detail the unique structural aspects of references, like the fact they allow governments to obtain judicial review without a live dispute, and explain why these features can be advantageous for political actors. Moreover, in discussing the behaviour of governments in reference cases, these chapters demonstrate how reference cases can be an effective political strategy that helps governments to achieve particular goals. For example, the finding that the reference power is used most often to deal with issues related to the constitutional division of powers speaks to the fact that the reference power is an effective mechanism of federalism and a means to deal with other governments.

Drawing on original interviews with individuals involved in past reference cases, Chapter 4 further examines the unique opportunities and advantages that the reference power provides governments. Analysis of the interview data reveals five themes that explain why governments are willing to give up decision-making power to the courts in reference cases. This analysis recognizes that references allow governments to capitalize on the institutional authority and the role of the courts within the Canadian constitutional framework, beyond simply using courts to avoid difficult decisions. I argue in Chapter 4 that by simply involving the courts, references provide governments with a unique strategic tool that affords them many political benefits.

Chapter 5 explores the reality that although the reference power can provide governments with several important political advantages, governments do not submit reference questions on every difficult political issue they face. Indeed, in comparison to all Canadian litigation, references are relatively uncommon. Through an examination of two statutes that prompted governments to consider seeking a reference but ultimately abandoned this option – Quebec's *Act to Protect the Province against*

Communistic Propaganda [*Padlock Act*] (1937) and its anti-blasphemy *Act Respecting Freedom of Worship and Maintenance of Good Order* (1953–54) – this chapter addresses the limitations of the reference power and engages with arguments against judicial review.[22]

Chapter 6 builds on the empirical findings of the book and, by conceptualizing the relationship between the courts and political actors in reference cases as one of delegation, provides a theoretical description of a government's decision to refer. The chapter makes an important normative contribution by analyzing how political actors empower the courts as a means of political strategy, which has two significant implications: first, reference cases present several important and unique problems for judicial independence; and second, the narrow access to the Canadian reference power is quite distinct compared to the advisory function of many European constitutional courts. However, I argue that advisory opinions and abstract review need not operate in such a centralized manner. A brief comparison of the Canadian case with four European constitutional courts that routinely engage in abstract review – those of France, Germany, Italy, and Spain – provides useful examples of institutional arrangements that avoid the concentration of power found with the Canadian reference power, thus suggesting possibilities for its reform.

The arguments presented in Chapter 6 are grounded in delegation theory. The central tenets and contributions of this theoretical framework, as well as its application to Canadian reference cases, are explored. Delegation provides a useful framework for understanding the relationship between the courts and political actors, as well as why empowering the judiciary is a viable political strategy. This perspective is grounded in the understanding that the decisions made by elected officials reflect a desire either to maintain power or to secure re-election. Based on this motivation, political actors will make decisions to engage in either credit claiming or blame avoidance. The courts provide an effective forum for this behaviour, and counterintuitively judicial review of political actions can be "friendly" and benefit political actors. Aside from blame avoidance, delegation scholarship explains that judicial review can be an effective means to overcome legislative opposition or gridlock and to provide position or policy legitimization. In sum, Chapter 6 argues that many of the elements of delegation theory are present in the use of reference cases.

Chapter 6 also notes the contradiction present in this understanding of the reference power: governments that use the reference power appreciate the advantages that can be gained from an authoritative constitutional interpretation in dealing with a political controversy, but at the same time, they do not recognize the threat that the reference power could pose for judicial independence. The chapter argues that for delegation to be effective, respect for the independence of the judiciary is essential – yet the delegation of political controversies to the courts in references cases can pose a direct threat to this independence. These tensions have been noted by the Supreme Court in the past,[23] as well as by scholarship that has examined the negative public reaction to salient or controversial decisions.[24]

Finally, the book's Conclusion concisely reviews the central findings of this study and invites readers to consider its broader implications. In particular, the Conclusion focuses on the relationship between political actors and the courts, as well as on the consequences of this relationship for Canadian politics. It emphasizes that when thinking about the Canadian reference power, it is crucially important to move beyond a narrow legal understanding of the power. It is clear that references have essentially become advisory in name only. Indeed, reference cases are not distinguished from other, more routine, types of litigation in practice. Yet, at their core, references are fundamentally different from all other types of litigation because a government can decide when and under what circumstances a particular policy (enacted or proposed) should be reviewed by the courts through a reference. As a result, it is vital to consider the underlying political nature of reference cases and the implications for the judiciary, the courts, and Canadian politics.

Origins and Implications of the Reference Power 1

The Canadian reference power was first adopted by the Parliament of Canada in a rather unremarkable manner. When creating the Supreme Court of Canada through the enactment of the *Supreme Court Act* in 1875, the Canadian government mirrored several provisions found in the United Kingdom's *Judicial Committee Act* of 1833. The provisions copied from the English law included section 4, which gave the Crown the ability to seek an advisory opinion from the judiciary on difficult questions.[1] Comparatively, section 52 of the *Supreme Court Act* provided the governor in council (effectively the first minister and Cabinet) the power to request the Supreme Court's advice on "any matters whatsoever as he may think fit."[2]

Beyond embracing the English tradition, the adoption of the reference power also served a uniquely Canadian purpose. Alongside the powers of reservation and disallowance,[3] references provided the federal government another tool to meddle with, and perhaps control, the provincial governments (Rubin 1960). Through the reference power, the federal government could protect its constitutional jurisdiction from provincial incursions by sending provincial legislation to the Supreme Court of Canada for review and, in some cases, invalidation. As Smith (1983, 126) explains, Prime Minister Sir John A. Macdonald understood that the reference power could supplement (or even replace) the power of disallowance and provide the federal government another means to "supervise provincial legislation." However, a reference need not be understood solely as an alternative to the powers of reservation and disallowance. Instead, Rubin (1960) notes that in the debates concerning the amendment of the reference power in the 1890s, some parliamentarians supported the use of a reference as a preliminary step prior to exercising the power of disallowance. The minister of justice, Sir John Thompson, explained that referring an issue that was followed by disallowance would give the decision to invalidate provincial legislation much more legitimacy because it would be supported by a judicial opinion and would not be simply a matter of the minister of justice acting alone (Rubin 1960, 172). Although Canada inherited a system based on the supremacy of Parliament, the creation of judicial review to adjudicate disputes concerning government jurisdiction and the reference power provided the courts an opportunity to engage in a form of judicial supremacy or, at the very least, created the space for judicial decisions to play an influential role in policy debates (Smith 1983; Lederman 1985).

In the early reference process, the Supreme Court of Canada was not obligated to provide reasoning for its decisions, nor were there any formal arguments submitted by the executive. Instead, when responding to reference questions, the court would state only whether the legislation was valid or invalid. As a result, the early Supreme Court reference cases provided little guidance to Parliament about the limits of its constitutional jurisdiction, which was most concerning when the court found that Parliament had acted outside the scope of its legal powers. As Strayer (1988) notes, in the first fifteen years following the adoption of the reference power, this structure remained in place, although the federal Cabinet's use of the power was relatively infrequent.

The deficiencies of the lack of written reasons provided by the Supreme Court in references was brought to light in an 1885 decision in *Reference re Sess Papers No 85a 1885 (Canada)* [*McCarthy Act Reference*], which found the federal regulation of liquor traffic ultra vires Parliament's constitutional jurisdiction. This invalidation by the court, without written explanation, sparked a backlash within the House of Commons, marking the first documented criticism of the reference power since its adoption.[4] Edward Blake, former attorney general and member of the

Opposition, argued that the reference power as it currently stood was illegitimate and problematic. Along with the concerns related to a lack of written reasons, the early reference process did not provide guidance regarding the inclusion of affected parties (often provincial governments) or a requirement of fact finding (House of Commons Debates 1890, 4089). Blake proposed to reform the reference power and suggested that it be limited to use in conjunction with disallowance and matters related to education (see Stayer 1988).

In response to this criticism, and shared dissatisfaction with the *McCarthy Act Reference,* Parliament, led by the Macdonald government, amended the reference power in 1891. This amendment required the Supreme Court to provide reasoning for its reference decisions, and if provincial legislation was implicated in the case, the appropriate attorney general would be notified and provided the right to represent provincial interests (Strayer 1988, 313). The amendments made it clear that for involved parties, reference opinions by the Supreme Court are considered a judgment and subject to appeal to the Judicial Committee of the Privy Council (JCPC) (313). However, these revisions to the reference power did not follow Blake's suggestion to narrow the scope of the power. Instead, the 1891 amendments expanded the application of the power to allow Parliament to seek a reference opinion on "any ... matter with reference to which he sees fit to exercise this power."[5] The 1891 amendments to the reference power have remained largely unchanged and continue to guide the present-day reference process at the Supreme Court of Canada.

Following the creation of the federal reference power, several provinces amended their judicature statutes to allow for the use of a similar power at provincial appellate courts. The provincial governments of Manitoba, Ontario, and Nova Scotia introduced reference legislation in 1890 that largely mirrored the provisions found in *An Act Respecting the Supreme and Exchequer Courts,* which granted the lieutenant governor in council the power to request a judicial opinion from a provincial court of appeal. The governments of British Columbia and Quebec followed suit, creating similar legislation in 1891 and 1898 respectively. By 1953, with the creation of a reference provision by the Government of Newfoundland (as it was then known), all provinces had the ability to initiate a reference case at the highest court within their jurisdiction. The *Supreme Court Act* was amended in 1922 to provide provinces a right of appeal to the Supreme Court.[6] As a result, the reference decisions of provincial appellate courts could be appealed, by right, to the Supreme Court of Canada and further appealed to the JCPC. Thus, unlike the federal government, provinces have multiple opportunities to obtain a favourable advisory opinion: first, at the provincial court of appeal; second, at the Supreme Court; and before 1949, at the JCPC.

Although the specificity and wording of each provincial government's reference legislation vary slightly, on the whole each achieves the common result of providing the executive the power to seek an advisory opinion from the bench. It is worth noting that the provincial and federal reference power is not the only form of reference or advisory opinion in Canada. The Federal Court of Canada has the ability to consider reference questions arising from the proceedings of federal commissions, tribunals, or boards. Questions can be submitted to the Federal Court through these various bodies or directly through Canada's attorney general.[7] British Columbia's reference provisions allow the provincial executive to refer questions to either the British Columbia Court of Appeal or the British Columbia Supreme Court, a lower court. Similarly, the Manitoba government has the ability to refer questions to the Manitoba Court of Appeal or the Court of Queen's Bench, a lower court. A recent example of a lower court reference is found in the British Columbia Supreme Court case regarding the constitutionality of polygamy.[8] For a complete list of reference legislation of Canadian appellate courts, please consult Appendix A.

Although references at provincial appellate courts and the Supreme Court of Canada show quite a bit of uniformity in terms of legislation, there is some variance across jurisdictions in terms of process and execution of reference questions.[9] In response to research requests, several governments refused to provide information on their reference processes, finding that the information fell within the realm of information protected by solicitor-client privilege and that guidelines outlining a reference process amounted to legal advice in litigation or contemplation of litigation.[10] As a result, no information on the reference process can be gathered from the attorneys general of Ontario, Quebec, and Canada, although responses to requests for information did confirm that procedural documents for reference cases do exist.[11] Several governments – British Columbia, Alberta, Saskatchewan, Manitoba, New Brunswick, and Nova Scotia – explained that their ministries of the attorney general do not have a defined formal procedure for initiating reference cases. Presumably, without a manual or set procedural guidelines, these governments initiate reference cases on an ad hoc or informal basis. The Saskatchewan Ministry of Justice and attorney general explained that the department has decided to engage in reference cases on a case-by-case basis.

Prince Edward Island (PEI) and Newfoundland and Labrador (NL) have no written guidelines for the operation of provincial reference cases, but officials from both of these provinces explained in separate interviews with the author that their process for reference cases is ad hoc. A senior solicitor in the PEI Department of Environment, Labour, and Justice explained that "decisions to use the reference process would be case by case" and that the process followed the "same procedure in bringing matters before Cabinet: a memorandum to Executive Council, including the facts and proposed reference questions, signed by the minister and deputy minister," with the final decision to proceed made by Cabinet alone.[12] Similarly, a senior official from the NL Department of Justice and Public Safety indicated that the province uses the reference power sparingly and that, as a result, the procedure surrounding its usage is informal and dependent upon the specific context of the reference being made. In that province, the Department of Justice and Public Safety drafts a request to Cabinet regarding the necessity of a reference by the lieutenant governor in council, with the creation of this memorandum done in consultation with other affected departments and other interested parties, such as the Law Society and Canadian Bar Association.[13] It is worth noting that consulting with interested parties means that in the case of Newfoundland and Labrador, the government would, in essence, consult interest groups on its political and litigation strategy.[14] However, it appears that, although bureaucratic officials and interested parties may be involved in the drafting of reference questions, the ultimate decision to proceed with a reference case is still concentrated in the executive through Cabinet, as outlined by the reference statutes.

Finally, although the Ministry of the Attorney General of Ontario found that documents outlining the reference procedure fall under solicitor-client privilege, the response to a request under the *Access to Information Act* provided a detailed description of the process as explained to the Australian High Commission in correspondence from 1983.[15] This letter explained largely the same process as that described by senior bureaucratic officials of the Governments of Prince Edward Island and Newfoundland and Labrador. However, the letter did contain one interesting caveat: "Although reservations about the efficacy and propriety of the reference case procedure has [sic] been expressed in academic writing, it has been our experience that those reservations are not shared by the government, the courts, nor by the practicing bar" (Ontario Ministry of the Attorney General 1983). This letter implies that most governments in Canada are likely aware that the reference power can be subject to criticism but have decidedly chosen not to concern themselves with these criticisms. Indeed, if the courts are generous in their engagement with reference cases, governments are likely to continue submitting reference questions.

Judicial Review of the Reference Power

Although the Canadian reference power has been in operation for approximately 140 years, the Supreme Court of Canada has ruled on the legality of the power in only two cases. Comparatively, the provincial reference power has never been subject to challenge (Hogg 2012). A review of the legal challenges to the reference power not only provides insight into how courts have understood and interpreted the legal foundations of the power but also highlights that some of the concerns regarding the executive's use of references from earlier periods in Canadian history are still relevant today.

The first challenge to the reference power in 1910 concerned the extrajudicial nature of reference cases and the proper role of the courts. In *Reference re References* (1910), a majority of the Supreme Court held that the federal government's reference power was constitutional.[16] This reference concerned several complex questions regarding the constitutional jurisdiction of provinces in regards to the incorporation of companies under section 92 of the *British North America Act, 1867* (as it was then known). In this case, six provinces argued that the Supreme Court should not hear this reference because the reference procedure was unconstitutional.[17] It is interesting to note that the majority of the provincial governments that made arguments regarding the legitimacy of the reference power had, by this time, already adopted their own reference power. The provinces argued that the reference power conferred original jurisdiction on the Supreme Court, which fell outside the court's jurisdiction as a general appeal court for Canada provided in section 101 of the Constitution.

In his decision, Chief Justice Sir Charles Fitzpatrick explained that by 1910 the reference procedure had become an established process within the Supreme Court's jurisdiction and that, when presiding over a reference case, "the members of this court are the official advisors of the executive in the same way as the judges in England are the counsel or advisers of the King in matters of law."[18] The Supreme Court rejected the arguments made by the provinces and found that because the reference power was based on a procedure similar to that used in the United Kingdom, it was legitimately enacted in Canada. Fitzpatrick recognized that in providing advisory opinions in a reference, a court was engaging in a role, albeit a legal role, that would ordinarily be fulfilled by Cabinet. This incursion into the routine role of Cabinet was not problematic for Fitzpatrick because the court is providing advice, not making binding decisions. Indeed, all of the justices participating in this reference agreed that the role of the courts in a reference case fulfils a legal function, albeit an extrajudicial one. In a concurring opinion, Justice Sir Louis Henry Davies agreed with Fitzpatrick that a reference case requires a court to step outside its routine function of adjudicating disputes between parties. Importantly, although this practice is extrajudicial, it is characterized as a legal function and is constitutionally permissible. This acceptance of the reference power by the majority in *Reference re References* was contingent on the fact that a reference opinion is advisory only. As Davies explained,

> These answers are simply to aid the Governor in Council in reaching conclusions for which they must be held entirely responsible. The answers do not bind the Governor in Council. He may act in accordance with them or not, as he pleases, giving them just such weight

> as he pleases. They are advisory only. They do not bind even this court as has been often said before if at any time it is called upon in its strictly judicial capacity to decide the very question asked.[19]

Echoing the reasoning of the other justices in the majority, Justice Sir Lyman Duff also focused on the nonbinding nature of references, explaining that a reference is technically not a judicial judgment and does not contribute to legal precedent set by the Supreme Court.[20] Regardless of how closely reference proceedings mirror routine litigation, reference decisions are markedly different from all other decisions rendered by appellate courts because they are advisory. For the majority, any potential problems for the independence of the judiciary and the implications that arise from the extrajudicial function of references are mitigated by the fact that reference opinions are simply advice and do not bind or dictate executive action.

This simple solution to the potential problems for the separation of the judiciary from the more political branches of government was not satisfactory for the dissenting justices in this case. Justice John Idington expressed concern that references might erode the separation of the legislative, executive, and judicial functions of government, which is not addressed by the safety valve of the advisory nature of references. He explained, "If we degrade this court by imposing upon it duties that cannot be held judicial but merely advisory and especially in the wholesale way submitted herein, we destroy a fundamental principle of our government."[21] Idington was concerned that the reference power imposes a duty on the courts that is outside the realm of judicial jurisdiction, requiring that courts fulfil a duty of the executive and legislative branches. For Idington, this imposition is a violation of the separation and independence of the judicial branch from the partisan branches of government. Unfortunately for Idington, no other justice in this case shared his concern about the separation of the branches of Canadian governance and the threat posed by the extrajudicial function in reference cases. In *Reference re References*, the Supreme Court declared the reference power constitutional.

The Province of Ontario appealed the Supreme Court's decision in *Reference re References* to the JCPC on behalf of several other provinces.

The JCPC unanimously upheld the Supreme Court's finding that the reference power is a valid exercise of the jurisdiction of the Parliament of Canada, not a violation of judicial independence. The JCPC relied on the same findings of the Supreme Court, reasoning that because references are advisory, they do not bind the executive or future courts. As a result, the JCPC found that references do not pose a threat to the independence of the judiciary and the separation of powers. The JCPC concluded its decision with the caveat that "mischief and inconvenience ... might arise from an indiscriminate and injudicious use of the Act," but it left the policing of the boundaries of the proper use of the reference power to the Canadian courts.[22]

The reference power was not challenged again until the *Secession Reference*. The amicus curiae appointed by the Supreme Court to represent the interests of Quebec in the *Secession Reference* made several arguments that questioned the legitimacy of the reference power.[23] The counsel argued that the federal reference power was invalid and ultra vires section 101 of the Constitution for three central reasons. First, in creating the reference jurisdiction for the Supreme Court, the Parliament of Canada had granted the court original jurisdiction. Conferring original jurisdiction on the Supreme Court is incompatible with the court's role as "a general court of appeal for Canada," as specified in section 101 of the 1867 Constitution.[24] In other words, the amicus curiae argued that section 101 limited the jurisdiction of the Supreme Court to reviewing the decisions of lower courts (i.e., appeals) and that a reference required the court to hear and decide a case. Second, the counsel argued that a reference case requires the court to engage in an advisory function that is not the duty of the judiciary but of the executive. Third, the amicus curiae claimed that the reference power infringes on the provincial jurisdiction over the administration of justice as provided in section 92(14) of the *Constitution Act, 1867*.[25]

In the *Secession Reference*, the Supreme Court found that the definition of the Supreme Court as provided by section 101 should not be viewed as restrictive. Instead, the court found that it is a common practice for appellate courts to exercise original jurisdiction on an "exceptional basis," as is permitted at the United States Supreme Court and the English Court of Appeal.[26] However, it should be noted that the court's comparison to the Supreme Court of the United States is arguably tenuous since the American Constitution explicitly confers original jurisdiction on its Supreme Court, whereas there is no comparable power given to the Canadian Supreme Court.[27] Finding that it is not unusual for an appellate court to exercise original jurisdiction, the court moved to consider the claim that the reference power infringes provincial jurisdiction as provided in section 92(14). In response to the challenge respecting the division of powers, the court found that the federal power under section 101 (a plenary power) takes priority over the provincial power. The priority afforded to section 101 implies that if there is a conflict over the reference power and the original jurisdiction of provincial courts, the federal capacity to create the reference power takes precedence. Given that the Parliament of Canada holds the power to confer original jurisdiction on an appellate court, the reference power is intra vires (within) the jurisdiction of Parliament and validly enacted by it.

The amicus curiae in the *Secession Reference* also challenged the reference power on the grounds that it is an extrajudicial function that requires the court to engage in a political role. The Supreme Court held that although engaging in an advisory function is outside of the routine role of appellate courts (i.e., the review of lower court decisions), it is nonetheless a legal function, which is legitimately exercised by the Supreme Court. The court explained, "There is no plausible basis on which to conclude that a court is, by its nature, inherently precluded from undertaking another legal function in tandem with its judicial duties."[28] Because the opinions provided in a reference case are advisory only and do not bind the actions of the referring parties, the court has no reservations about engaging in this advisory role. Furthermore, the court explained that nothing bars governments from rejecting the advice of the courts as provided in reference cases.[29] The court supported this conclusion on the grounds that reference cases are an established and accepted practice in Canada and that many other courts, including some American state courts and many European constitutional courts, engage in a similar function. In the *Secession Reference,* a unanimous Supreme Court found section 53 and the reference power of the *Supreme Court Act* constitutionally valid. The reference power is an enduring feature of the

Canadian legal-political landscape, and it is unlikely that the Supreme Court will invalidate the reference power in the future.

As mentioned above, the provincial reference power has not been subject to a constitutional challenge. Although the provincial reference legislation largely mirrors the *Supreme Court Act* provision, the creation of this power flows from the provincial power over the administration of justice as provided in section 92(14) of the *Constitution Act, 1867* rather than from section 101. Since the provincial constitutional jurisdiction in relation to the reference power is different, the Supreme Court's declaration regarding the constitutionality of the reference power in the *Secession Reference* does not preclude a legal challenge to the provincial power. That being said, mounting a challenge to the provincial power would certainly be difficult in light of the Supreme Court's ruling in the *Secession Reference* and in *Reference re References,* as the court made it clear that it is acceptable for a court to engage in the extrajudicial function of rendering advisory opinions. Furthermore, provinces have the constitutional authority to grant original jurisdiction to courts and thus would not be subject to a challenge on this ground.

References as Abstract Review

Governments can use the reference power to ask courts to consider legal questions in the abstract, without the context of real litigants and a live dispute. For example, in *Reference re Same-Sex Marriage* [*Same-Sex Marriage Reference*],[30] the Supreme Court was asked whether the *Proposal for an Act Respecting Certain Aspects of Legal Capacity for Marriage for Civil Purposes* was consistent with the Charter and within the constitutional jurisdiction of the Parliament of Canada.[31] Importantly, the court was not presented with a same-sex couple who wished to be married and were challenging the government restriction on nonheterosexual marriage. Reference cases require courts to engage in a type of judicial review that is fundamentally different from its routine role in adjudicating live cases and controversies. Indeed, a reference case can require that courts engage in abstract, rather than concrete, review. That is because a reference is the product of the referral of questions by a government to the courts rather than a live dispute between two parties. It is this practice of abstract review by Canadian courts in references that sets the Canadian case apart from other common law countries such as the United States and Australia. Abstract review does, however, link the Canadian case to the work of civil law constitutional courts in Europe, and an understanding of European constitutional courts can provide important insight into the many political and legal contours of abstract review.

In the civil law tradition, judges were prohibited from constitutional interpretation to preserve a Rousseauian notion of democracy that relied on the sovereignty of the people through the supremacy of Parliament. The maintenance of parliamentary supremacy became increasingly difficult with the spread of new written constitutions following the Second World War (Stone Sweet 2003; Merryman and Pérez-Perdomo 2007). Additionally, following the rise of a powerful court in the United States, the European aversion to judicial review was also an attempt to avoid the United States' so-called governance by judges. However, following the many tragedies of the war in Europe, several countries adopted constitutions that placed an emphasis on human rights, and they created constitutional courts to interpret those rights and ensure their protection.[32] The new European constitutional courts were designed to reflect the Kelsen model, named after Hans Kelsen, a legal scholar and the architect of the Austrian constitutional court. This model rests on a separation of the constitutional court from the rest of the country's judicial structure as a means of protecting the separation of powers and "to ensure the normative superiority of the constitutional law" (Stone Sweet 2003, 2745). Unlike the American and Canadian models, Kelsenian courts exercise centralized review insofar as these courts are the sole interpreters of the Constitution and given that lower courts cannot engage in constitutional review (Sadurski 2005).

Abstract review involves the judicial pronouncement of constitutionality without reference to the factual circumstances that may have brought the particular law or rule in front of the court. Abstract review also involves the consideration of laws that have been adopted by Parliament but not yet promulgated, as in France, or laws that have been promulgated but not yet enforced, as in Germany, Italy, and Spain (Stone Sweet 2000). This pre-promulgation or pre-enforcement review protects the "sovereign character of [a] statute within the legal system afterwards," as it significantly limits the number of statutes that will be found unconstitutional at a later date (Stone Sweet 2003, 2768) or even be subject to review by a court. Pre-promulgation review greatly limits the number of statutes struck down and prevents judges of the constitutional court from engaging in this form of judicial activism.[33] Not only does abstract review protect the sovereign character of legislation, but it also fosters a level of stability within the system, as it prevents future statutory constitutional review. At the same time, the limitation of judicial activism curtails the ability of constitutional courts to engage in policy making, eliminating one of the longstanding fears of judicial review in Europe (Sadurski 2005).

The abstract review system is open to strategic manoeuvring by opposition legislators within Parliament, as it can allow them to stall or even block the legislative agenda of the governing party through the initiation of abstract review. That being said, for the architects of the European constitutional courts, the stability and continuity within the public policy realm that abstract review promotes are central and cannot be achieved through models that rely solely on judicial invalidation of statutes after promulgation, as in the American system. Abstract review reconciles the historically grounded aversion to judicial review and the necessity for constitutional protection in continental European countries.

The ability to engage in abstract review increases the judicialization of politics. Kommers (1994) explains that abstract review transforms political conflicts into constitutional issues, thus involving a third party – the court – in addition to the governing party and the opposition, which significantly alters the power structure. In his assessment of several constitutional courts, Stone Sweet (2000, 45) finds that abstract review increases the level of judicialization of politics compared to systems that do not engage in such a process: "Abstract review harnesses the (virtually continuous) struggle between parliamentary majority and opposition over policy outcomes to a particular end: the progressive development of constitutional constraints on law-making." Abstract review allows politicians direct access to constitutional courts through litigation, thus increasing the power of the courts, while forcing them to mediate highly political disputes concerning salient issues (Merryman and Pérez-Perdomo 2007).

In his assessment of the effect of abstract review on the politics of constitutional review in Germany, Vanberg (2005) posits that courts must not be understood as solely nonpartisan and technical actors. Instead, analyzing the strategic interplay between courts and legislatures shows that constitutional courts have demonstrated the capability to directly influence policy making in a strategic manner. Thus the *mutual* strategic actions of the legislature *and* the court must be taken into consideration. Akin to other political actors, not only will the German Constitutional Court act on the basis of the preferences of the individual justices as shaped by the institution, but it will also make decisions in anticipation of the reactions of other actors and institutions. In this view, the German Constitutional Court has moved beyond the strictly legal role of apolitically applying the Constitution, instead adopting a mode of interpretation that reflects, to some extent, the goal of maximizing preferences and minimizing costs, both real and perceived.

The concern over creating constitutional courts in Europe stems largely from the desire to avoid powerful courts that implicate themselves in political debates. The abstract nature of the review helps to ease these concerns regarding the separation of powers between the political and partisan branches of government and the judiciary. That being said, many of the safeguards created to preserve the separation of powers and judicial independence in the European context of abstract review are not present in the Canadian system. These differences are examined further in Chapter 6, which engages in a more in-depth comparison of the European abstract review process and the Canadian reference process.

References as Strategic Litigation

Scholars studying the political implications of abstract review in the context of European constitutional courts have recognized that the model favouring separation of powers does not operate in its pure form in practice. Instead, accountability is often blurred, and difficulties arise in identifying which institution or actor is responsible for actions taken or decisions made because the routine activities of courts can veer into policy making and legislatures frequently arbitrate between opposing factions (Stone Sweet 2000, 130). The diffusion of power that takes place with the separation of powers also diffuses responsibility between institutions (Lovell 2003). When power is separated, institutions can attempt to relinquish responsibility for decisions and blame other branches for a specific outcome. In other words, when paired with a separation of the executive (or any other primary decision maker) from the judiciary, abstract review increases, and perhaps in some instances incentivizes, strategic behaviour. This problem can be materialized by the use of the reference power, where political actors shift decision-making responsibilities to the court through a reference, which could make it difficult to know which institution is responsible for the policy outcome.

For example, the response to the *Same-Sex Marriage Reference* often credits the Supreme Court for the legalization of same-sex marriage in Canada, even though the court simply advised the federal government that its legislation was constitutionally sound. The technical and formal legalization came from the passage of the *Civil Marriage Act* by Parliament,[34] a fact that political actors used to their advantage when commenting on the controversy surrounding same-sex marriage (see Russell 2009). This pivot toward the judiciary to resolve political disputes not only complicates the notion of a separation of the judicial branch from the executive and legislative branches but also demonstrates how policy makers can rely on judicial advice (or judicial approval) to serve strategic and political goals.

With regard to the judicialization of politics in Canada, some scholars have speculated that political actors will turn to the courts to resolve political disputes with the goal of blame avoidance, or engage in "buck passing" to skirt responsibility, or receive legitimization from the courts through the reference power (Hausegger, Hennigar, and Riddell 2015). Even Supreme Court justices have surmised that the reference tool has been employed as a means of "political opportunism" (Macfarlane 2013; Makin 2013). Whereas there are several examples of scholarship that examines the litigation of rights-based interest groups seeking redress through the courts for strategic purposes (see Olson 1990; Scheppele and Walker Jr. 1991; Manfredi 2004; Morton and Knopff 2000; and Hein 2001), much less data pertain to the government as a litigant and its use of the courts to obtain strategic political goals. Moreover, there is little analysis of how litigation could be used pragmatically aside from avoiding blame.

We do have some understanding of government's litigation behaviour (specifically its propensity to appeal) in routine cases. Like other litigants, the government's decision to litigate is one that is shaped by finite resources, and the decision to initiate legal action, whether proactively against another party or simply to defend its own legislation, must be considered in light of the costs of litigation. Hennigar (2002) has demonstrated that the government must be cognizant of the costs that can be incurred when engaging in litigation (specifically the decision to appeal unfavourable outcomes in lower courts), such as the loss of resources like political capital, personnel, and time, as well as a loss of control over policy. Thus the government's decision to appeal is not solely determined by the facts of the case or by the fact that a government policy is subject to challenge. Rather, it is a product of strategic cost-benefit analysis and calculated decision making.

Institutional constraints also shape a government's decision to litigate. Unlike other private litigants, the government must consider not only its own costs and benefits of legal action but also the interests of the Canadian public, and it must not be seen as wasting public funds on unnecessary litigation (Hennigar 2007). With these factors under consideration, Hennigar finds that the government's decision to appeal is the result of strategic decision making that considers the likelihood of success, the salience of the facts of the case, and potential costs, such as invalidation or judicial amendment of government legislation (245). However, that the decision to engage in a reference can limit a government's policy-making capability makes governmental litigation strategy in regards to the reference power even more perplexing.

In his analysis of a realist conception of the judicialization of politics, Hirschl (2008) explains that judicialization from above (i.e., from those in power) can take place when political actors engage in strategic deference to the judiciary as a means of resolving political conflict. Taking the *Secession Reference* as one of his examples, Hirschl postulates that the judicialization of politics is not necessarily the by-product of activist judges; rather, politicians can attempt to deflect responsibility by opening up conflicts to judicial review (106). Additionally, governments may turn to the judicial branch to mediate conflicts that they lack either the capacity or the willingness to resolve themselves.

Focusing on the Canadian reference power, Hennigar (2009) has attempted to answer similar questions regarding the government's decision to use a reference question to deal with the constitutionality of same-sex marriage. In this analysis, which uses Tsebelis's (1990) concept of "nested games" to consider the multiple arenas in which the government operates, Hennigar looks at how the seemingly counterintuitive decision of the government to ask a reference question and thus render itself virtually powerless in defining the constitutionality of same-sex marriage was actually the product of governmental strategy. Hennigar finds that a reference case was the most viable strategy for Jean Chrétien's government to deal with the competing demands of voters, lower court decisions in favour of extending rights to same-sex couples, party members, the parliamentary caucus, and partisan competition. Although Hennigar's work is focused on a single case study, one can assume that similar analysis and strategic calculation by political actors have taken place in other contentious reference cases.

Engaging in a reference case and thus delegating decision making may provide the government a means of strategic litigation. Although most scholars examining references from a case study perspective have not explicitly conceptualized this process as a form of delegation,[35] there is quality analysis that looks at individual reference cases as a means of strategic litigation. In their consideration of *Reference re Exported Natural Gas Tax* [*Alberta Gas Tax Reference*],[36] Riddell and Morton (2004) examine how the Alberta provincial government was able to use the reference procedure as a political tactic to push back against a federal government program that ran counter to the political interests of the province. The authors assert that the reference power provides governments a unique ability to engage in litigation that aids political strategy in a manner that cannot be achieved by other litigants, such as individuals or nongovernmental interest groups. Riddell and Morton demonstrate how the Alberta government was able to manufacture favourable facts to present to the court in its reference against the energy policy of Pierre Trudeau's government, a tactic that would not be possible through routine litigation within a live dispute. Through their study, the authors provide strong evidence of how reference questions could provide governments a means of strategic litigation.

Similarly, as previously mentioned, in his analysis of the *Same-Sex Marriage Reference,* Hennigar (2009) claims that executive interaction with the courts can be a means to blur responsibility for public policy that could alienate a portion of the electorate. Moreover, Hennigar points to the high level of public support for the courts as one of the motivating factors behind the strategic use of the courts to seek legitimization of public policy by the judicial branch. When the Chrétien government was faced with addressing same-sex marriage, the legalization of same-sex marriage was not supported by a majority of Canadians, and the Liberal Party caucus was divided internally on the issue. However, with several provincial appellate courts ruling in favour of same-sex marriage, the Chrétien government could not simply ignore the issue. As a result, the government was confronted with responding to an issue that, no matter how it was decided, would leave some of its supporters unhappy, making it a no-win decision. Hennigar finds that delegating decision making over same-sex marriage through a reference case provided the government with a viable political strategy to deal with the pressing issue of the constitutionality of nonheterosexual marriage.

The work by Hennigar, like that of Riddell and Morton, provides the initial theoretical pieces of the puzzle respecting strategic litigation and delegation by the executive in reference cases. This book builds on this work and carries it forward with a comparative approach that assesses multiple reference cases to take into consideration different situational and institutional factors that may cause a government to litigate strategically. That being said, this work helps to further show that the simple conception of activist courts as a force that runs counter to the goals of democratically elected officials in Canadian politics is not wholly accurate. Indeed, the strategic use of the reference power poses several theoretical problems for the role of judicial review in political disputes and in the delegation of decision making to courts.

The Possibilities of "Mischief and Inconvenience" Raised by the Reference Power

Although the reference power has been the subject of judicial scrutiny on only two occasions – *Reference re References* and *Secession Reference* – the courts noted in both cases that the power poses some complications for executive-judicial relations and judicial independence. Given how the reference process functions and the important role that many reference cases have played in many significant debates and controversies of Canadian politics, the reference power highlights several concerns.

First, in the absence of a live legal dispute, the reference power requires that the judiciary provide legal advice to the executive on existing or simply proposed government action in the abstract. Providing this advice is within the legal sphere, but it is a function routinely filled by the minister of justice/attorney general. Additionally, without a live case or controversy, this role is extrajudicial and is thus outside the routine adjudicative function of courts. This extrajudicial nature of references raises questions for the separation of the judiciary from the partisan branches of government, which poses complications for the separation of powers in Canada and the preservation of judicial independence.

Second, when the executive refers matters of public policy to the courts and then follows their advice, it effectively delegates its decision-making authority to the courts. At first glance, this delegation appears to run counter to the goals of a rational political actor that is primarily motivated by power attainment and maintenance. However, delegation to the courts can be a valuable political strategy that can provide means for political actors to avoid blame or legitimize their position. This delegation involves the courts in political and partisan debates, which like the extrajudicial nature of reference cases, can have negative implications for judicial independence. Moreover, this process helps to facilitate the use of reference litigation as a political strategy.

Third, unlike with routine litigation, courts do not have the power to grant leave in the case of references. Instead, courts must accept and hear any reference question put forward by the executive, regardless of whether the question conflicts with the standards of justiciability. Justiciability is best understood as the "set of judge-made rules, norms and principles delineating the scope of judicial intervention in social, political and economic life" (Sossin 2012, 7). In practice, when courts apply the standards of justiciability, they exercise a gatekeeping function to prevent the courts from wading into political controversies that lack substantial legal disputes. When we consider some of the political and highly salient matters that can become the subject of reference cases, the inability to apply the standards of justiciability and thus reject inappropriate reference questions elicits further concerns for the independence of the judiciary and the proper boundaries between courts and the partisan institutions of government.

Finally, relying on courts to deal with controversial issues or to avoid a difficult process in Parliament can result in a marginalization of the legislature in the policy-making process. If political and partisan disputes are considered by courts instead of legislatures, one of the implications is that these disputes are no longer the domain of democratically accountable legislators in a forum that is publicly accessible. Additionally, when executives circumvent the legislature and pivot to the courts to deal with political controversies, it furthers the centralization of power in the executive (i.e., the first minister and Cabinet) at the expense of the legislature. Not only does the resulting process further the judicialization of politics, but it also does so in a manner that subordinates legislators in the policy-making process.

Each of these concerns, or more pessimistically "mischiefs," that arise from the Canadian reference power and from the manner in which it is used by Canadian governments animates the discussion in the chapters that follow.

Contestation and Reference Cases 2

With its creation in 1875, the Canadian reference power has been a feature of Canadian politics almost since Confederation. During this time, governments have confronted a diverse array of political and social problems: two world wars, an economic depression, Quebec separatism, constitutional reform, the legal status of women, and the constitutionality of same-sex marriage, among many others. Such salient political and social issues often lead to legal controversies and constitutional questions, and Canadian governments have, on many occasions, sought the counsel of the courts through a reference case. Indeed, provincial and federal governments have resorted to the reference power over two hundred times since 1875. Many of these reference cases emerged from the leading political issues of the day. For example, during the period of constitutional reform spurred by the governments of Pierre Trudeau and Brian Mulroney in the 1980s and early 1990s, *Reference re Resolution to Amend the Constitution* [*Patriation Reference*], *Reference re Authority of Parliament in Relation to the Upper House* [*Upper House Reference*], and *Reference re Amendment to the Canadian Constitution* [*Quebec Veto Reference*] played an instrumental role in framing both the context and outcomes of political debates.[1]

The reference option has been an important dynamic that has shaped Canadian politics and the decisions made by Canadian governments.

As a result, it is important to understand the circumstances in which governments will rely on the reference power to help navigate the challenge of governing. In an attempt to ascertain the relationship between reference cases and the dynamics of Canadian politics over time, this chapter considers and analyzes all reference cases from 1875 to 2017, a total 209 cases, by engaging in a within-case analysis.

This analytical description of reference cases demonstrates that the number of references has varied greatly in a manner unrelated to the global expansion of judicial power that occurred in the latter half of the twentieth century (see Tate and Vallinder 1995). Instead, the variation in reference cases corresponds to important societal and economic events in Canadian politics rather than simply to the judicialization of politics, indicating the importance of temporality and context. In particular, the 1930s and the 1980s were two periods with a flurry of reference activity. Both decades saw significant transitions in Canadian politics and governance, which resulted in an increase of conflict between levels of government. Each of the high-reference periods examined below provides insight into the major concerns facing Canadian governments during the two decades, demonstrating how these concerns translated into reference case episodes. To explain the peak instances of Canadian reference cases, an appreciation for temporality and an understanding of concurrent events in Canadian politics are essential. This analysis is grounded in an understanding that timing and process are important to explaining a phenomenon that has multiple factors (Pierson 2004). In other words, it is necessary to recognize that the peaks in the use of reference cases over time do not exist in a vacuum; instead, they are reflective of other events taking place in Canadian political and constitutional history, such as the economic crisis of the 1930s and the mega constitutional politics of the 1980s.

Detailing the use of the reference power over time demonstrates that governments will seek an advisory opinion during periods of great political contestation to deal with a diverse range of issues – from banking regulations to constitutional amendment to labour policy – highlighting the many ways a reference case can be useful to a government when dealing with a political controversy. Finally, this chapter presents an overview of all Canadian reference cases across time, which provides an essential foundation for the empirical and theoretical analysis in subsequent chapters.

Canadian References over Time: 1875 to 2017

This chapter considers 209 reference cases, which include all references adjudicated by provincial appellate courts, the Supreme Court, and the Judicial Committee of the Privy Council (JCPC) from 1875 to 2017. The majority of cases in this dataset are from the Supreme Court of Canada (44 percent, 92 cases), whereas cases from provincial appellate courts comprise 29 percent (61 cases), with most cases coming from the appellate courts of Ontario (8.1 percent, 17 cases), Alberta (5.7 percent, 12 cases), and British Columbia (4.3 percent, 9 cases). These statistics mean that in almost 30 percent of the cases, a provincial government did not exercise its right to appeal to the Supreme Court following a decision of the provincial appellate court. Finally, cases from the JCPC comprise a total of 27 percent of the references (56 cases).

With regard to the distribution of cases across the various appellate courts, it is important to keep in mind that the federal reference power has been in operation longer than the provincial power and that many cases that begin in the provincial appellate courts will eventually end up in the Supreme Court of Canada. In this dataset, 41 of the Supreme Court cases (44.5 percent) originated in provincial appellate courts. Similarly, prior to 1949, many decisions of both the Supreme Court and the provincial appellate courts were further appealed to the JCPC. All JCPC cases in this dataset are appeals from either a provincial appellate court or the Supreme Court, as no government held the power to refer questions directly to the JCPC. Of the 56 references that were appealed to the JCPC, a majority (69.7 percent, 39 cases) originated at the Supreme Court of Canada, with 30.3 percent (17 cases) originating at provincial appellate courts.

Whereas the data above illustrate the most frequent sources for reference cases, they do not demonstrate the frequency with which each government initiated references. Figure 2.1 details the proportion of reference cases originated by each government. These data indicate that the federal government has been the most frequent initiator of reference cases from 1875 to the present. This finding should be expected given

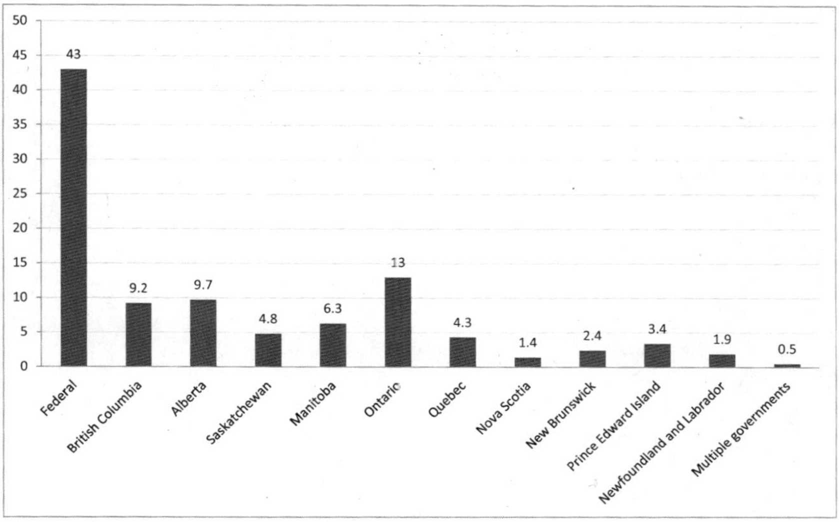

Figure 2.1 Percentage of reference cases initiated by each government, 1875–2017

Note: The category "multiple governments" refers to instances in which several provincial references were combined upon appeal to the Supreme Court or the JCPC, such as *Reference re Resolution to Amend the Constitution*, [1981] 1 SCR 753 [*Patriation Reference*].

that the federal reference power has existed longer than the provincial power and that the federal government has more legal resources and capacity compared to the provinces. The different rates of reference power usage between the federal and provincial governments are further discussed below.

To fully appreciate the trends associated with reference use by governments, it is best to look at the provinces collectively. This approach is taken for two reasons. First, grouping the provincial governments together allows for a better understanding and analysis of reference use over time. Second, a great number of references concern the constitutional division of powers between the federal government and all provincial governments, and to recognize the full implications of this dynamic of federalism, it is best to consider the provinces as one group. This collective assessment of provincial reference use is detailed in Figure 2.2. These data indicate that although the federal government initially used the reference power at a greater rate than the provinces, the provinces have begun to outpace the federal government.

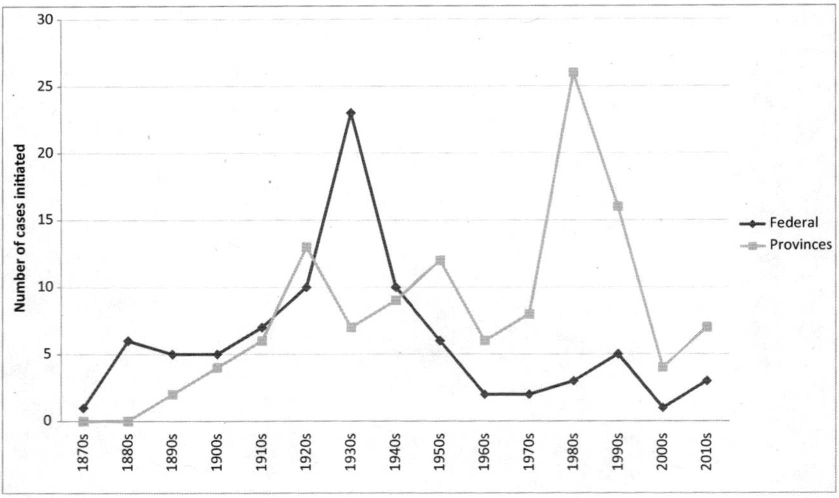

Figure 2.2 Federal and provincial references, 1875–2017

Three features of Figure 2.2 are important to note. First, even though the federal government created the reference power with the intention of using it, alongside the powers of reservation and disallowance, to limit the provinces, the reference power was generally used by the provinces at a rate similar to that of the federal government until the 1930s. Figure 2.2 demonstrates that the differences between the rate of use of the reference power by federal and provincial governments between the 1870s and 1890s are explained by the nonexistence of a provincial reference power until 1890. Since the creation of a provincial reference power in 1890, the difference between federal and provincial use has been minimal. Second, Figure 2.2 illustrates a stark increase in reference use by the federal government during the 1930s. The reference activity in the 1930s is a reflection of several circumstances unique to this period of Canadian political history, stemming largely from the economic crises of the Great Depression and the Dust Bowl. This era of reference use is the subject of an in-depth investigation below. Third, beginning in the 1940s, provincial governments began to use their reference powers at a much greater rate than the federal government. This is a trend that spiked in the 1980s and 1990s and carries through to the present day.

The more frequent use of the reference power by the federal government until 1940 could reflect several things. First, from Confederation to the mid-twentieth century, the federal government had more bureaucratic capacity than the provinces, providing it with greater legal, financial, and other resources than provincial governments, which can generally influence a government's decision to litigate (Hennigar 2007). Second, most obviously, that a greater proportion of cases originated with the federal government in the earlier period is consistent with the fact that the statute establishing the federal reference power has simply existed longer than comparable provincial statutes. Finally, the greater use of references by the federal government in the early era may reflect the original intent behind its creation of the reference power. As mentioned, the federal reference power was enacted as a means to control provincial legislation either instead of or in combination with the powers of reservation and disallowance (Rubin 1960; Smith 1983). A reference concerning provincial legislation can provide the federal government with the same ends as the disallowance power if the court invalidates the provincial law on the grounds that it is ultra vires. Thus the greater use of the reference power by the federal government is evidence of the larger trend in Canadian intergovernmental relations during this period toward a federal government that was more powerful than the provincial governments (Cameron and Simeon 2002). That being said, even with these explanations under consideration, it is important to note that the difference between provincial and federal use of the reference power from 1875 to 1940 is relatively minimal – excluding the significant anomaly of the 1930s.

Table 2.1 helps us to understand the rate at which governments have referred the actions of other governments to the courts for review. It demonstrates that both provincial and federal governments are quite willing to refer the legislation or action of the other government to the court – herein referred to as a cross-governmental reference. As displayed in Table 2.1, the federal government has referred provincial legislation in approximately 9 percent of all references, whereas provinces have referred federal government legislation in over 12 percent of all references. Taken together, these data demonstrate that 21.8 percent of all references

Table 2.1 Government initiating reference and statute or action referred

		Reference-initiating government		
		Provinces	*Federal*	*Total*
Statute or action under consideration	**Provincial**	85 (40.6%)	19 (9.2%)	104 (49.8%)
	Federal	27 (12.6%)	60 (29%)	87 (41.6%)
	Other[a]	6 (2.9%)	8 (3.9%)	14 (6.7%)
	Both[b]	2 (1%)	2 (1%)	4 (1.9%)
	Total	120 (57%)	89 (43%)	209 (100%)

Note: This analysis does not consider interprovincial reference cases as a separate category, where one province refers the action of another. This is a limitation of the binary coding used in this analysis.

a The *Secession Reference* is an example of a case coded as "other," as the Supreme Court was asked to assess, in the abstract, whether a province could unilaterally secede from the federation. The court was not referred a piece of legislation that provided a government the power to secede. Instead, the Supreme Court was asked to consider this question in light of domestic Canadian law and international law. Another example is *Reference re Mineral and Other Natural Resources of the Continental Shelf*, [1983] 145 DLR (3d) 9, 119 APR 27 [*Newfoundland Continental Shelf Reference*], where the Court of Appeal for Newfoundland and Labrador was asked to decide whether the province held authority over particular lands off the coast of Newfoundland and Labrador.

b Cases coded as "both" include those where a court was referred a series of questions that asked it to consider both provincial and federal legislation, as with *Reference re Agricultural Products Marketing Act*, [1978] 2 SCR 1198. In this case, the Supreme Court was referred questions that concerned the *Agricultural Products Marketing Act*, RSC 1970, c A-7, a federal statute, and the *Ontario Egg Order and Egg Marketing Levies*, SOR 72-743, a provincial statute.

have been cross-governmental references. This shows that governments regularly use the reference power to ask the courts to review the actions of other governments, illustrating an essential dynamic of federalism that characterizes a large portion of reference cases.

A recent example of a provincial government submitting the legislation of the federal government for review is *Reference re Bill C-7 Concerning the Reform of the Senate (QC)* [*Quebec Senate Reform Reference*].[2] In this case, Quebec referred the federal government's plan to reform the Senate by introducing term limits and consultative elections to the

Quebec Court of Appeal for constitutional review. The submission of the federal government's legislation provided the Government of Quebec an option to try to thwart or delay the federal government's unilateral attempts at Senate reform. The most recent example of a federal government using its reference power to send provincial government action to the Supreme Court for review also involved Quebec. In 1993 Kim Campbell's government referred Quebec legislation providing for a provincial sales tax that paralleled the newly enacted federal sales tax to the Supreme Court of Canada, arguing in *Reference re Quebec Sales Tax* [*Quebec Sales Tax Reference*] that the legislation was ultra vires the power of the province.[3] In both of these examples of cross-governmental reference cases, the courts sided with Quebec, with the Quebec Court of Appeal finding Bill C-7 unconstitutional and the Supreme Court of Canada finding Quebec's tax legislation a valid exercise of provincial constitutional power.

Other recent examples of a federal government referring the legislation or action of a provincial government are rare. It appears that federal governments have shied away from using references to challenge the legislation of provinces. Aside from the 1994 *Quebec Sales Tax Reference*, the next most recent examples include the 1992 and 1985 references concerning language rights in Manitoba.[4] However, aside from the Manitoba language references, to find another example of a federal government submitting provincial legislation to the Supreme Court, one must go back to 1957, when Louis St. Laurent's government referred Ontario legislation concerning the marketing of farm products within the province.[5]

To be sure, this does not mean that the federal government has not challenged the provinces in reference cases by intervening against provincial legislation, as in *Reference re Public Schools Act (Man)*, or by directly opposing provinces to defend its own legislation, as in *Reference re Assisted Human Reproduction Act*.[6] However, it does demonstrate that the overtly confrontational act of referring provincial legislation has largely fallen out of favour. This movement away from directly challenging provincial legislation mirrors the abandonment of the powers of reservation and disallowance by the federal government: disallowance has not been exercised since 1943, and reservation has not been used since 1961. According to Heard (2014), although the powers of reservation and disallowance have not been formally abolished, despite several attempts (e.g., the Charlottetown Accord of 1992), in practice they are essentially unavailable to the federal government. The effective termination of reservation and disallowance and the disuse of cross-governmental references by the federal government speaks to the change in the relationship between the provinces and Ottawa that occurred over the course of the twentieth century. The powers of reservation and disallowance and the federal use of cross-governmental references harken back to a period in Canadian federalism when the balance of power was in favour of the federal government and when provinces were in many ways subservient. The movement away from federal cross-governmental references also highlights the progression toward a collaborative approach to intergovernmental relations, where federalism is understood to be a relationship between two equal and autonomous orders of government (Cameron and Simeon 2002). As a result, cross-governmental references by the federal government may be less politically palatable in an era when the federal government is less likely to engage in a confrontational approach to intergovernmental relations.

This trend away from overtly challenging the legislation or action of another government in cross-governmental references is not present when assessing the actions of provincial governments in recent years. Since 2000, provincial governments have challenged Government of Canada legislation five times in provincial courts of appeal. Interestingly, four of the five examples involve Quebec challenging the federal government on a diverse range of legislative initiatives.[7] Along with the most recent example of the Senate reform legislation, Quebec has challenged Government of Canada policy concerning technologies of assisted human reproduction in *Reference re Assisted Human Reproduction Act,* unemployment insurance in *Reference re Employment Insurance Act (Can) ss 22 and 23,* and the reform of youth criminal justice in *Reference re Bill C-7 Respecting the Criminal Justice System for Young Persons (QC)*.[8] The last example of a provincial government engaging in a cross-governmental reference since 2000 is *Reference re Firearms Act (Can)* [*Firearms Reference*].[9] In this reference, Alberta challenged federal legislation providing for a national gun registry, claiming that it was not a valid exercise of the federal power over criminal law and that the legislation encroached on the provincial power related to property and civil rights. However, it is important to keep in mind that the practice of governments referring the statutes or actions of other governments is relatively uncommon. Indeed, the data provided in Table 2.1 demonstrate that the vast majority of references do not concern cross-governmental appeals.

The use of reference cases by Canadian governments has ebbed and flowed over time, as demonstrated in Figure 2.3. Clearly, some governments have been much more likely to refer questions to the courts in some periods than in others, with peak reference use in the 1930s and the 1980s. With respect to the trends in references over time, the high periods of cases do not appear for a single decade and then disappear; rather, the level of cases gradually peaks over time. As Figure 2.3 illustrates, the other high points in reference cases flank the two decades with the highest number of reference cases: the 1930s are preceded by the third highest number of references (1920s), and the 1980s are succeeded by the fourth highest number (1990s). The discussion that follows details the political dynamics of each peak reference decade, providing insight into the specific motivations that prompted governments to submit reference questions to appellate courts at a greater rate compared to all other periods in Canadian politics.

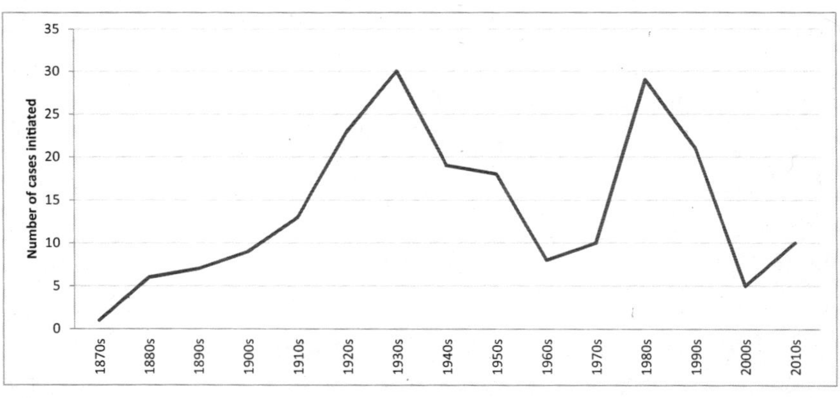

Figure 2.3 Canadian reference cases, 1875–2017

Reference Case High Point I: 1930s

In the 1930s both the federal and the provincial governments struggled to deal with the Great Depression, which led governments to use the reference power at a much greater rate than in all other decades since the power's inception in 1875. The policy choices by governments attempting to ameliorate the disastrous effects of the Depression within the confines of the Constitution characterize many of the political conflicts of this period and, of course, reference case jurisprudence. Political conflicts of this era spilled into the courts through references concerning many aspects of the New Deal legislation of R.B. Bennett's government and the Social Credit legislation of Alberta premier William Aberhart, most often at the hands of the government of Mackenzie King. It is not surprising to find that of all first ministers in Canada, King is credited with the highest number of reference cases, at 32 of 209 cases (15.3 percent) – a count that reflects not only the political environment of the period examined here but also the longevity of King's time as prime minister.[10]

The majority of cases during the 1930s (21 of 30 cases, 70 percent) asked the courts to consider the constitutional jurisdiction of the federal and provincial governments as provided in the *Constitution Act, 1867*, demonstrating that the reference jurisprudence of this decade was largely centred on issues of federalism.[11] In an effort to bring clarity to the many contours of Canadian federalism, disputes regarding constitutional jurisdiction or the division of powers ask the courts to consider whether a particular policy either proposed or enacted is intra vires or ultra vires the jurisdiction of the enacting government. This focus on the division of powers indicates that the references of this era were largely concerned with the powers of governments rather than with individual, group, or minority rights. Governments were not in the habit of asking the courts how a particular policy would impact individuals and their rights. During this decade, there were two cases that concerned the *Constitution Act, 1867*, but they did not present a question about division of powers: *Reference re Meaning of the Word "Persons"* [*Persons Case*] and *Reference re the Power of the Governor General in Council to Disallow Provincial Legislation and the Power of the Reservation of a Lieutenant-Governor of a Province* [*Powers of Disallowance and Reservation Reference*].[12] That being said, both cases were primarily concerned with the powers of governments. The *Persons Case* was a statutory interpretation case that concerned the powers of the federal government to appoint senators. The *Powers of Disallowance and Reservation Reference* also concerned the powers of governments, as it originated in the dispute between the Alberta Social Credit government and the King government. Both of these cases are considered in greater detail below.

The Great Depression References

In an attempt to deal with the economic depression of the early 1930s, the Bennett government introduced several statutes often referred to as Bennett's "New Deal," a reference to similar policy efforts put forward by President Franklin D. Roosevelt in the United States. The Bennett government introduced eight different pieces of New Deal legislation. The early Bennett New Deal involved two acts that attempted to protect agricultural producers. The *Farmers' Creditors Arrangement Act* allowed farmers to negotiate a compromise with creditors that would allow them to stay on their land when falling into debt, to be enforced through the courts.[13] The *Natural Products Marketing Act* aimed to improve the distribution and marketing of produce through the enforcement of legally binding marketing schemes, with the goal of decreasing the discrepancy between the price paid by consumers and the producer's production costs (McConnell 1968).[14]

Other pieces of the Bennett New Deal involved four statutes enacted in 1935 that were aimed at implementing conventions adopted by the General Conference of the International Labour Organization, an aspect of the *Treaty of Peace between the Allied and Associated Powers and Germany* [Treaty of Versailles]. The *Weekly Rest in Industrial Undertakings Act*, the *Limitation of Hours of Work Act*, the *Employment and Social Insurance Act*, and the *Minimum Wages Act* introduced various protections for workers, including the creation of national labour standards and unemployment insurance.[15] The *Weekly Rest in Industrial Undertakings Act* required that workers be provided with a twenty-four-hour rest period per every seven days worked. The *Limitation of Hours of Work Act* provided for an eight-hour workday and a forty-eight-hour workweek for industrial labourers, with exceptions for urgency. The *Employment and Social Insurance Act* provided unemployment benefits to workers who had previously contributed to the fund for a minimum of forty weeks. And the *Minimum Wages Act* provided the governor in council the power to establish a minimum wage in "rateable trades," a category that could be defined by the governor in council. These acts comprised the treaty-related New Deal legislation.[16]

The last aspects of the Bennett New Deal included the government's two statutory responses to the 1935 report of the Royal Commission on Price Spreads. The first involved an amendment to section 498A of the *Criminal Code of Canada*, which prohibited discriminatory and predatory trading practices.[17] The second statute, the *Dominion Trade and Industry Commission Act*, was primarily concerned with creating a commission with jurisdiction over the *Combines Investigation Act* and other statutes related to the regulation of trade.[18]

While in Opposition in Parliament, the Liberal Party led by King was opposed to the New Deal legislation as a matter of partisanship and out of concern regarding the legality of the legislation (McConnell 1968). However, the Liberals framed their opposition to the various legislative schemes within a constitutional argument, contending that many of the provisions encroached on provincial jurisdiction (McConnell 1968; Neatby 1976). The early New Deal legislation was enacted on questionable constitutional grounds, as the *Natural Products Marketing Act* and the *Farmers' Creditors Arrangement Act* appeared to regulate local transactions, a matter of provincial jurisdiction.[19] The treaty-related legislation also raised questions regarding constitutionality, as it concerned property and civil rights, a power solely under the jurisdiction of the provinces. Finally, the price-spread enactments were problematic for two reasons. First, even though the federal government has an expansive power over criminal law, the amendments to the Criminal Code appeared to infringe on "property and civil rights" and on the regulation of individual industries and trades, both matters of provincial jurisdiction. Second, the *Dominion Trade and Industry Commission Act* raised concerns because it appeared to engage in the administration of justice and to intervene in the "contract and civil rights of individuals and corporations," again a provincial responsibility (Hart 1991, 44).

The Liberal Party struggled with how to deal with its opposition to the Bennett New Deal. King did not want to appear opposed to labour reform regardless of his partisan opposition to Bennett and his uncertainty about the constitutionality of the legislation (Neatby 1976, 93). To deal with the tensions between the concerns over the constitutional compliance of the New Deal and the equally important concerns over public opinion, the Liberals promised in the 1935 election campaign to send the New Deal legislation to the Supreme Court for review in a reference case. After winning a majority government, King and the Liberals returned to power and shortly thereafter referred the eight statutes to the Supreme Court, resulting in six different reference cases.[20]

To be sure, using the reference power to test the constitutionality of the New Deal was not the only option available to the King government. Alternatively, it could have waited for the provinces to challenge the legislation themselves through references in the provincial courts of appeal. If the King government had not wanted to wait for the provinces to act, it could simply have repealed or amended the legislation through an act of Parliament. Of course, the latter is almost always an option for a government faced with statutes it opposes. Instead, for several reasons, the more optimal political strategy was to refer the legislation to the Supreme Court. First, it allowed the King government the power to shape and frame the dispute, as it could draft the questions and structure the terms of the reference. If King had waited for the provinces to challenge the legislation, the cases would have been framed by the provincial governments and might not have reflected the specific concerns of the King government. Second, a reference at the Supreme Court would address the issue in a more direct and timely manner, as the provincial appellate decisions would have been almost certainly appealed to the Supreme Court in the end. Finally, simply repealing the legislation would have exposed the government to anti-labour criticism and would likely have required the government to fill the void left by the repealed laws by putting forward its own response to the Depression. As McConnell (1968) explains, the references not only placed the decision out of the hands of the government but also provided it time to create an alternative legislative scheme for dealing with the economic crisis.

In the six New Deal references, eight Acts were subject to judicial scrutiny, and only two Acts emerged from the Supreme Court unscathed. The Supreme Court found the *Farmers' Creditors Arrangement Act* and section 498A of the Criminal Code to be fully within the constitutional jurisdiction of the federal government. Two Acts, the *Employment and Social Insurance Act* and the *Natural Products Marketing Act,* were found to be entirely ultra vires the jurisdiction of the Parliament of Canada, with a unanimous court in the latter reference. The court unanimously found several sections of the *Dominion Trade and Industry Commission Act* to be ultra vires, effectively nullifying the legislation in practice. In the *Labour Conventions Reference,* the court was divided three to three on the constitutionality of the remaining three pieces of legislation – the *Minimum Wages Act, Limitation of Hours of Work Act,* and *Weekly Rest in Industrial Undertakings Act* – all of which originated in the International Labour Organization and therefore hinged on the interpretation of the treaty-making power of the Parliament of Canada.[21] As only six justices heard the references, the final pieces of New Deal legislation remained at a standstill.

The Supreme Court decisions were appealed to the JCPC, not because the King government was unhappy with the result at the Supreme Court but because the final appeal would end all uncertainty about the constitutionality of the New Deal legislation.[22] Moreover, the government was confident that the decisions of the Supreme Court would be affirmed by the JCPC, which turned out to be an accurate prediction. The JCPC found five pieces of the Bennett New Deal to be ultra vires the jurisdiction of the Parliament of Canada. Both the *Natural Products Marketing Act* and the *Employment and Social Insurance Act* were again found to be constitutionally invalid. Unlike the Supreme Court's even divide in the *Labour Conventions Reference*, the JCPC's finding that all three statutes were ultra vires provided clarity. The *Farmers' Creditors Arrangement Act* and section 498A of the Criminal Code were again found to be valid, affirming the previous findings of the Supreme Court. However, there was one point of departure from the Supreme Court, as the JCPC found the *Dominion Trade and Industry Commission Act* to be valid, reversing the Canadian high court.

Even though the JCPC decisions effectively limited federal powers, making it difficult for the federal government to pursue social reform in the future,[23] King took satisfaction in the confirmation that he was "correct" regarding the constitutionality of Bennett's New Deal (Neatby 1976).[24] Through effective (and politically savvy) use of the reference power, the King government was able to achieve its goal of largely voiding the Bennett legislation, while not having to appear anti-labour in the process. However, reaction to the JCPC decision was not all favourable. Instead, the imperial judicial body appeared to be preventing the Government of Canada from responding to the economic disaster that was the Depression. Indeed, the undoing of much of the New Deal legislation by the JCPC fuelled sentiment for the abolition of appeals to the JCPC (McConnell 1968; Cairns 1971).

The New Deal references demonstrate how political actors can rely on the judiciary to deal with politically contentious matters, instead of using more routine political channels. The New Deal references allowed the Liberal government to achieve its goal of invalidating the previous government's legislation without having to take a public stance against labour and employment protections that could have been politically disastrous. As Snell and Vaughan (1985, 165) argue, the references allowed the King government not only to avoid any public backlash but also to redirect public discord toward the court, resulting in a "political exploitation of the reference system." Despite the fact that the King government had referred Government of Canada policy and lost at the Supreme Court and the JCPC, King did not appear disappointed with the invalidations by the courts (Cairns 1971). King would resort to the strategic use of the reference power again in his clashes with the Social Credit government in Alberta.

The Social Credit References

When the courts invalidated several parts of the Bennett New Deal, there was a legislative void left behind. Provincial governments were faced with the challenge of filling the gap in national social and economic policy left by the Great Depression references, often without the fiscal capacity to do so. To this end, the Alberta Social Credit Party, led by William Aberhart with a commanding majority (56 of 63 seats), introduced a series of sweeping legislative reforms in the Alberta legislature. The Social Credit Party supported a policy program based on distrust and hostility toward financial institutions and the interests of creditors. Support for the Social Credit Party was largely comprised of lower-middle-class and agrarian individuals. One of the goals of the party was to increase individual purchasing power on the grounds that all individuals have a right to communally produced wealth (Mallory 1976, 183).

The Social Credit legislative program began to take shape in 1937 through the introduction of three acts: the *Credit of Alberta Regulation Act*, the *Bank Employee Civil Rights Act*, and the *Judicature Act Amendment Act*.[25] Each of these Acts raised serious questions of constitutionality. The *Credit of Alberta Regulation Act* transferred control over licensing of banks to the province and created a Social Credit Board to oversee the activities of the banks. The *Bank Employee Civil Rights Act* prevented bank employees and banks from seeking legal redress from the courts. And the *Judicature Act Amendment Act* prohibited the courts from questioning any provincial government legislation. Whereas the first two pieces of legislation were a direct attack on the federal power over banking provided by section 91 of the *British North America Act, 1867*, the third Act was a direct affront to the rights of individual Albertans. Although this questionable legislative triad had received royal assent from the lieutenant governor general of Alberta, it resulted in the resignation of the provincial attorney general, John Hugill (Mallory 1976).

More importantly, the three pieces of legislation caught the attention of the King government, which disallowed all three Acts after they had been in force for a mere ten days. Aberhart reacted to the disallowance by passing a resolution that the federal power of disallowance no longer existed. Following Aberthart's resolution, the Social Credit government reintroduced the *Credit Act* but changed the bodies affected by the Act from "banks" to "credit institutions" and passed the *Bank Taxation Bill*, which imposed a substantial levy on reserve funds and paid-up capital, with the goal of eliminating or severely limiting banks in the province (Neatby 1976).[26] To silence dissent, Aberhart took the additional step of passing the *Accurate News and Information Bill*, which required newspapers to provide sources for any news item at the request of the government and to publish any governmental statement in full (Mallory

1976; Neatby 1976).[27] Once again, the Aberhart government had gained the unwanted attention of Ottawa, which responded by reserving the three new pieces of provincial legislation.

This chain of political events provoked the referral of the reserved bills to the Supreme Court by the King government, accompanied by a separate reference case that asked the court to rule on the constitutionality of the powers of reservation and disallowance.[28] The six-member panel of the Supreme Court unanimously held that the federal powers of reservation and disallowance were valid powers that were not in disrepute, regardless of their infrequent use in recent years. Furthermore, the federal powers of disallowance and reservation were largely unfettered and subject to few limitations. For the specific statutes referred, the court held that the Acts were ultra vires and voted unanimously to strike them down, which was later affirmed by the JCPC. Like the New Deal references, the Supreme Court was placed directly in the middle of a political conflict by King, and once again it vindicated the political goals of King and the federal government.

Strategic Litigation in the 1930s

The references by the King government to the Supreme Court in the 1930s confirmed not only the utility of the reference power but also the political utility of the court itself (Mallory 1976; Snell and Vaughn 1985). Through these two episodes, with the aid of his extremely capable minister of justice, Ernest Lapointe, King was able to measure the constitutionality of the legislative schemes of opponents and reap the benefits of a reference from the Supreme Court of Canada. In the first instance, referral of the New Deal legislation not only enabled the King government to challenge the Acts of the previous government but also allowed it to avoid appearing anti-labour. By submitting the references to the Supreme Court, the King government was able to shape the terms of the debate with a greater amount of power than would have been possible if provinces had initiated references at provincial courts of appeal or if the laws had been repealed in Parliament. Similarly, effective use of the reference power by the King government in its response to the Alberta Social Credit government not only quashed the legislation that challenged the jurisdiction of the federal government but also allowed

King to shape the debate while relying on the courts to sort out the political conflict.

The federal government is credited with the majority of references during the 1930s: only 7 of the 30 references during this decade were instigated by provincial governments.[29] Other cases of note during this decade involve *Reference re the Regulation and Control of Aeronautics in Canada* [*Aeronautics Reference*], which concerned the scope of the federal residual power held in the "Peace, order, and good government" clause of the *British North America Act, 1867*.[30] The *Aeronautics Reference* was a favourable decision for the federal government, holding that the negotiations of the Treaty of Versailles by the federal government concerning the regulation of aerial navigation were constitutional. The JCPC's decision in the *Aeronautics Reference* provided support for federal paramountcy when conflicts arise regarding the division of powers between the federal government and the provinces, and it is an example of the national dimensions test of the "Peace, order, and good government" clause.[31] It was this reading of the treaty-making power that Bennett believed supported his government's legislation regarding minimum wage and hours of work, which was tested by the courts in *Reference re Minimum Wages Act, Limitation of Hours of Work Act, Weekly Rest in Industrial Undertakings Act* (Neatby 1976).[32] However, the Supreme Court and the JCPC found that the treaty-making power did not extend to civil matters. The JCPC decisions on the New Deal legislation signalled the move away from the interpretation of federal power provided by the *Aeronautics Reference* and a greater respect for provincial constitutional jurisdiction.

Another important reference of this era was *Reference re Meaning of the Word "Persons"* [*Persons Case*], which was considered by the JCPC in 1930, making it one of the earliest cases in this decade. As a case that concerned individual and minority rights, this case stands apart from other cases of this era. The *Persons Case* asked whether women were considered "qualified persons" in the Canadian Constitution, with a focus on the provision that outlined appointments to the Senate. That being said, as L'Heureux-Dubé (2000b) notes, this case made very little mention of the real issue of the case: discrimination against women. What is most influential about this case is the means by which the JCPC concluded that women are indeed considered "persons." Instead of relying on legislative intent, the author of the decision, Lord Chancellor John Sankey, explained that the Constitution can be viewed as a "living tree capable of growth and expansion within its natural limits."[33] This reasoning was based on the fact that Parliament had not explicitly used the word "men" but instead had used "person," a term that could also include women. Additionally, by this time most women could vote (except for most Indigenous women and except in Quebec provincial elections) and were entitled to sit as members of Parliament. The living tree approach first described in this reference has expanded far beyond its immediate use in the *Persons Case* and has become an influential line of constitutional interpretation. The living tree approach has influenced a broad reading of "civil rights," as provided in the *Constitution Act, 1867,* as a means to foster provincial human rights codes in a manner far beyond its original purpose. Furthermore, it underpins much of the jurisprudence respecting the *Canadian Charter of Rights and Freedoms* that has taken a broad interpretation of rights (Manfredi 2001, 190).

In comparison to Canadian reference cases across all decades, the *Persons Case* stands as an anomaly, as it is one of the only examples where a reference case has been used to protect the rights of a minority and one of the few cases in the 1930s that did not exclusively focus on the powers of governments. However, it should be noted that this was not the intended effect of the case. Instead, the JCPC's decision was primarily concerned with interpreting the meaning of the word "persons" and with determining whether this term could include women as well as men. As a result, if the law under consideration by the JCPC had explicitly stated "men," not "persons," it is likely that women would not have been protected by its decision. Furthermore, it is important to remember that even though this case effectively extended a right to a minority group, this case was still essentially about government power – specifically the power (and indeed the right) of the governor general to appoint women to the Senate.

During the 1930s, governments in Canada found it necessary or a valuable political strategy to seek a reference opinion from Canadian courts at a greater rate than in any other decade. As detailed above, a significant number of these references were the result of the political manoeuvring of the King government, which was able to effectively use the reference power to achieve several political goals. First, the King government was successful in blocking the implementation of Bennett's New Deal legislation without appearing anti-labour and anti-reform. In this instance, the reference acted as a stopgap measure because it invalidated the legislation and did not require the government to immediately fill the legislative void. References were also used efficiently by King to respond to three policies of the Social Credit government that invaded federal jurisdiction. These cases prevented the Aberhart government from implementing its policies and made it clear that the federal government was willing to protect its legislative jurisdiction through the courts.

The high number of cases during the 1930s fundamentally reflected the political episodes of that decade. Regarding this period, Mallory (1976, 181) explains, "A particular judicial decision in a particular case, or even a body of case-law made up of a series of decisions, does not take place in a vacuum in which the result is a simple arithmetical conclusion from purely abstract data." Instead, the references of the 1930s not only reflected the central priority of the period – the Depression and economic regulation – but also demonstrate the difficulties of applying the constitutional division of powers to various problems, such as the making of treaties, the recognition of minority rights, and the expansion of social reform. Beyond the fact that the cases often concerned major debates between governments, their increase in number reflected a period of greater political contestation when more issues were open for consideration. Use of the reference power by governments to initiate judicial review as a means to deal with political conflicts was carried forward in Canadian political history and is again demonstrated in the following discussion of the other high period of Canadian reference cases, the 1980s.

Reference Case High Point II: 1980s

During the 1980s, governments sought a reference opinion from either an appellate court or the Supreme Court of Canada on 29 separate occasions. Looking at this period in combination with the successive decade (see Figure 2.3) shows that the spike in reference case activity directly corresponds to a period that Russell (2004) associates with "mega constitutional" politics. Mega constitutional politics refers to a specific period in Canadian politics when constitutional politics were highly emotional, intense, and concerned with issues at the very foundation of the political community. Many of the issues that arise during times of mega constitutional politics relate to questions of identity and the stability of the nation-state. This style of politics is distinguished from routine constitutional politics because it concerns large theoretical questions, instead of addressing more technical constitutional reform (Russell 2004, 75). Mega constitutional politics in Canada has four different sources: Canadian nationalism, Quebec nationalism, regionalism, and Indigenous self-government (Lusztig 1994; Russell 2004). These four forces are often in conflict with one another, seeking distinct ends. With the competing understandings of sovereignty, constitutional discussions become intense and passionate, and constitutional change is incredibly difficult (Lusztig 1994; Manfredi and Lusztig 1998).

The height of mega constitutional politics in Canada was during the 1980s and the 1990s (Russell 2004, 74–75). Three different constitutional proposals and negotiations took place during this period. First, there were the 1981 constitutional negotiations and the proposals adopted in the Meech Lake Accord of 1987 and the Charlottetown Accord of 1992. Second, Quebec nationalism and separatism were intensified with the 1995 referendum, the reference case regarding the legality and constitutionality of the secession of Quebec, and the resulting *Act to Give Effect to the Requirement for Clarity as Set Out in the Opinion of the Supreme Court of Canada in the Quebec Secession Reference* [*Clarity Act*].[34] Regionalism was also a key factor, with the 1993 election seeing the emergence of the Bloc Québécois, a separatist party, as the official Opposition and the electoral breakthrough of the Reform Party of Canada, a party rooted in sentiments of alienation in the western provinces (Flanagan 2009). Third, Indigenous self-government and rights made inroads into national debates through the rejection of the Meech Lake Accord under the leadership of Elijah Harper in Manitoba, the Oka Crisis in Quebec, and the participation of Indigenous groups in patriation and the drafting of the *Constitution Act, 1982,* which included a recognition of Aboriginal and treaty rights in section 35.[35]

In this era of mega constitutional politics, political episodes spilled over into the courts both directly and indirectly through 50 reference cases, almost one-quarter of the entire number of reference cases in Canadian history. The indirect impact of mega constitutional politics is reflected in cases that concerned some of the same issues that gave rise to disputes between the provinces and the federal government during the constitutional negotiations, such as disagreements over natural resources. The direct impact is reflected in references that originated directly out of a mega constitutional episode, like *Reference re Resolution to Amend the Constitution* [*Patriation Reference*].

Another important feature of this era, which influenced not only the number of reference cases but also the subject of cases, was the rise in executive federalism. Executive federalism involves a process of intergovernmental negotiation between the executives (i.e., prime minister, premiers, and members of Cabinet), which is often removed from both public participation and scrutiny (Watts 1989; Meekison, Telford, and Lazar 2003). Executive federalism relies on high-level discussions between executives of governments often in the form of first ministers' conferences. Along with a lack of public participation, executive federalism contributes to the centralization of power within Canadian parliamentary government, as it often does not provide a role for the legislative branch and backbench parliamentarians (Savoie 1999). Indeed, it is executive federalism that provides the vehicle for the many episodes of mega constitutional politics, best illustrated through the 1981 constitutional negotiations and the Meech Lake and Charlottetown Accords.[36] The expansion of executive federalism has occurred alongside the growth of government activity and priorities in policy spheres that cut across jurisdictional boundaries. This expansion not only distorts the division of constitutional jurisdiction between governments but also means that a policy change at one level of government can have a significant impact on another government and its legislative agenda (Meekison, Telford, and Lazar 2003).

Given these features, it is not surprising that there was a corresponding increase in reference cases during the height of executive federalism. The reference case process shares many of the features of executive federalism and extends this style of intergovernmental relations into the courts. As mentioned previously, the decision to pursue a reference is made at the highest level of the executive through Cabinet and does not involve the participation of members of the legislature or the public. Additionally, as constitutionally defined jurisdictions become less clear, an advisory opinion can prove to be an extremely valuable policy-making tool that provides guidance to governments. As discussed below, the majority of references during this era concerned governmental power and the relations between governments, regardless of the fact that the Charter became an intervening factor during this decade. This finding further demonstrates that the reference procedure is an effective tool of political elites rather than rights-seeking Charter groups (see A.C. Cairns 1992).

The focus on the powers of governments in references during the 1930s is a trend that was carried through into the 1980s. A majority of the 29 reference cases (over 55 percent) during the 1980s concerned the *Constitution Act, 1867* and disputes over federal and provincial jurisdiction. With the focus on constitutional questions and the powers of governments, only a small portion of the cases (just under 14 percent) concerned issues of statutory interpretation. Although the Charter became an important factor during this decade in Canadian politics, it did not have a big impact on the references of this era, comprising approximately one-quarter of the cases (24.1 percent). This finding is interesting given the important arguments made by A.C. Cairns (1992) regarding the differences between Canada's two constitutional documents. According to Cairns, the *Constitution Act, 1982* is the citizens' Constitution, being concerned with individual and collective rights and with limiting governmental power. In comparison, the *Constitution Act, 1867* is centrally a government Constitution, being primarily concerned with defining the power of governments and the division of powers between governments, thus leaving no room for citizens. Cairns argues that following the introduction of the 1982 Constitution and the Charter, the debate shifted by opening up to include the participation of individual citizens and groups. This democratization of constitutional debates, which occurs in non-reference Charter-based litigation, was not replicated within the reference cases of this era. Indeed, as the reference power is solely the tool of governments, it continued to be a site of executive federalism and did not demonstrate the greater shift toward individual rights and post-materialist values that occurred in the courts in general following the Charter's adoption.

References on the Politics of Constitutional Negotiation and Reform

Reference re Authority of Parliament in Relation to the Upper House [*Upper House Reference*] was the first case of the 1980s, and as a case considering the complete transformation of Parliament, it set the tone for the constitutional reform cases of the 1980s. This case is one of the first examples of discussions of constitutional reform making their way into the courts during the era of mega constitutional politics. Yet this case did not appear out of a void. The provincial election of the Parti Québécois in the fall of 1976 and the very real prospect of Quebec separatism pushed the Canadian Constitution back into the public debate, leaving the federal and other provincial governments with little choice but to participate (Russell 2004, 92). The Trudeau government introduced Bill C-60, a unilateral attempt by the federal government to launch constitutional change and reform of the Senate, as little progress was being made during negotiations with the provinces (McMurtry 1982). Bill C-60 was quite ambitious: not only did it propose to fundamentally change the Senate to a "House of Federation" that would split appointments between the provinces and Ottawa,[37] but it also proposed a charter of rights, a domestic constitutional amending formula, constitutionally entrenching the Supreme Court of Canada, and limiting the power of the executive (see Desserud 2009).

The *Upper House Reference* was born out of the conflict over constitutional reform between Ottawa and the provinces. In this case, the Supreme Court of Canada was asked two multipart questions that concerned the reform of the Senate through various mechanisms, such as the selection method of members, tenure, and the representation of provinces and territories. Although the Trudeau government submitted the reference questions, this action was in response to the opposition of provincial governments to the proposed reform package (Mendelsohn 2013). Ultimately, this reference provided the Supreme Court with one of the first opportunities to advise the federal government on how to amend the Constitution vis-à-vis the amending powers of Westminster.

In a unanimous decision, the court found the unilateral reform of the Senate by the federal government to be outside its constitutional jurisdiction. The court found, contrary to the arguments put forward by the attorney general of Canada, that section 91(1) does not provide Parliament the power to unilaterally amend the Constitution in regards to the Senate.[38] Instead, Parliament's ability to amend the Senate is limited to "housekeeping," as provinces have a legitimate interest in the functioning of the Senate since its role is (ostensibly) regional representation. The implication of this finding is that changes to the constitutional role of the Senate cannot be duly enacted without the participation of the provinces.

The *Upper House Reference* essentially blocked the Trudeau government's plan for constitutional change, but it did not quell the desire for constitutional reform. Although the calls for constitutional change became more subdued following the reference, the re-election of the Trudeau Liberals in Ottawa and the lead-up to the 1980 referendum campaign in Quebec pushed constitutional reform back onto the bargaining table, this time with more force than ever before (Russell 2004). Speaking at a rally just days before the referendum vote in Quebec, Trudeau promised that a "No" vote for sovereignty would ensure the return to constitutional negotiations and a renewal of the Constitution. Executive-level negotiations did resume following the success of the "No" campaign, but they were ultimately ineffective. The impasse in negotiations was met with a public announcement from Trudeau that the federal government would proceed unilaterally with constitutional reform and patriation. It should be noted that, prior to Trudeau's declaration, although provinces were often consulted when constitutional amendments affected their powers, the provincial role in amendment was subject to dispute, and the federal practice of obtaining provincial consent was inconsistent (Brandt 1982; Hogg 1992). Although some argued that a convention requiring provincial consultation had developed, the necessity of unanimity among the provinces was contested (Lederman 1966; Knopff 1981).[39] To be sure, it was generally accepted that Trudeau's proposed amendments, specifically the charter of rights and a constitutional amending formula, had clear implications for provincial powers (Hogg 1992).

Understandably, the public declaration by Trudeau was not met with enthusiasm by the governments of several provinces. Quebec, Manitoba, and Newfoundland submitted references to their respective provincial appellate courts, which questioned the constitutionality of the federal government's declaration of unilateral amendment as a matter of both law and constitutional convention (Mandel 1994). These references are remarkable for two reasons. First, it was generally agreed that the proposed amendments did conventionally require the consent of the provinces (Hogg 1992; Mandel 1994). As a result, the three provinces were seeking a reference opinion from the courts to confirm what was generally already accepted. This manoeuvre not only directly implicated the courts in the political conflict but also spoke to the power of a pronouncement from the courts as a strategic mechanism for protecting a particular position within a political debate. Second, these references mark the first time that courts were asked to make a ruling on the existence of a constitutional convention (i.e., a norm of political behaviour that has been accepted over time), which in Canadian law is considered nonjusticiable and outside the purview of the courts (Russell 1983; Mandel 1994).

The provincial appellate courts returned conflicting answers to the reference cases: Quebec and Manitoba, in divided decisions, ruled in favour of the unilateral move, whereas Newfoundland was unanimously opposed.[40] All three provincial references were further appealed to the Supreme Court and combined in the *Patriation Reference*. This case garnered more attention from the public and media than any other episode in the court's history up to this point (Snell and Vaughan 1985). As Russell (2011) notes, this case marks the first and last instance in which the court released a decision on live television. In the end, the *Patriation Reference* did not fully propel the federal government forward with amendment, nor did it block the unilateral movement by Trudeau. Neither side could be fully satisfied with the outcome.[41]

The court unanimously held that the constitutional reform package concerned provincial power, but this was the only aspect of the decision that provided a clear direction. The court was asked whether either law or constitutional convention prohibited the patriation of the Constitution without provincial consent. Addressing constitutional conventions, six of the justices found that "a substantial degree of provincial consent" was necessary but did not define what constituted "a substantial degree." The majority found that the federal government could legally submit a resolution to the United Kingdom's Parliament to unilaterally amend the *British North America Act, 1867,* but doing so would offend the constitutional convention of needing "significant" provincial consent. More specifically, because the formal power to amend the Canadian Constitution (technically a British statute) still resided with Westminster, the majority's decision was limited to examining the power of the Canadian Parliament to pass such a resolution without the participation of the provinces. The majority concluded that there was no limit on the power of the Parliament of Canada to submit such a resolution.

The Supreme Court's decision in the *Patriation Reference* was highly criticized by scholarly commentators (see Snell and Vaughan 1985; Mandel 1994; and Russell 2004, 2011) largely because of the opacity of the court's reasoning, which did not provide a clear direction to either party in the debate. Additionally, many commentators disapproved of the court's willingness to address matters of constitutional convention, which are not enforceable by law. The court's consideration of convention not only occurred with a lack of precedent (Mandel 1994) but also inserted the court into a highly political debate on the basis of addressing conventions, an extrajudicial matter that was thought to be beyond the purview of courts (Snell and Vaughan 1985; Russell 2011). The opaqueness of this decision did not stop political actors, including Trudeau, from respecting the findings of the court (Russell 2004). Even though the decision did not find a clear winner in the political conflict over patriation, it forced the parties back to the bargaining table. The return to negotiation eventually resulted in a constitutional package that received the support of all provinces, except Quebec, in November 1981.

The absence of Quebec support for the 1981 agreement led to the final constitutional negotiation reference case of this era, *Reference re Amendment to the Canadian Constitution* [*Quebec Veto Reference*]. As a result of the November 1981 agreement, the Government of Quebec sent the following question to the Quebec Court of Appeal: "Is the consent of the Province of Quebec constitutionally required, by convention, for the adoption by the Senate and the House of Commons of a resolution the purpose of which is to cause the Canadian Constitution to be amended."[42] Additionally, Quebec asked the Court of Appeal whether unanimity for constitutional amendment was required, even though the Supreme Court had already considered this specific issue in the *Patriation Reference*. The Court of Appeal found that, as a matter of convention, the consent of Quebec was not required for the constitutional amendment. This ruling was then appealed to the Supreme Court. Unlike in the previous decision regarding constitutional amendment, the Supreme Court provided a unanimous decision with a clear direction in the *Quebec Veto Reference:* Quebec did not hold a veto over constitutional amendments. As the *Constitution Act, 1982* was already in place by the time the Supreme Court rendered its decision, the *Quebec Veto Reference* did not receive the same attention as its predecessor, the *Patriation Reference*. That being said, according to Russell (2011), the decision helped to provide the impetus that led to the highly contested 1995 sovereignty referendum. The *Quebec Veto Reference* demonstrates that reference cases and episodes of mega constitutional politics are often part of a much larger political dispute beyond the specific legal questions decided by courts in the immediate case.

Intergovernmental Conflict References

The constitutional negotiation cases are part of a larger trend in disputes between governments in Canada in the 1980s. Indeed, conflicts between governments resulted in several federalism-based reference cases during this decade. One recurring theme in these cases is a dispute over the division of powers as concerns the management and ownership of natural resources. This pattern is indicative of the disputes between provinces and the federal government over natural resources that began in the 1970s and were intensified by the 1973 OPEC oil crisis. As Cairns, Chandler, and Moull (1985) explain, when negotiations between governments stalled or a strong case could be made, legal actions in the courts (including references) were an essential "bargaining chip" in disputes over natural resources. Six references during this decade concerned disputes over the division of powers and the control, ownership, and regulation of natural resources, often between the federal and provincial governments.[43] However, *Reference re Upper Churchill Water Rights Reversion Act* was a dispute between Newfoundland and Quebec, and

Reference re Mining and Mineral Rights Tax Act [*Mining and Mineral Rights Reference*] was a reference born out of a conflict between Newfoundland and several corporations.[44]

Three cases – *Reference re Mineral and Other Natural Resources of the Continental Shelf* [*Newfoundland Continental Shelf Reference*]; *Reference re Seabed and Subsoil of the Continental Shelf Offshore Newfoundland* [*Seabed and Subsoil Reference*]; and *Reference re Ownership of the Bed of the Strait of Georgia and Related Areas* – concerned the ownership of specific areas of land and the natural resources associated with those areas of land.[45] The first two considered the coast of Newfoundland and Labrador, whereas the third concerned the coast of British Columbia. Each case asked the courts to grant ownership over the lands to either the federal or provincial government, as jurisdiction over the specified areas would be an economic asset with the expansion of oil and gas development (Hildreth 1991). These cases are symptomatic of the Canadian approach to offshore federalism and demonstrate that because of jurisdictional disputes, Canadian governments have relied on a patchwork, or case-by-case, approach rather than comprehensive legislation (Hildreth 1991; Juda 2003). The case-by-case approach has encouraged litigation on behalf of the provinces to settle disputes over jurisdiction, which has proven a profitable strategy for coastal jurisdictions with lower political capital and economic status.

In the *Newfoundland Continental Shelf Reference*, the Supreme Court ruled in favour of the federal government, finding support for its position that provincial powers are confined by section 92 of the Constitution and that the area under debate extends beyond the provincial geographical boundaries. In the *Newfoundland Continental Shelf Reference*, a case that was decided prior to the *Seabed and Subsoil Reference*, the Newfoundland Court of Appeal largely sided with the federal government. The Court of Appeal found that the federal government holds jurisdiction over the continental shelf, with its potential for natural resource development, but that the province did retain power over the seaward limit of the waters adjacent to Newfoundland, extending 12 nautical miles from the coast baseline (also known as the territorial sea). Despite these rulings, once Prime Minister Brian Mulroney and the Progressive Conservative Party came to power in 1984, the government moved away from combative negotiations (and thus from the courts) and adopted the cooperative-federalist agreement in the Atlantic Accord of 1985 (R. Cairns 1992).

The *Alberta Gas Tax Reference* and the *Mining and Mineral Rights Reference* are two reference cases that concerned the regulation of natural resources. In the *Mining and Mineral Rights Reference*, Newfoundland referred the *Mining and Mineral Rights Tax Act* to its Court of Appeal to verify the Act's constitutionality in response to strong opposition from several corporations that would be subject to the new taxation under the Act.[46] The Newfoundland Court of Appeal found the Act to be a valid exercise of the provincial power over direct taxation in section 92 of the *Constitution Act, 1867* and intra vires the jurisdiction of the province. This ruling was upheld on appeal to the Supreme Court of Canada. Similar to the *Mining and Mineral Rights Reference*, the *Alberta Gas Tax Reference* was also a response to opposition regarding a new tax on a natural resource. This case effectively demonstrates how a reference can be used effectively to attain a political goal (in the same vein as the references of Prime Minister King) and how it can provide a means to adjudicate jurisdictional disputes. In opposition to the Trudeau government's National Energy Program, Alberta launched a reference at the Alberta Court of Appeal to challenge Ottawa's proposed export tax on the province's petroleum.

When negotiations over energy policy between the Province of Alberta and the federal government stalled, the Trudeau government introduced the National Energy Program, which included a tax on exported gas, something that the government of Premier Peter Lougheed vehemently opposed. Alberta submitted reference questions regarding a hypothetical contract with an American company respecting a nonexistent pipeline as a means of testing the constitutionality of the proposed federal tax. This case demonstrates a highly strategic use of the reference power, as the Alberta government manufactured hypothetical facts, favourable to its position, to achieve a desired outcome in the courts, something that would not be possible with routine litigation (Riddell and Morton 2004). Thus, like the Alberta Social Credit references in the 1930s, the reference power was effectively used to block another government from legislative action, even though the legislation was not yet in force. Furthermore, in both instances, reference-initiating governments were able to achieve their political goals through the courts when negotiations between governments had stalled.

The 1930s and 1980s: References Become a Tool of the Provinces

The two decades highlighted in this analysis mark two unique periods of significant transition and challenge in Canada. Addressing the Depression and creating new ways to regulate the economy consumed Canadian politics in the 1930s, whereas national unity and a new constitutional regime dominated the political landscape of the 1980s. These two moments of profound transition inevitably led to conflict between levels of government and an increase in the number of reference cases. One feature of the reference cases during the 1980s that stands in stark contrast to the 1930s is the fact that provincial governments initiated the overwhelming majority of the cases during this period: 26 of 29 cases, or 89.7 percent. In the 1930s this figure was almost completely reversed, with the federal government initiating 23 of the 30 reference cases during this decade, or 76.7 percent.

In the 1930s the greatest proponent of the reference power was the King government. King's strategy to annul the Bennett New Deal legislation was to refer it to the courts with the expectation that it would be found ultra vires. Given that the central constitutional concern regarding the New Deal package was the incursion into matters of provincial jurisdiction, it is quite likely that provincial governments would have challenged the legislation. Instead of waiting on a reaction from the provinces, the King government challenged Government of Canada policy, and thus the references were not rooted in an opposition to the powers of the provinces. Instead, by submitting the New Deal legislation to the courts, with the belief that the legislation would be ultimately found ultra vires, the federal government inadvertently strengthened provincial jurisdiction. Although it is unknown whether the provinces would have eventually challenged the Bennett New Deal, the King government's opposition to this legislative scheme increased the number of federal government references, while limiting the provincial reference totals.

It is important to note that during the Depression, the provinces simply lacked the financial capacity to effectively manage the economic turbulence. As Russell (2004, 61) explains, "provinces were going bankrupt and it was evident that only a strong central government could deal effectively with the economic and social consequences of a worldwide depression." The provincial governments' inability to effect legislative change contributed to centralization in the federal system. Indeed, from this time until the 1950s, the Canadian system was highly skewed toward Ottawa, and the provinces were unable to effectively protect their own constitutional jurisdiction (Smiley 1962; Cairns 1977; Russell 2004).

The strong centralist nature of the Canadian political system was furthered by the outbreak of the Second World War and by the corresponding rise in nationalism and postwar reconstruction led by the federal government (Russell 2004). This era is often referred to as one of cooperative federalism – a period when the federal government (largely with the consent of the provinces) established itself as the provider of the welfare state and national standards, reflecting the strength of the federal public service and Ottawa's economic abilities (Stilborn 1997; Cameron and Simeon 2002). Cooperative federalism inherently results in a decrease in provincial autonomy. Indeed, provinces contribute to this decrease of autonomy either through inaction or through a lack of opposition to the expansion of federal power. As a result, the provincial governments of the 1930s were less likely to challenge federal incursions into their constitutional jurisdiction simply because they could not fill the void themselves, making it less likely that the provinces would initiate reference cases. Instead, the provinces generally acquiesced to the federal government's development of many social programs. This centralist orientation was furthered by the 1937 Rowell-Sirois Commission on federal-provincial relations, which recommended shifting provincial debt to the federal government and amending section 91.2(a) of the Constitution to transfer the jurisdiction over unemployment insurance to Ottawa (Smiley 1962). As a result, the provinces were less likely to use the reference power when they were not engaging in the type of policy making that provokes constitutional questions. Moreover, the provinces were less likely to challenge the federal government through a reference, as during this period federal incursions into provincial jurisdiction were often accepted and, at times, welcomed.

The increase in provincial use of the reference power following the 1950s is reflective of the expansion of provincial autonomy and the move toward a more collaborative style of federalism (Cairns 1977; Cameron and Simeon 2002; Baier 2006). This transition toward an increase in provincial power, also referred to as the province-building movement, was influenced by the awakening of Quebec through the Quiet Revolution. Quebec's campaign to be *maîtres chez nous* (masters of our own house), coupled with the search for a "made in Canada" amending formula, reinvigorated provincial powers across Canada, leading to a movement away from the cooperative federalism that had prioritized the central government (Russell 2004). Federal-provincial relations were now either collaborative or competitive, with the provinces viewed as an equal partner or adversary of the federal government in the production and delivery of Canada-wide policy and national standards (Cameron and Simeon 2002; Meekison, Telford, and Lazar 2003).

The increase in provincially initiated references took place not only because the provinces were simply legislating more, which provided more opportunities for litigation, but also because the increase in provincial power created a greater capacity to challenge federal incursions into provincial jurisdiction through a reference. Indeed, when analyzing reference cases in the 1980s, we are presented with many instances where provinces challenged the federal government and attempted to protect provincial jurisdiction. Alberta's challenge to the federal National Energy Program and Newfoundland's challenge to the federal assertion of jurisdiction over the continental shelf effectively demonstrate this change in relationship.

Following the 1950s, provincial powers were expanded, stemming from the increased importance of areas of provincial jurisdiction, like healthcare and education. At the same time, relations between the federal and provincial governments became more collaborative (with provinces as equals) or competitive (with provinces actively protecting their jurisdiction). These changes are mirrored in the use of references by governments over time. Following the 1950s, the provincial governments became much more active in their use of the reference power and began to use references as a strategy either to protect legislation from jurisdictional challenge by another government or to challenge the constitutionality of another government's policy. Given that references can be used to achieve such ends, it is not surprising to find a growth in the use of the reference power by the provinces during the instances of increased provincial autonomy in intergovernmental relations that followed the 1950s and peaked in the 1980s. Through the increased importance of the constitutional powers of the provinces and the evolution of intergovernmental relations, the provinces have come to use references – a power that was created to control them – as a way to effectively attain their own goals.

Conclusion

This chapter discusses the foundation of the reference power via an analytical description of this power from its creation through to its current use. Employing a within-case analysis, this chapter provides a comprehensive assessment of references across time, with specific analysis of two periods when more references were initiated by governments (both federal and provincial) than at any other time. This analysis demonstrates that the fluctuations in the number of reference cases are both reflective of and directly related to other events taking place within Canadian politics, such as the Depression, the Social Credit experiment in Alberta, mega constitutional politics, and evolutions in federal-provincial relations.

In tracing the roots of the Canadian reference power, this chapter demonstrates that the federal government created this power as a means to supplement reservation and disallowance. Parliamentarians believed that references would provide important legitimacy to the invalidation of provincial legislation in a way that simply could not be achieved by simply exercising disallowance. Indeed, if a court found provincial legislation to be ultra vires through a reference, with that legislation subsequently being disallowed, the disallowance would be supported by the constitutional advice of the Supreme Court and therefore be more legitimate. This early strategic use of the reference power as a source of legitimization is one benefit of the reference power that has been carried through to the present day, becoming more powerful with the increasing independence and authority of the Canadian Supreme Court.

Aside from creating the reference power to supplement or replace the powers of reservation and disallowance, the Parliament of Canada intended for the reference power to be a means of challenging the constitutionality of another government's policy without the federal government having to partake in routine litigation that would require a concrete dispute and a set of facts. Governments have demonstrated that a reference case can be used to sort out constitutionality and that a finding of intra vires in a reference can help to insulate the legislation from future legal challenges. With respect to which governments (federal or provincial) have initiated references over time, these data demonstrate that the reference power has shifted from being a tool created by the federal government to being a tool more routinely utilized by the provinces. An appreciation of the contemporaneous events taking place in Canadian politics provides context and explains the changes in reference cases across time. Although there are few restrictions on what governments can ask courts in reference cases, references have remained largely about the powers of government. Only a small portion of references have asked the courts about government responsibility regarding individual or group rights, and the introductions of the *Canadian Charter of Rights and Freedoms* and section 35 of the *Constitution Act, 1982* have had little impact on the reference power.

This historical evaluation of reference cases lays an essential foundation for the analysis that follows. Relying on this analysis, the next chapter undertakes a detailed examination of reference cases after 1949 and compares these findings to more general trends associated with Canadian appellate courts in the recent era.

3 Routine Politics and Nonroutine Litigation: References after 1949

In 1949 the Supreme Court of Canada became the apex in the Canadian judicial system and the final arbiter of all legal matters in Canada. Prior to this change, the Supreme Court was viewed only as a step on the way to the Judicial Committee of the Privy Council (JCPC), and its decisions (and often its members) were not afforded the respect and stature associated with the court in the more recent era (Snell and Vaughan 1985). Indeed, provincial governments often appealed directly to the JCPC and bypassed the Supreme Court altogether, further contributing to its subservient status within the Canadian legal system. In 1949 the membership of the court was increased from seven members to the current nine, and the jurisdiction of the court was expanded to reflect the jurisdiction previously held by the JCPC. The quality of individuals appointed to the Supreme Court after 1949 substantially increased, and the court was no longer viewed as a place of patronage (Snell and Vaughan 1985). The judiciary was now understood to be an independent and separate branch of government, and interactions between members of the court and members of the executive and legislative branches became much less frequent (Russell 1987).

The previous chapter provided a broad sketch of the trends in Canadian references over time from the reference power's inception in 1875 to 2017; however, this does not give any insight into how the actors in references – the courts, governments, and third-party interveners – have responded to these cases. For example, is the behaviour of the judiciary more restrained in responding to reference questions? Are certain types of governments more likely than others to use the reference power? Do reference cases attract similar levels of participation from third-party interveners? Answering these questions requires comparing "usual" or "routine" litigation and the behaviour of the courts in nonreference cases, and given all the changes made to the Canadian judicial system in 1949, it makes sense to focus on the post-1949 era.

The context provided in this chapter increases our ability to engage in descriptive inference in order to assess how reference cases relate to litigation in Canadian appellate courts in general. However, this comparison must be done with acknowledgment that the scholarship on Canadian courts is disproportionately focused on the Supreme Court of Canada and often does not include provincial appellate courts. As Hausegger, Riddell, and Hennigar (2013) note, this focus on the Supreme Court is understandable given its position in the Canadian judicial hierarchy. However, since the Supreme Court hears only approximately one hundred cases per year (and often far fewer), provincial appellate courts are the final court of appeal for the majority of legal matters in Canada and thus warrant greater scholarly analysis. The inclusion of data on provincial courts in the present study is thus done with the intention of furthering our understanding of these important, but underexamined, courts. This analysis not only expands our understanding of reference cases and how the reference power is used but also provides insight into any distinctions between reference cases and routine litigation in Canadian appellate courts.

Laying the Groundwork: An Overview of References after 1949

This chapter analyzes 97 reference cases adjudicated by provincial appellate courts and the Supreme Court of Canada; any remaining JCPC decisions that were released after 1949 are excluded.[1] The majority of post-1949 reference cases focus on constitutional questions, asking the courts to interpret either the *Constitution Act, 1867* or the *Constitution Act, 1982* (see Table 3.1). Most cases consider the *Constitution Act, 1867,* with the greatest proportion focusing on government jurisdiction and

Table 3.1 Case type, 1949–2017

Case subject area	*Primary issue*	*Secondary issue*
***Constitution Act, 1867* (total)**	**51 (52.6%)**	**8 (8.4%)**
Division of powers	45 (46.4%)	4 (4.2%)
Nondivision of powers	6 (6.2%)	4 (4.2%)
***Constitution Act, 1982* (total)**	**17 (17.5%)**	**5 (5.3%)**
Charter of Rights and Freedoms	17 (17.5%)	3 (3.2%)
Non-Charter		2 (2.1%)
Statutory interpretation	26 (26.8%)	15 (15.8%)
Other	2 (2.1%)	4 (4.2)
Missing data	1 (1%)	63 (66.3%)[a]
	N = 97	

a Not all cases concern more than one issue.

the division of powers between the federal and provincial governments. *Reference re Securities Act* [*Securities Reference*] is an example of a case concerning the division of powers.[2] In this reference, the federal government asked the Supreme Court whether its proposal for a national securities regulator was a valid exercise of its power to regulate trade and commerce, as provided by section 91 of the *Constitution Act, 1867*. A small number of references concern the *Constitution Act, 1867* but do not consider issues related to the division of powers. An example of such a case is *Reference re Education Act (Que)*, in which the Government of Quebec referred a question to the Quebec Court of Appeal (subsequently appealed to the Supreme Court) regarding the constitutionality of the province's proposed plan to change from religion-based school boards (i.e., Catholic and Protestant) to school boards based on language (i.e., French and English).[3]

When the number of cases is averaged over the years that each document has been in existence, references under the *Constitution Act, 1867* still occur at a greater rate. The rate of reference cases per year for the *Constitution Act, 1867* is 0.75 from 1949 to 2017, whereas references under the *Constitution Act, 1982* occur at a rate of 0.49 per year from 1982 to 2017.

That a greater number of cases concern the 1867 Constitution rather than the 1982 Constitution reflects two things. First, the *Constitution Act, 1867* has obviously existed longer. That being said, the second explanation for fewer references regarding the *Constitution Act, 1982* is that many of the issues that can arise concerning the compatibility of government legislation with the Charter are often dealt with by courts through routine litigation (Kelly 1999). Indeed, there has been no shortage of individuals and groups willing to litigate constitutional issues that arise under the Charter, and thus the need for abstract review through reference cases to address Charter-based issues has been reduced.

The references regarding statutory interpretation in Table 3.1 are not concerned with the Constitution but ask courts to interpret whether a new piece of legislation conflicts with existing and related statutes. For example, in *Reference re Canada Assistance Plan (BC),* British Columbia challenged the legality of the federal government's cancellation of the Canada Assistance Plan on the grounds that it went against an agreement between the province and the federal government made in 1967.[4] Other nonconstitutional questions include instances where governments asked the courts to review a criminal conviction when doubt was raised about the guilt of individuals convicted and other means of appeal were not available, such as in *Reference re R v Truscott* [*Truscott Reference*].[5]

As regards the post-1982 era exclusively, the majority of cases still concern the division of powers and the *Constitution Act, 1867* (28 cases) rather than the Charter (17 cases). This finding is interesting given that, since 1982, Charter cases have consistently comprised a majority of the Supreme Court's decisions on constitutional law (Hausegger, Hennigar, and Riddell 2015, 60–61). This situation reflects the fact that a substantial amount of the Charter has been litigated in routine cases through the legal action of individual citizens rather than through governments asking reference questions that open themselves up to Charter review by the courts. Furthermore, this finding demonstrates that the reference power is still primarily used to deal with controversies between governments, fulfilling the original intent of the reference power. To be sure, governments can disagree about interpretation and application of the Charter; however, it appears that when it comes to the Charter, governments are less likely to proactively seek judicial advice regarding constitutionality through a reference and more likely to deal with Charter-based claims in a reactive manner through routine litigation. That a greater number of questions asked by governments in reference cases concern federalism rather than the Charter demonstrates that governments are much more likely to initiate a reference case out of concern for violating the constitutional jurisdiction of another government than out of concern for protecting the rights of individual citizens or groups.

How Courts Respond When Governments Seek Judicial Advice

A decision in a reference case can block or facilitate a government's desire for policy change, derail or advance campaign promises, and obstruct or expedite negotiations between governments. Reference decisions can profoundly shape the powers of governments and can hinder further government action in a policy area – like any other decision made by a high appellate court. Yet courts are keenly aware that reference cases are fundamentally different from all other types of litigation. As a result, it is pertinent to understand how courts respond to reference questions. Do courts see their role as limited by the abstract nature of many reference questions? Are references more likely to be unanimous compared to routine litigation? Are reference cases more likely to be anonymous and unanimous per curiam (by the court) decisions? Answering these questions provides important insight into judicial behaviour in reference cases compared to routine litigation and allows us to appreciate how courts understand their role in references.

One of the most important measures that helps us to understand the judicial role in references is the rate at which courts invalidate government actions. On the one hand, a low rate of invalidation could signal that courts view their role as limited by the unique nature of reference cases.[6] On the other hand, a high rate of invalidation could speak to the well-documented trends regarding the judicialization of Canadian politics, as it shows that the courts are willing to participate in debates over public policy (Kelly and Manfredi 2009). In all references after 1949, when a statute or action was found to be invalid, it was seen as either ultra vires the jurisdictional power of the enacting government or in violation of one of the sections of the Charter. If a statute or action was deemed invalid *in part*, the court pointed to specific sections of the legislation

Table 3.2 Disposition of reference cases

Disposition by the court	*Frequency*
Invalid or potentially invalid in full	20 (20.6%)
Invalid or potentially invalid in part	15 (15.5%)
Valid	45 (46.4%)
Not applicable	17 (17.5%)
Total	97 (100%)

or aspects of a government action, instead of finding the legislation or action invalid in its entirety.

From 1949 to 2017, courts most often sided with the government initiating the reference case, finding both enacted and proposed legislation to be compliant with the Constitution in approximately 46 percent of all cases examined (see Table 3.2). However, when viewed in insolation, this validation rate is misleading. It is important to examine the first two categories – invalidation in full and in part – together in order to obtain a true measure of the judicial power to block government action in references. When these categories are combined, we see that courts were a roadblock to government action in 35 instances, or 36.1 percent of reference cases. This rate of invalidation or partial invalidation largely reflects the Supreme Court's disposition of all cases in general (Manfredi and Kelly 2004). For example, the Supreme Court heard 177 cases concerning division of powers, including both reference and nonreference cases, from 1950 to 1984 and invalidated 65 governmental statutes, almost 37 percent of cases (Manfredi and Kelly 2004).

The disposition of reference cases reveals two things. First, given that this finding is comparable to the outcome of routine litigation before the Supreme Court, it demonstrates that in references the courts do not view their role in finding government policy unconstitutional to be any different from their role in routine litigation. Courts do not see their power as limited by the fact that some reference cases do not arise out of concrete disputes between two opposing parties, as they are quite willing to find government actions to be invalid. Second, that Canadian appellate courts have blocked the goals of legislators in over one-third of all reference cases suggests that the courts can play an important role in the legitimation and creation of public policy. If we assume that unlike with the *Egg Reference* and the actions of the King government in the New Deal references, most governments do not ask reference questions with the goal of invalidation by the courts, this finding provides further evidence that the judiciary can be an important policy actor and can divert power away from elected political actors, furthering the judicialization of politics.

Understanding the unanimity rate in references provides some insight into how courts view their role in reference cases. A high rate of unanimity could reflect that the individual preferences of the justices were less important than achieving consensus (Songer et al. 2012). A unanimous opinion could demonstrate that a court found it important to set a clear precedent on an issue of high political salience. A low number of divided opinions could reflect the genuine agreement of the court, or it could be evidence of strategic decision making by the justices, whereby a justice agreed to sign on to a colleague's opinion in one case in exchange for agreement on another issue or case.[7]

In the period 1949–2017, references had a 55.7 percent unanimity rate (54 cases). Although the courts provided unanimous decisions in more than half of all cases, this rate of unanimity is actually lower than the Supreme Court's overall unanimity rate and likely much lower than the unanimity rate for appellate courts. Although a unanimity rate for provincial courts of appeal is not available, in their study of Canadian appellate courts, Greene et al. (1998, 17) note that "the great majority of appellate decisions in Canada are unanimous." With respect to the Supreme Court of Canada, from 1982 to 2003 the unanimity rate for the court hovered at 70 to 80 percent. In 1984 unanimity reached a rate of almost 90 percent during a period when the court first started making decisions under the Charter (Songer et al. 2012, 154). Looking at pre-Charter rates, Muttart (2007, 95) finds that unanimity dipped as low as below 30 percent from 1949 to 1954, with a high of just over 60 percent from 1963 to 1973. Following the passage of the Charter, the Supreme Court's unanimity rate increased (L'Heureux-Dubé 2000a), and thus one might expect Charter-based references to reflect this trend by demonstrating a higher unanimity rate than that seen with cases concerning division of powers and statutory interpretation. Although there are a relatively low number of Charter references to examine, this trend does not hold: of the 17 cases, slightly more than half were unanimous, at 10 cases (58.9 percent). The unanimity rate of highly visible Supreme Court of Canada decisions is actually lower than the unanimity rate of all Supreme Court cases together (Macfarlane 2013). Thus, although courts may wish to prioritize speaking with one voice in high-profile cases, these cases often consider more difficult and contentious issues, making consensus more challenging than in other, less visible, cases (L'Heureux-Dube 2000b).

It is important to note that a divided decision does not necessarily mean that dissenting opinions were issued. Instead, 30.2 percent of the 43 divided opinions were dissenting opinions, whereas 44.2 percent were concurring opinions. In 25.6 percent of divided opinions, the court issued both a concurring and a dissenting judgment. Judges may write a concurring opinion for a variety of reasons, such as in instances where they agree with the result of the majority opinion but rely on different law to support their opinion. Judges may write a concurring opinion because they wish to emphasize or clarify a particular issue (see Hausegger, Hennigar, and Riddell 2015, 110). Furthermore, Belleau and Johnson (2008) demonstrate that a decision to concur or dissent can also reflect personal characteristics and identity rather than solely the issue before the court. Although a concurring opinion does not signify a great disagreement respecting the outcome of a case, it can have important implications for future decisions and the development of legal doctrine. Hausegger, Hennigar, and Riddell (2015) note that although concurrences are quite uncommon in lower appellate courts, they are also not a routine practice at the Supreme Court, occurring on average approximately ten times per year under the leadership of Chief Justice Beverley McLachlin. With this being considered, the high rate of concurrence in reference cases is noteworthy, and the possible explanations for this rate are worth exploring further.

The high rate of divided opinions issued by courts in references could be demonstrative of the abstract nature of many reference questions (see more on abstract review below). In routine litigation, appellate courts address issues that have already been examined by at least one lower court judge, and they are expected to address questions of the law rather than questions of fact. This position in the judicial hierarchy means that appellate courts ordinarily have the benefit of at least one previous judicial opinion to guide their assessment of the case, including the articulation of relevant facts and applicable law. When appellate courts engage in abstract review, as they do in many reference cases, they do not have the benefit of a previous decision or a factual context to help shape and inform their decision. Therefore, justices participating in reference cases can have a broader scope for analysis, which could foster a more diverse understanding of the issues and varied reasoning.

In the reference decisions that were unanimous, a court may have issued an anonymous decision because the case was highly salient and/or partisan. Macfarlane (2013) argues that when the Supreme Court is concerned with protecting its institutional legitimacy, as in the *Secession Reference,* this style of authorship may be a priority for the justices. Moreover, this authorship style demonstrates that rather than giving voice to the individual justices who currently fill its bench, the court finds it important to speak as one voice, emphasizing the legitimacy of the court as an institution (L'Heureux-Dubé 2000a). If this reasoning holds true, one can assume that the unanimous reference decisions are more likely to be anonymous per curiam decisions. That is because references can ask the courts to step outside of the traditional institutional role of adjudicating concrete cases and engage in the abstract review of public policy. The institutional role of a court may be threatened when a case blurs the line between interpretation of law and interpretation of policy or political action. This separation between legal and political considerations can become even more obscured when a case lacks a concrete controversy and courts must therefore make considerations in the abstract. As a result, when reaching a unanimous decision in a politically sensitive reference case, a court may be more likely to render that decision as authored by the court.

Under the leadership of Chief Justice Bora Laskin, the Supreme Court adopted the practice of issuing per curiam decisions in a select number of cases (McCormick and Zanoni 2015). This practice is not very common, with this authorship style occurring at a rate of 1.6 percent of all decisions by the Laskin court and 9.8 percent of all decisions by the court of Chief Justice Brian Dickson (L'Heureux-Dubé 2000a). That being said, there is relatively little known regarding the Supreme Court's use of anonymous and unanimous per curiam decisions. In a study of the emergence of this style of authorship at the Supreme Court of Canada, McCormick and Zanoni (2015) note that its origins are relatively unknown and that its use by the Supreme Court does not fit a specific pattern. Whereas the Canadian case suffers from a lack of academic analysis, American scholarship on the use of per curiam decisions by the United States Supreme Court explains that this practice has evolved to be employed in the most challenging, complex, and politically charged cases, such as *Bush v Gore* (Ray 2000).[8] However, McCormick and Zanoni (2015) find that in the Canadian case, decisions rendered as authored by the court are not a reliable indicator of major cases, disconfirming their initial hypothesis regarding the practice.

From 1949 to 2017, 24.7 percent of the decisions in Canadian reference cases were attributed to the court as the author. This number is much greater than the percentages of per curiam decisions under the chief justiceships of Laskin and Dickson, and it is remarkably higher than the percentage of such decisions by the Supreme Court in general. Indeed, McCormick (2016) notes that less than 1 percent of Supreme Court decisions are rendered as being by the court. This high rate of per curiam decisions in references certainly reflects the belief that in politically salient cases, courts may be concerned with protecting their institutional legitimacy and may resort to an anonymous authorship style to convey a greater degree of authority. However, the high rate found in references compared to Supreme Court cases in general may also reflect that the present data do not exclusively look at the Supreme Court but also include decisions of provincial appellate courts. Unfortunately, just as there is a paucity of analysis of the Supreme Court's use of per curiam decisions, there are no available data on provincial courts of appeal. Nonetheless, if provincial appellate courts are more likely to be unanimous, it is likely that provincial appellate courts are more likely to rely on per curiam authorship. The lack of data on per curiam rates for provincial appellate courts and the Supreme Court makes it difficult to draw significant conclusions about this finding.

Refusing to Answer and the Justiciability of References

Unlike in routine litigation, courts do not have to grant leave to hear a reference case. Instead, they must accept reference questions from the lieutenant governor in council – Cabinet in practice. As a result, through the reference procedure, the executive can force issues onto the dockets of provincial appellate courts and the Supreme Court. A court can gain some control over the reference process when it refuses to answer all the questions referred. Some justices who have sat on reference cases have noted their disagreement with participating in abstract review, and this disagreement has resulted in the courts or individual justices refusing to answer some of the questions referred to them in reference cases.

Although there has been scholarly debate over the capacity of courts to refuse to answer reference questions (see McEvoy 2005; Huscroft 2006, 2010), this scholarship does not empirically investigate the actual number of times courts have refused to answer reference questions and their reasons for doing so. That being said, in his coverage of the reference power, Hogg (2012) surmises that the courts have refused to answer questions in instances where the issue had become moot, where the questions did not concern any real controversy of interpretation, where the questions concerned an issue that was not legal, or where the court did not have enough information to formulate an opinion, although he provides no analysis of how often the courts have used these reasons to refuse to answer.

Hogg's hypothesized reasons for the courts' refusal to answer revolve around the issue of justiciability. Even though governments that refer questions to courts are not bound by the limitations of standing and leave, courts can informally consider whether the questions are justiciable and appropriate for judicial analysis. The practical implications of justiciability impose "a set of judge-made rules, norms and principles delineating the scope of judicial intervention in social, political and economic life" (Sossin 2012, 2). If an issue is justiciable, it is ripe (i.e., it cannot be solved through other means), and it is not moot (i.e., it is a live dispute).[9] Moreover, questions that are deemed too political or not to involve a legal controversy can be found to be nonjusticiable by a court. The assessment of justiciability by a court must be done in tandem with three factors: "(1) the capacities and legitimacy of the judicial process, (2) the constitutional separation of powers and (3) the nature of the dispute before the court" (Sossin 2012, 2). When granting leave to a case or deciding whether to answer reference questions, a court bears the responsibility of ensuring that the particular case (or questions) will not have serious negative consequences for its position within the Canadian institutional framework, which is inherently related to judicial independence.

In the *Secession Reference,* the Supreme Court was presented with arguments that criticized the reference procedure and claimed that the issues before the court were of a political nature and therefore nonjusticiable. This argument provided the Supreme Court the opportunity to explain why it might refuse to answer questions. First, it will refuse to answer questions that require it to engage in a role that is "beyond its own assessment of its proper role in the constitutional framework of our democratic form of government."[10] Second, it will refuse to answer questions that fall outside the court's expertise, which is the interpretation of law, broadly construed.[11] In this case, the Supreme Court concluded that it was acceptable for it to answer the questions referred in the *Secession Reference*. Because the court deemed its participation acceptable in the politically charged context of the *Secession Reference,* it arguably set quite a liberal standard for future participation in highly political references.

This focus on the appropriateness of the question referred was echoed in *Reference re Canada Assistance Plan (BC)*. In a more deferential decision, after assessing British Columbia's *Constitutional Questions Act,*[12] the Supreme Court noted that the lieutenant governor general has the power to ask *any* question of the court and that the court has the duty to attempt to answer the question as long as the question is justiciable, regardless of whether the question is confusing and unclear.[13] The court considered the possibility that some reference questions could involve courts in the legislative process and/or a political controversy. The Supreme Court explained, "In considering its appropriate role the Court must determine whether the question is purely political in nature and should, therefore, be determined in another forum or whether it has a sufficient legal component to warrant the intervention of the judicial branch."[14]

Another aspect of justiciability is the concept of mootness. If the issue that gives rise to a reference has already been resolved, thereby making a decision by a court unnecessary, the court can refuse to answer the reference on account of mootness (Hogg 2012). A refusal based on mootness can be fairly apolitical. It will most likely be clear to the parties involved that the issue has already been resolved. According to Sossin (2012), the Supreme Court has a liberal approach to issues of justiciability, and it is uncommon for the court to refuse to hear a case on the grounds of mootness. Due to the structure of the reference procedure, it is less probable that a reference question will be declared moot. Often cases become moot upon appeal to a higher court due to the amount of time it takes for a case to be heard, which can provide an opportunity for the parties to resolve their dispute. This is often not a factor in references, as they are subject to a relatively quick process compared to routine litigation, and it is unlikely that an issue will resolve itself before a court has the opportunity to hear a reference case.

However, with this understanding, the reference case in which the Supreme Court explained the discretion over "mootness refusals" was more controversial than one might expect. In the *Quebec Veto Reference*, the Supreme Court explained that courts hold the discretion to refuse to answer reference questions where the issue before them has been rendered moot or the legal controversy no longer exists. A discussion of mootness in reference cases was of particular importance in the *Quebec Veto Reference*, as this case asked the Supreme Court whether the Province of Quebec had a constitutionally protected veto over constitutional amendment, as discussed in Chapter 2. When the *Quebec Veto Reference* reached the Supreme Court, the *Constitution Act, 1982* was already in force and therefore made the question of a Quebec veto moot – a fact conceded by the Supreme Court. Although the court maintained that it held discretion to refuse reference questions that were moot, in this particular case, the constitutional controversy was of great importance and deserved an answer. Furthermore, prior to the adoption of the *Constitution Act, 1982*, the Quebec Court of Appeal had rendered an opinion on the *Quebec Veto Reference*, and the Supreme Court explained that it was duty bound to review this constitutionally important case. As explained in Chapter 2, the Supreme Court rejected the notion of a Quebec veto in this case.

In appellate court reference cases from 1949 to 2017, courts answered all the questions referred in the majority of cases. In 81.4 percent of references (79 cases) courts answered all the questions submitted by governments. Courts refused to answer one or more questions in 17.5 percent of references (17 cases).[15] In terms of all cases during this period, an average of 3.33 questions per reference were asked, with a response rate of 2.84 questions answered. In 17 reference cases, courts found it to be within their discretion to refuse to answer some of the questions posed to them. Courts have refused to answer reference questions for one of the following three reasons: (1) the questions were unnecessary to answer, (2) the court had a lack of information that prevented it from answering, or (3) the questions could be considered inappropriate and/or of a political nature.[16]

First, a court will most often not answer a question because answers to previous questions asked in the same reference preclude it from answering additional questions. In this instance, the refusal to answer the remaining questions is due to practicality rather than a clear rejection by the court. Courts may refuse to answer reference questions simply because, once they have responded to the first question in a case, the remaining questions may not warrant an answer. Courts have relied on this explanation in 11 cases.[17] It is interesting to note that courts answer reference questions in the order of referral, which can have significant implications for the questions that courts refuse to answer. For example, in many references that centre on a statute's conformity with the Constitution, the first question asks whether the entire Act is ultra vires or intra vires the jurisdiction of a particular government, and any remaining questions ask the courts to consider specific sections in isolation. In answering the first question, if a court finds that the entire Act is either ultra vires or intra vires, it will likely refrain from answering the remaining questions. Basing the survival of the entire statute on the answer to the first question can impede the court from providing specific guidance on the legality or constitutionality of the specific sections and can restrict the court's assessment to the Act in its entirety. It is important to note that narrowing the court's focus to assessing the entirety of the Act in such instances is a restriction that the court has imposed upon itself.

The Supreme Court refused to answer a reference question for practical reasons in *Reference re Upper Churchill Water Rights Reversion Act*. In this case, the Supreme Court was asked nine different questions related to the constitutionality of legislation that was aimed at reasserting the Province of Newfoundland and Labrador's right over Churchill Falls. In finding the entire Act ultra vires by answering the first question, the court declined to answer the remaining eight questions, which concerned the constitutionality of specific portions of the Act. This refusal by the court to answer all the questions was a reflection of circumstance rather than an assertion of power. In a similar manner, the Saskatchewan Court of Appeal refused to answer the second question in *Reference re Freedom of Informed Choice (Abortions) Act (SK)*, as doing so would have been "purely academic" because of its answer to the previous question, namely that the act in question was ultra vires the jurisdiction of the province.[18]

Second, a court may refuse to answer a question because it lacks the proper amount of information to provide a well-informed answer. Courts have provided this reasoning for refusing to answer either when the questions were unclear or when the government had not provided enough related information or facts (if applicable) to permit clear judicial analysis. In 6 cases, courts have refused to answer reference questions because the questions were too abstract or hypothetical.[19] Cases that fall into this category are illustrative of the pitfalls of abstract review: courts have found in some instances that without the facts or context of a concrete dispute, categorical answers to reference questions are too difficult or require too much speculation.

For example, in *Reference re Goods and Services Tax*, the Supreme Court refused to answer one of the six questions referred. The refusal was due to the fact that it was "a hypothetical question which cannot be answered with any assurance of correctness."[20] Instead of admonishing the Government of Alberta for posing such a question, the court simply stated that it is "entitled to exercise its judgment on whether it should answer referred questions if it concludes that they do not exhibit sufficient precision to permit cogent answers."[21] In making this assertion, the court supported its refusal by citing other instances where it refused to answer questions on similar grounds but did not provide any statutory basis for this power of denial. The Government of Alberta did not respond by resubmitting the unanswered questions to the court for review. The failure of governments to challenge courts when they refuse to answer has helped to further the court's inclination to believe it has the prerogative to refuse.

Whereas courts have refused to answer questions due to a lack of information, that did not happen in *Reference re Court of Unified Criminal Jurisdiction*, where the Supreme Court noted that the very questions referred "suffered from excessive abstractness."[22] In this case, the Government of New Brunswick referred three questions that asked the courts to consider the constitutionality of creating a unified criminal court in the province. New Brunswick did not submit draft legislation with the reference, nor was any explanatory material provided. This lack of factual aids caused the Supreme Court to explain its discretion to refuse reference questions that "do not exhibit sufficient precision to permit cogent answers ... irrespective of the fact that the reference power is couched in broad terms."[23] The Supreme Court defended this reasoning through an examination of other instances where courts had refused to answer reference questions because the questions lacked "specificity." Although the Supreme Court criticized the questions referred by New Brunswick for being based on "extremely flimsy material," the court explained that it would not abort the questions referred in this case, as the "Court has enough of the essential features of the proposed scheme" to permit judicial analysis.[24] The court went on to answer the questions in this reference, but its reasoning clearly directed governments to pose reference questions with as much specificity as possible.

The third reason for refusal to answer a reference question stems from the court's understanding that the question is inappropriate or asks the court to go beyond its role of interpreting the law. This category includes refusals to answer based on the overt political nature of the question. Whereas the first two reasons are largely practical, this type of refusal involves the analysis of the place of the judiciary within the constitutional framework and sensitivity to the fact that the independence of the judiciary can be threatened if the court entertains questions that are overtly political and partisan. Although arguably all decisions by high courts can be viewed as political in some sense, as they often supervise and impact the actions of political actors, we expect courts to be sensitive to a separation of questions of law from questions of politics (Sossin 2012).

In considering the divide between questions of law and questions of politics, courts have refused to answer for political reasons in only two cases.[25] In the *Same-Sex Marriage Reference,* some of the interveners argued that the subject matter – the legalization of same-sex marriage – was too political and thus not justiciable.[26] One area of particular concern was Question 4. It is worth noting that it was submitted approximately five months after the first three questions were referred to the Supreme Court, after Paul Martin replaced Jean Chrétien as prime minister and leader of the Liberal Party. The Martin government added this question: "Is the opposite-sex requirement for marriage for civil purposes, as established by the common law and set out for Quebec in section 5 of the *Federal Law–Civil Law Harmonization Act, No. 1,* consistent with the *Canadian Charter of Rights and Freedoms*? If not, in what particular or particulars and to what extent?"[27] Essentially, the fourth question asked whether a heterosexual definition of marriage violates the Charter. This question is noteworthy given that the other questions in this reference were aimed at enacting legislative change to allow for same-sex marriage,[28] whereas Question 4 contemplated the reverse: the preservation of the opposite-sex definition of marriage. Although it is quite possible that it is constitutionally valid to provide for the right to same-sex marriage, governments may not be constitutionally *obligated* to provide for this right, making it also constitutional to take no action on same-sex marriage. If in answering Question 4, the Supreme Court had found that the Constitution required governments to provide the right to same-sex marriage, it could have made the court a target for opponents of same-sex marriage, allowing the government to avoid this criticism.

After considering Question 4, and perhaps realizing this strategy on behalf of the government and engaging in some strategic behaviour of its own, the Supreme Court refused to answer. The court explained that it held the discretion to refuse questions that are "inappropriate" or that prevent a "complete or accurate answer."[29] The court found it inappropriate to answer the final question, regardless of the fact that the question had the required legal content to be justiciable. The court explained that there were several unique circumstances surrounding this case that would have made answering Question 4 imprudent. First, the attorney general had accepted the lower court rulings in favour of same-sex marriage and had made it clear the government was intent on proceeding with the legalization of same-sex marriage, regardless of the outcome of the reference.[30] Beyond statements made by the attorney general during the proceedings, the court found further evidence that Canadian governments were moving toward acceptance of same-sex marriage in the fact that at the time of its decision, half of the provinces and one territory had moved away from limiting marriage to opposite-sex couples.[31] Second, the attorney general's decision not to appeal the lower court rulings granting same-sex marriage provided a notion of finality regarding the issue, and thus many jurisdictions were now in the practice of granting marriage to same-sex couples. The court noted that answering Question 4 could place the court in the position of jeopardizing rights that had already been granted.[32] Finally, because the attorney general did not exercise the right to appeal, making the reference a discrete legal proceeding, answering Question 4 would have put the Supreme Court in the unusual position of reviewing the appropriateness of several provincial appellate court decisions, without actually participating in a direct appeal of those cases.[33]

Writing in response to the Supreme Court of Canada's refusal to answer Question 4 in the *Same-Sex Marriage Reference,* McEvoy (2005, 36) is highly critical of the court, arguing that the "will of Parliament is manifestly clear ... No margin of appreciation or discretion is conferred on the Court." Huscroft (2006) joins McEvoy in critiquing the actions of the court, finding that the discretion the court has afforded itself in refusing to answer questions lacks any statutory foundation in the *Supreme Court Act*. As a result, according to Huscroft, the governor in council can push the court on a refusal and resubmit unanswered questions to the court in order to force their consideration if so desired. Hogg (2012) posits that the refusal of the court to answer a question posed in a reference is an exception rather than the norm. He believes that the court has not "made sufficient use of its discretion not to answer a question posed on a reference" (8-20).

The Supreme Court's refusal to answer the fourth question in the *Same-Sex Marriage Reference* is not indicative of the majority of reasons why courts refuse to answer reference questions. Yet it is the *Same-Sex Marriage Reference* that consumes the scholarship on refusal. That being said, the refusal in the *Same-Sex Marriage Reference* is cause for concern if it has created a precedent for the courts to refuse to answer reference questions in the future on similar grounds. Such a precedent would afford the court a great deal of discretion in reference cases, fundamentally altering the relationship between the court and governments submitting reference questions. Nevertheless, considered in relation to all reference cases, the important context for the Supreme Court's refusal to answer Question 4 in the *Same-Sex Marriage Reference* demonstrates that this case is an anomaly and that courts do routinely comply with the request to answer reference questions.

How Governments Ask for Judicial Advice in References

A survey of the statutes that grant reference powers demonstrates that there are few parameters respecting what governments can ask courts in reference cases. For example, the federal power outlined in the *Supreme Court Act* provides the governor in council the ability to ask the court to consider "important questions of law or fact concerning any matter."[34] The statutes of Alberta, British Columbia, Manitoba, Newfoundland and Labrador, and Saskatchewan provide the lieutenant governor in council the power to "refer any matter to the Court of Appeal ... for hearing and consideration" (see Appendix A). The statutory provisions of some provinces state that the lieutenant governor in council may ask "any question," as with Prince Edward Island and Ontario, or address any matter that "he [sic] thinks fit," as with Nova Scotia. The New Brunswick statute requires that the issue be "important," and the Quebec provision explains that the questions must be deemed "expedient," but what is considered either "important" or "expedient" is not defined (see Appendix A). With few or no restraints on the type of questions that can be asked, it is unsurprising that there is great variation in the nature of the questions submitted to courts in references.

Abstract review requires the adjudication of an issue or controversy entirely in the absence of a live dispute or case. In many instances, abstract review asks a court to rule on the constitutionality or legality of hypothetical government action or a piece of legislation that may or may not be in force. This style of review requires the court to consider questions in the absence of facts that result from a dispute between two or more parties. Concrete review, in contrast, is what most would envision as the routine role of courts. It often involves the litigation of a dispute between two parties, either both private individuals or an individual and the state, in which one alleges the violation of a law or rights protected in the Constitution by the other and seeks redress from the courts (Stone Sweet 2000).[35]

The reference cases were analyzed to determine whether the questions being referred asked the court to engage in either concrete or abstract review.[36] As will be discussed, there are some instances where a clear concrete dispute preceded the referral of questions to the court, but the questions were asked in a general and abstract manner, without reference to this specific dispute. Such cases are considered abstract review, as the questions put before the court were still abstract and did not ask the court to consider the related factual situation.[37] To be sure, a "concrete" reference case is still at its core abstract review when compared to routine litigation because the case does not originate with the appeal of a genuine live legal controversy. That being said, reference cases vary in their level of abstractness, with some cases having clear roots in a live controversy, whereas other cases are divorced entirely from facts.

In more than two-thirds of all references from 1949 to 2017 (64.9 percent, 63 cases), the reference questions asked courts to engage in some form of abstract review, whereas approximately one-third of the references (32 percent, 31 cases) asked the courts questions that were more concrete.[38] This finding means that in approximately one-third of all references, governments used the reference power to deal with a live dispute, instead of pursuing the routine routes to litigation. In some instances, a concrete application of the reference power was used because a reference was the only avenue available to governments to receive a judicial ruling on a matter, notably in several criminal law references.

Concrete Review Reference Cases

In the *Truscott Reference,* the attorney general of Canada referred a question regarding the guilt of the accused, Steven Truscott, when his conviction became questionable in the eyes of the public. Following the publication of a national bestselling book, *The Trial of Steven Truscott* (LeBourdais 1966), the public became increasingly doubtful of Truscott's guilt. Many parliamentarians became interested in the Truscott case, prompting action by the government (Snell and Vaughan 1985). However, the Supreme Court had already rejected Truscott's application for leave to appeal. With no available avenues for appeal remaining, a reference provided the attorney general a means to have the case heard by the court, regardless of its previous rejection of leave. The attorney general referred the following question to the Supreme Court: "Had an Appeal by Steven Murray Truscott been made to the Supreme Court of Canada ... what disposition would the Court have made of such an Appeal on consideration of the existing Record and such further evidence as the Court, in its discretion, may receive and consider?"[39]

In a unique use of the reference procedure, the *Truscott Reference* marks the first time in the Supreme Court's history that new evidence was presented, including witness testimony, thus requiring the court to act not as an appellate court but as a trier of fact (Snell and Vaughan 1985). Unfortunately for Truscott, even with a reconsideration of his case and the acceptance of new evidence, a majority of the Supreme Court found the original verdict of guilty to be valid.[40] However, the court's opinion in the *Truscott Reference* was re-examined in 2007 by the Ontario Court of Appeal, which declared the original guilty verdict a miscarriage of justice.[41]

This case demonstrates the unrestricted nature of the reference power, specifically how it can provide governments the ability to seek judicial review in virtually any circumstance, including live cases with significant implications for the parties involved. The *Truscott Reference* provided a means to circumvent the usual restrictions on litigation and force the issue before the Supreme Court. Using the reference power in this manner – to obtain judicial review where it has previously been denied – highlights the complications that the reference power can raise for a separation of the judiciary from the political branches of government, implicating judicial independence. In this case, the Supreme Court had already determined that the conviction of Truscott should stand, yet through the reference power a government was able to force a court to reconsider its ruling.[42] Perhaps in this case, more than any other, the ability of a government to use a reference to force matters onto a court's docket is apparent.

This practice of using a reference to compel the Supreme Court to reassess a criminal case, where leave has been previously denied, occurred more recently in *Reference re Milgaard*.[43] As in the *Truscott Reference*, the government was concerned that a criminal conviction constituted a miscarriage of justice. This case asked the court to examine fresh evidence and decide whether a new trial for David Milgaard was warranted. The court's decision in *Reference re Milgaard* had significant implications for the convicted. Finding that a miscarriage of justice had occurred and that Milgaard had likely been wrongfully convicted, the Supreme Court's reference decision prompted the Government of Saskatchewan to stay proceedings against Milgaard. As a result of this decision, Saskatchewan ceased pursuing a retrial in the case, resulting in Milgaard's release from prison. Milgaard was later exonerated through DNA analysis and compensated by Saskatchewan (MacCallum 2008).

Not all concrete reference cases concern the re-examination of verdicts in criminal cases. For example, in *Reference re Ng Extradition (Can)*, the attorney general of Canada asked the Supreme Court to consider whether the decision of the minister of justice to surrender an accused person, Charles Chitat Ng, to the United States to stand trial for homicide, without seeking assurances regarding the application of the death penalty, constituted an error of law and a violation of sections 7 and 12 of the Charter.[44] Other examples of concrete review concern noncriminal matters. For example, in *Reference re Broome v Prince Edward Island*, the Government of Prince Edward Island referred several questions that asked the court to consider whether the province owed a general duty of care to a group of children who had suffered abuse at a private orphanage, the grounds for the decision being an agreed statement of facts describing the events that had taken place at the orphanage.[45] In *Reference re Provincial Electoral Boundaries (Sask)*, the Supreme Court was asked to assess whether changes to the provincial electoral boundaries in

Saskatchewan, namely conforming urban ridings to existing municipal boundaries, would violate the right to vote provided by section 3 of the Charter and, if so, whether the limitation was reasonable under section 1 of the Charter.[46] More specifically, the central concern in this reference was whether the right to effective representation, provided by section 3 of the Charter, was compromised by changes in electoral districts that resulted in an overrepresentation of rural areas and an underrepresentation of urban areas.[47] In this case, the Supreme Court was provided with maps of the electoral constituencies and was asked to contemplate the effect of the proposed changes within the province. Other examples of concrete reference cases have asked courts to consider the regulation of bypass pipelines by a province and the application of rights respecting minority language education to a specific school district.[48]

Abstract Review Reference Cases

Governments have asked the courts reference questions in an abstract manner, even though the questions have had a clear connection to a live dispute or current event. For example, in *Reference re Supreme Court Act, ss 5 and 6* [*Nadon Reference*], the Supreme Court was asked to consider the legality of filling one of the three seats on the Supreme Court reserved for Quebec jurists by appointing a justice from Quebec who was not a member of the Barreau du Québec at the time of appointment.[49] This controversy stemmed from the appointment to the Supreme Court of Justice Marc Nadon, a semi-retired justice from the Federal Court of Canada. The federal government asked the following reference questions:

(1) Can a person who was, at any time, an advocate of at least 10 years standing at the Barreau du Québec be appointed to the Supreme Court of Canada as a member of the Supreme Court from Quebec pursuant to sections 5 and 6 of the *Supreme Court Act*?

(2) Can Parliament enact legislation that requires that a person be or has previously been a barrister or advocate of at least 10 years standing at the bar of a province as a condition of appointment as a judge of the Supreme Court of Canada or enact the annexed declaratory provisions as set out in clauses 471 and 472 of the Bill entitled *Economic Action Plan 2013, No. 2*?

Table 3.3 Nature of action under review in abstract references

Status at time of reference	*Frequency*
No bill	4 (6.3%)
Draft bill	12 (19%)
In force[a]	43 (68.2%)
Both draft and in force	4 (6.3%)
Total	**63 (100%)**[b]

a Includes bills that are promulgated and have received royal assent but are not yet in force.

b Table figures equal 99.8% due to rounding.

These two questions made no mention of Justice Nadon and did not ask the Supreme Court whether Nadon in particular was qualified for appointment to the court. Instead, the questions were posed in an abstract manner.

Based on the questions referred to the court, Table 3.3 provides a description of the nature of action under review in the abstract reference cases. The categories are arranged from most abstract (i.e., the court was asked questions that did not make reference to any legislation or bill) to less abstract (i.e., the court was asked questions that related to a bill in force). The categories of both draft and in force capture references where courts were asked one question that referred to a specific law and other questions that did not. The key difference between the category of in force and the categories of no bill and draft bill is that the latter are references that asked the courts to weigh in before the legislative (and democratic) process took place. Comparatively, references that considered bills already in force asked the court for an opinion after the routine legislative process had occurred.

References that asked for a court's advice prior to the legislative process – the draft bill references – ostensibly provided a court the opportunity to have a greater impact on legislative outcomes (depending on whether the court's advice was followed or not) compared to references that considered legislation already in place. *Reference re Bill 30, An Act to Amend the Education Act (Ont)* provides a good example of a draft bill reference case, as the Ontario Court of Appeal was asked to determine whether the proposed law, Bill 30, which would extend provincial funding to Roman Catholic high schools, was consistent with the Charter.[50] In this case, Bill 30 was adopted by the Legislature of Ontario only after it was found to be constitutionally compliant by the Ontario Court of Appeal – a decision later affirmed by the Supreme Court of Canada. If the Ontario Court of Appeal had ruled that the proposed changes to funding Catholic high schools violated the Charter, it is reasonable to assume that the bill would have been amended or abandoned by the legislature.

As discussed previously, in *Reference re Court of Unified Criminal Jurisdiction,* the Supreme Court was asked whether it was within the legislative authority of the Parliament of Canada to amend the *Criminal Code of Canada* to allow provinces to create a unified criminal court to hear all indictable offences. Although the referred question made a general reference to the Criminal Code, it did not ask the court to consider any particular section that might require amendment to allow for the creation of a unified court. In addressing the questions referred to the court in the reference, the Supreme Court first considered whether it should even answer the reference questions, noting the "excessive abstractness" of the questions.[51] When references are used in this manner, they ask courts to engage in abstract review in the purest sense, as not only are there no concrete facts for the court to address, but there is also no legislative scheme for it to interpret. When references are used to seek judicial input on a legislative proposal that has not yet been subject to the legislative process, the role of the court becomes quite similar to that of the many European constitutional courts, like those of Italy, Germany, and Spain, that are restricted to engaging in the review of laws that are not yet in force.

Frequently, abstract reference cases have asked courts to engage in statutory interpretation, which involves the referral of a particular piece of legislation, either a draft bill or a law that is already in force. In the *Securities Reference,* the Supreme Court was referred a series of questions that concerned a bill that was simultaneously being considered in Parliament. In this case, the federal government asked the Supreme Court whether the proposed *Securities Act* was within the legislative jurisdiction of the Parliament of Canada. Although several provincial governments opposed the federal government's move to create a national securities regulator, there was no concrete dispute for the Supreme Court to sort out, as there was no wrongdoing alleged by one party against another. As a result, the court was required to engage in an analysis of the proposed statute based solely on an interpretation of the Act and its compliance with the Constitution. Moreover, because the Act was not in force, the court had to assume how the Act would operate in practice if it were adopted.

In some abstract reference cases, governments have exercised great effort to pursue a case in the abstract, even if a concrete dispute and possible grounds to initiate routine litigation existed. A clear example is *Reference re Manitoba (AG) v Manitoba Egg and Poultry Association* [*Egg Reference*]. As detailed in the Introduction, with the restriction of imports in Ontario and Quebec, which are two of the largest provincial markets in Canada, Manitoba claimed that its agricultural exports were injured by the restrictive legislative schemes. Instead of challenging the constitutionality of the provincial legislation through routine litigation, the Manitoba legislature adopted parallel legislation based on the Quebec model, with the sole purpose of referring it to the courts. This legislation was promptly referred to the Manitoba Court of Appeal and then further appealed to the Supreme Court. The reference made no mention of Manitoba's agricultural discrimination; instead, the courts were asked to assess the constitutionality of the legislation in the abstract. As a result, the Supreme Court's decision in the *Egg Reference* is puzzling, as the court was required to assess the impact of the regulatory scheme and its possible discriminatory effects without any facts. The use of abstract review in this particular case resulted in a confusing and highly criticized decision by the Supreme Court (see Hogg 2012).

In other references, governments have submitted questions to courts in an abstract manner regardless of the fact that there was routine litigation concerning the same issue already in progress. This was the case when the *Same-Sex Marriage Reference* was referred to the Supreme Court of Canada. Prior to the reference, the British Columbia Court of Appeal had ruled in *EGALE Canada Inc v Canada (AG)* that denying homosexual couples the right to marry was a violation of the equality rights guaranteed under section 15 of the Charter.[52] Similarly, the

Ontario Court of Appeal had ruled in *Halpern v Canada (AG)* that the definition of marriage as between one man and one woman in the common law was a violation of section 15.[53] The attorney general of Canada had the ability to appeal to the Supreme Court in both cases. In fact, the attorney general had previously hinted that his government would appeal the decision in the *EGALE* case (Hennigar 2009). However, the government did not follow through on its intention to appeal the cases from the British Columbia and Ontario appellate courts. Instead, Jean Chrétien's government drafted a bill providing for the legalization of same-sex marriage and then submitted the draft legislation along with several reference questions to the Supreme Court of Canada.

In the *Same-Sex Marriage Reference*, the questions referred to the Supreme Court did not mention the concrete *EGALE* and *Halpern* cases; instead, they were referred in an abstract manner without any connection to the particular facts or circumstances of the two lower court decisions. To be sure, the court's decision in this reference did not take place in a vacuum: the individuals involved in the *EGALE* and *Halpern* cases appeared before the court as interveners. However, the Supreme Court considered their particular circumstances only when it refused to answer the final question in the reference. The court acknowledged that if it chose to answer Question 4, its answer could invalidate the marriages of the interveners and the other individuals who had been granted same-sex marriages in British Columbia, Ontario, and Quebec, depending on how it answered the question. The court recognized that its abstract decision could have tangible consequences for concrete cases regardless of the fact that these immediate cases were not included in the terms of the reference.

Parties in References I: Governments

Given that all reference cases result from a decision by a government to pursue a case, it is important to know whether there are any patterns regarding the types of governments that initiate references. For example, after relative time in power is considered, have more references come from governments led by the Conservative Party or the Liberal Party? Similarly, are governments more likely to refer

Table 3.4 Governments initiating four or more references, post-1949

First minister	*Party*[a]	*References*	*Days in power*[b]	*Yearly average*[c]
Davis (ON)	PC	6	13 years, 10 months	0.46
Lougheed (AB)	PC	5	14 years, 2 months	0.36
P. Trudeau	LP	5	15 years, 5 months	0.33
St. Laurent	LP	5	8 years, 7 months	0.63
W.A.C. Bennett (BC)	SC	5	20 years, 1 month	0.25
Peckford (NL)	PC	4	10 years	0.40
Hatfield (NB)	PC	4	16 years, 11 months	0.25

a PC = Progressive Conservative; LP = Liberal Party; SC = Social Credit.
b Including multiple terms if applicable; rounded to the nearest month.
c Rounded down to a full year.

questions in a minority Parliament compared to a majority Parliament? As mentioned in Chapter 2, Prime Minister Mackenzie King is credited with the most references, at 32 cases, a number that certainly reflects King's lengthy time as prime minister but also his willingness to rely on reference cases to deal with disputes with both provincial and previous federal governments. However, at over 30 reference cases, the King government stands as an outlier. In the post-1949 era, Premier Bill Davis of Ontario is credited with the most references, at 6 cases. Table 3.4 details the governments that asked the most reference questions during the post-1949 era, listing all governments that referred four or more cases.

What is most interesting about the findings in Table 3.4 is that the government with the shortest time in power referred the second highest number of cases. Prime Minister Louis St. Laurent was in power for just over eight and half years but referred as many cases as the government of Premier W.A.C. Bennett (in power longest, at over twenty years), the government of Premier Peter Lougheed (in power for over fourteen years), and the government of Prime Minister Pierre Trudeau (in power for over fifteen years). When the number of reference cases initiated by a government is averaged over the number of

Table 3.5 Reference case by party, 1949–2017

Party[a]	*Cases*	*Percent*
Progressive Conservative Party	42	43.3
Liberal Party	31	32.0
Social Credit Party	8	8.2
New Democratic Party	6	6.2
Conservative Party of Canada	3	3.1
Parti Québécois	2	2.1
Liberal Progressive Party	2	2.1
Co-operative Commonwealth Federation	2	2.1
Saskatchewan Party	1	1.0
Total	**97**	**100**

a Federal and provincial parties are combined to reflect research documenting that the linkages and vertical integration between federal and provincial associations of the same party are much closer than previously believed (see Pruysers 2014).

years in power, the St. Laurent government still used the reference power at a much greater rate than the other governments listed, at 0.63 references per year. Although no Conservative or Progressive Conservative prime ministers appear in Table 3.4, as they did not have the requisite number of references, it is interesting to note that the rates of reference power use for conservative prime ministers serving at minimum one full year – Brian Mulroney and Stephen Harper – is relatively comparable to the rate of Liberal Party prime minister Pierre Trudeau. Indeed, Harper initiated reference cases at a rate of 0.33 per year in office, and Mulroney used the reference power at a rate of 0.38 per year in office, as both are responsible for 3 reference cases during their tenure. Table 3.5 also demonstrates that the majority of reference cases have been initiated by governments led by the Progressive Conservative Party.

From 1949 to 2017, just over 46 percent of reference cases were initiated by federal and provincial conservative parties – either the Progressive Conservative Party (both federal and provincial) or the Conservative Party of Canada. The second highest number can be attributed to the Liberal Party (again both federal and provincial), with 32 percent. For context, from 1949 to 2017, Social Credit governments referred just over 8 percent of all reference cases, and the New Democratic Party referred just over 6 percent. The domination of conservative and liberal parties (78 percent of cases) demonstrates that both parties are willing to initiate judicial review through a reference case. This finding also reflects that conservative and liberal parties (both federal and provincial) have governed in Canada more than other political parties. It is interesting to note the limited number of reference cases from parties that have governed provincially for lengthy periods of time. For example, from 1949 to 2017, Social Credit governments presided in Alberta and British Columbia for a combined fifty-eight years and account for only approximately 8 percent of reference cases. New Democratic governments led Manitoba and British Columbia for a combined thirty years and referred just over 6 percent of cases. Finally, the Parti Québécois governed in Quebec for eighteen years and initiated only about 2 percent of all reference cases during this period.

It is also interesting to note that governments are much more likely to ask reference questions when in a position of parliamentary strength. From 1949 to 2017, majority governments were the source of 88.7 percent of references, whereas governments in minority parliaments initiated just 11.3 cases. Looking at both provincial and federal legislatures since 1910, Thomas and White (2015) find that Canadians are more likely to be governed by a minority government. Addressing just federal parliaments, Russell (2008) finds that half of the elections since 1957 have produced minority governments. Indeed, minority governments are a frequent occurrence in Canadian politics. The frequency of minority parliaments reflects both the single member plurality electoral system and the fact that Canadian voters do not strongly support any single political party (Russell 2009; Dufresne and Nevitte 2014). As a result, it is noteworthy that majority governments have instigated references at a much greater frequency than minority governments.

Minority governments likely do not participate in reference cases for the central reasons of time and uncertainty regarding government survival. Although Canadians have elected many minority governments, these governments have a shorter shelf life than majority governments.

The reference process is relatively quick compared to routine litigation, but decisions in reference cases can still take several months to over a year from the time of referral. A government that is uncertain about its future survival may be reluctant to initiate a reference case, as it may be out of power by the time the court renders a decision. Furthermore, the uncertainty of a minority government has direct implications for public policy outputs and governmental policy plans. The public policy of minority governments is developed with short-term goals and on an urgent basis (Bourgault 2011). The types of large constitutional questions (especially those addressing issues of mega constitutional politics) that have given rise to many reference cases do not align with the short-sighted public policy mindset of a minority government and do not become a priority for governments that are preoccupied with legislative survival. The finding that minority governments are reluctant to turn to judicial review through a reference case may seem counterintuitive given the claims made by some delegation scholars, like Ginsburg (2003) and Hirschl (2000, 2004), who posit that governments are more willing to delegate decision making to the courts when faced with uncertainty regarding their political survival. If this claim were true regarding reference cases, we would expect to see a much higher rate of use of the reference power by minority governments. Instead, the data demonstrate that the reference power is most often a power used by majority governments that have a high degree of stability in the legislature.

Parties in References II: Third-Party Interveners

The participation of third-party interveners signals that a case has gained the interest of groups that are not direct parties to the dispute and that the court's decision may have wider political or public policy effects. Third-party interveners can include other governments (both provincial or federal), business or corporate-based groups, unions, and rights-based interest groups such as LEAF (Women's Legal Education and Action Fund) and the Canadian Civil Liberties Association. The participation of an intervener typically includes the filing of a legal brief that details the group's arguments and opinions regarding the case. Additionally, groups are often permitted to make oral arguments and respond to questions during the case proceedings, although they are typically afforded less time than the direct parties. These groups often provide expertise or legal arguments not addressed by the direct parties in the case. In some instances, intervening groups represent individuals or groups that could be affected either directly or indirectly by the decision of the court. For example, the Canadian Association of the Chiefs of Police and the Law-Abiding Unregistered Firearms Association intervened in *Reference re Firearms Act* [*Firearms Reference*], a case concerning the constitutionality of the Canadian Firearms Registry, because the Supreme Court's decision would directly affect the members of both associations, even though neither group was a direct party in the case. It is important to note that both provincial attorneys general and the federal attorney general have the automatic right to intervene in any reference case at the Supreme Court, provided by section 53(5) of the *Supreme Court Act*.[54]

Some scholars argue that the participation of interveners signals that a court exerts a great deal of influence on the society within which it operates and that a higher or increased number of interventions is indicative of a court that has either become politicized or has moved toward a policy-making role, signifying judicialized politics (Epp 1998; Manfredi 2004). Moreover, Radmilovic (2013) finds that government intervention in Charter cases is strongly associated with, and has an impact on, whether or not the Supreme Court finds a statute unconstitutional, showing that intervention can have a tangible impact on case outcomes. However, contrary to Radmilovic's findings, interviews with justices of the Supreme Court demonstrate that the justices generally welcome the participation of intervening groups but doubt that interveners influence their decisions (Songer et al. 2012; Macfarlane 2013).

Nevertheless, there is no clear pattern of how many groups are granted access to intervene at the Supreme Court, and unfortunately there are no data that consider provincial appellate courts. Songer et al. (2012) find that the number of applications to intervene at the Supreme Court varies from year to year, without any discernable pattern. However, the success rate of groups applying to participate as third parties at the Supreme Court has dramatically increased since 1987 due to changes in the court's rules governing participation, and now the rate of success is often over 90 percent (Songer et al. 2012, 86). According to Muttart (2007, 21), this high acceptance rate can be viewed as reflecting a self-reinforcing cycle.

Now that the Supreme Court is in the practice of granting rather than denying applications to intervene, any refusals of interventions can be viewed as political or a pre-judgment of the case, and thus courts are more likely to grant access (Muttart 2007, 21). Interviews and public statements by Supreme Court justices appear to confirm Muttart's hypothesis. Macfarlane (2013, 51) finds that justices are sensitive to public perception respecting which groups are granted access as interveners and that they make an effort to appear objective and not to overtly favour particular groups in granting access.

In Canadian appellate court references from 1949 to 2017, approximately 93 percent of cases included the participation of an intervener group, either another government or an interest group. In total, 66.3 percent of cases included governmental interventions (2.3 per case), and 72.6 percent included nongovernmental interveners (3.1 per case), with several cases including the participation of both nongovernmental and governmental groups. Only 7 cases did not include the participation of a third party or another government. However, of the 7 cases, 4 included the appointment of a third-party nongovernmental group by the court to present arguments in opposition to the government in the case.[55] These cases still demonstrate the participation of an outside group, albeit in a different (and more direct) capacity. Fifteen cases included the participation of ten or more third-party intervener groups, including both governmental and nongovernmental parties,[56] and 6 cases included the participation of more than fifteen intervening groups (see Table 3.6). *Reference re Bill 30, An Act to Amend the Education Act (Ont)*, a 1987 Supreme Court case concerning the funding of a separate Catholic school board in Ontario, had the highest number of third-party participants in this dataset, with twenty-four nongovernmental groups and two governments.

When the participation of interveners in reference cases is compared to their participation in all cases heard by the Supreme Court of Canada, the results are striking. Epp (1998) finds that between 1985 and 1990, only 30 to 40 percent of all Supreme Court cases included third-party interveners. Hausegger, Hennigar, and Riddell (2015, 228) document trends regarding intervener participation after 1986 at the Supreme

Table 3.6 Cases with the greatest number of third-party interveners

Case	*Subject*	*Nongovernmental interveners*	*Governmental interveners*	*Total*
Reference re Bill 30	Is the funding of a separate Catholic school board constitutional?	24	2	26
Reference re Same-Sex Marriage	Constitutionality of same-sex marriage	23	2	25
Reference re Education Act of Ontario and Minority Language Education Rights	Minority language education rights	18	1	19
Reference re Senate Reform	Can the Parliament of Canada amend or abolish the Senate without provincial consent?	5	12[a]	17
Reference re Firearms Act	Is the *Firearms Act* intra vires the criminal law power of the federal Parliament?	8	7	15
Reference re Securities Act	Is the *Securities Act* intra vires the federal Parliament's power to regulate trade and commerce?	8	7	15

a Including territorial governments.

Court, excluding reference cases, finding an increase in participation of both nongovernmental and governmental interveners over time. However, the percentage of cases that include the participation of an intervening group (both governmental and nongovernmental) does not surpass 55 percent (Hausegger, Hennigar, and Riddell 2015, 228). Thus the finding that over 90 percent of references include the participation of an intervening group demonstrates a stark difference between reference cases and routine litigation.

The higher rate of intervener participation in reference cases compared to routine litigation may be the result of several factors. First, along with signalling the importance of reference cases, this participation is indicative of the unique nature of reference cases. When a piece of legislation either proposed or not yet in force is the subject of a reference, the parties intervening have the opportunity to participate in the shaping and perhaps writing of this legislation. For example, in the *Same-Sex Marriage Reference*, the court was asked to consider the constitutionality of proposed legislation that had not been introduced to Parliament, let alone enacted as law. The groups that intervened in this case would have been motivated by the opportunity to shape the civil definition of marriage. Participation in a reference thus provides access to the legislative process that may otherwise be unavailable. Similarly, given that many reference cases centre on statutory interpretation, intervening groups have a unique opportunity to argue how a particular statute or provision should be understood. This influence has the potential to be substantial when questions are referred to the courts in the absence of a factual dispute. In the absence of facts, parties can approach their legal arguments in a broad manner, moulding the interpretation to a particular situation that best suits their preferences for interpretation and eschewing the need to rely on a parliamentarian or political party to present their views. Ostensibly, the high rate of government interveners could reflect that all governments are invited to participate in a reference once questions are referred to a court.

Conclusion

This chapter has detailed the central trends in reference cases from 1949 to 2017 and contextualized the findings with existing scholarship on Canadian courts and judicial politics. During this time, the majority of references still concerned the *Constitution Act, 1867*, regardless of the introduction of the *Constitution Act, 1982* and the *Charter of Rights and Freedoms*. This finding reflects the fact that although the 1982 Constitution simply did not exist during the earlier period of this study, after 1982, references that consider this Constitution are still quite uncommon. Additionally, this finding demonstrates that the reference power still serves largely the same purpose for which it was created: to sort out constitutional controversies regarding the division of powers between governments. The reference power has not been used extensively by governments to assess whether government legislation violates the protected constitutional rights of individuals or groups. The rights revolution spurred by the Charter, which has greatly impacted other areas of Canadian governance, is not present in reference cases.

The findings of this study demonstrate that courts do not view their role in reference cases as markedly different from their role in other types of litigation, regardless of the unique characteristics of references. Indeed, appellate courts have been quite willing to invalidate government action, either proposed or enacted, and do not appear to limit themselves in reference cases despite the technically advisory nature of these cases. If judicial activism is understood as the invalidation of governmental action by courts, the findings of unconstitutionality and statutory invalidation in reference cases demonstrate this principle. However, the unique characteristics of references require a reconsideration of how judicial activism is framed and understood. Indeed, if governments self-initiate references, they are inviting the judicial branch to participate in political debates regarding the legality and constitutionality of government action and legislation. Activism in this sense cannot be framed as the judicial branch usurping the powers of elected officials; instead, political actors have realized some benefits of inviting the courts into debates and relying on the bench to make decisions on complex normative and legal issues.

Although reference cases reach courts in a manner that is entirely distinct from routine litigation, the analysis in this chapter demonstrates that courts do not view their role differently in these cases. This fact becomes apparent when analyzing the unanimity rate of reference cases. Given the high-profile and controversial nature of many reference cases, it might be assumed that references generally have a high rate of unanimity, as a court may prioritize speaking with one voice to set a clear precedent. However, this assumption is not supported by the data. The high rate of divided opinions in reference cases may reflect that many references can be normatively difficult to resolve and that many references are abstract, which may result in more divided opinions. Unlike the routine litigation normally heard by appellate courts, reference cases do not come with a trial record, and the justices do not have the benefit of a previous decision by a lower court judge. Moreover, unlike with a routine appeal, justices are not bound by the analysis of the issues raised on appeal. As a result, it may be that references can allow for judicial creativity and a wider breadth of legal analysis.

One feature of reference cases that distinguishes them from all other types of litigation in Canada is the ability of governments to refer questions that do not arise from a concrete dispute. This lack of a concrete dispute requires the courts to engage in abstract review. However, as the present analysis has demonstrated, not all reference cases concern abstract problems. Approximately one-third of all appellate court reference cases are much closer to routine concrete judicial review. That reference cases have been used to sort out live legal disputes is a previously understudied finding and has implications for understanding why governments refer questions to the courts in this manner. When a government initiates a reference case in an instance where there is a concrete dispute, it makes a deliberate choice to avoid routine litigation and to opt for a reference instead.

The majority of reference cases from 1949 to 2017 were abstract. That being said, many of the abstract references had clear connections to ongoing concrete disputes, as did the *Nadon Reference*. However, instead of referring narrow questions based solely on the specific dispute, governments referred questions in an abstract manner. This use of abstraction potentially allows the parties involved to receive a broad judicial decision that could be used in future cases instead of being limited to the specific case at hand. Yet reliance on abstract review can raise important issues for the role of the judiciary within the political system. First, abstract review can have the effect of requiring courts to hypothesize the effects of legislation without having a factual context. Second, the reliance on abstract review can cause governments to partake in unusual legislative behaviour, such as passing legislation that conflicts with the public policy goals of the government for the sole purpose of challenging it in the courts through a reference, as in the *Egg Reference*. This type of legislative manoeuvring results in a distortion of both the policy-making process and the reference question procedure.

Third, abstract review furthers the judicialization of politics. Abstract review embroils the courts and policy makers in a direct interaction, and sometimes conflict, over the Constitution's meaning and its constraints on the creation of public policy (Stone Sweet 2000, 51). When judicial review is abstract, it can serve as an extension of the legislative process. More specifically, when governments refer legislation that is not in force to the courts through a reference case, judicial review becomes another stage in the policy-making process, as legislators will wait for judicial approval before taking further action. Unlike concrete review, which takes place after the policy enactment, abstract review can actively involve the courts in the legislative process, ultimately contributing to judicialization. Finally, abstract review has the ability to place the courts in the position of dictating the acceptable parameters of public policy in a manner that is much more direct compared to concrete review. Without the benefit of a concrete case or controversy, abstract review places the courts in the position of directly questioning the wisdom of policy makers, instead of reviewing the implementation and application of a public policy, as in routine litigation.

The tension surrounding the proper role of the courts vis-à-vis reference cases is also evident in the debate concerning the ability of the courts to refuse to answer reference questions. To be sure, most of the time, courts refuse to answer questions for practical reasons, as answers to other questions within the same case render the remaining questions unnecessary. However, there are several instances where the courts have found the referred questions too abstract to permit worthwhile judicial analysis or where the questions have placed the court in a role that is contrary to the separation of the judiciary from the partisan branches of government.

The final section of this chapter has analyzed the behaviour of parties in reference cases, specifically governments and third-party interveners. The findings show that governments are more likely to initiate reference cases from a position of parliamentary strength. Majority governments are much more likely to refer questions to the courts compared to minority governments. Furthermore, the reference power is a tool used by governments led by parties of all political stripes, both conservative and liberal. References have not been strongly associated with one particular party over others. With respect to the participation of third-party intervener groups, the rate of participation of intervening groups is much higher in references than in routine litigation. This situation could reflect that courts may be more willing to grant access and that more groups may apply to participate due to the unique nature of reference cases. What can be established from this finding is that intervening groups have deemed participation in reference cases to be worthwhile, as they would not dedicate their (often limited) resources to references if they did not believe reference cases had any impact outside the courtroom. Intervening groups may believe that reference cases provide a unique opportunity to influence the policy-making process in a manner that is not possible through regular parliamentary channels. Finally, the high level of participation by interveners in reference cases further demonstrates that although references are advisory opinions in theory, they can have important implications for public policy and governance in practice.

Given these findings, it becomes apparent that there is a disconnect between how courts and participants understand reference cases. Several different measures of how courts have responded to references, such as unanimity rate and authorship, show that the trends are not markedly different from those of routine litigation. Although it is reasonable to assume for a variety of reasons – including the high-profile nature of many reference cases and the unique structural characteristics of this form of abstract and advisory judicial review – that courts will respond to these cases in a manner distinct from routine litigation, this is simply not the case. Instead, on the whole, Canadian appellate courts have not altered their behaviour when hearing reference cases.

That being said, the overwhelming participation rate of third-party interveners (both interest groups and other governments) demonstrates that these parties understand reference cases in a different manner. Although this rate is contingent on the courts granting access, it also reflects a higher level of interest among third parties, who still must apply to participate in these cases. Finally, it is important to consider that the initiation of a reference case is entirely at the will of the government. Comparatively, governments are most often in a reactionary role in routine litigation, whereas self-initiated references enable the government to be proactive by placing the power over initiating litigation entirely in the hands of the court.[57]

"It's Always a Little Bit of Politics": Why Governments Ask Reference Questions

4

As we have seen, the Canadian reference power has been used by governments to address a highly diverse range of issues. Governments have sought judicial advice on matters related to institutional reform, such as the amendment or abolishment of electoral districts, the reform of the Senate, and the patriation of the Constitution.[1] Canadian courts have issued reference opinions on many contentious issues (sometimes with moral implications), including the unilateral secession of a province, the criminalization of prostitution, the criminalization of bigamy, and the constitutionality of same-sex marriage.[2] Additionally, decisions rendered in reference cases have played a key role in disputes between governments over constitutional jurisdiction in a variety of policy spheres, including agriculture, natural resources, human reproduction, and the national regulation of firearms and securities.[3] And of course, the reference power has frequently been used to deal with matters related to economic and labour regulations, best demonstrated by the many references that took place in the throes of the Great Depression.[4] Although there is virtually no limit on what governments can ask the courts to consider through a reference, there is also effectively no discernable pattern or similarity that links the diverse range of issues on which governments have sought judicial advice through reference cases. Indeed, governments have found the reference power to be an attractive response to a wide array of issues.

Evidence presented in the two preceding chapters has provided some further insight into how the reference power has been used. We now know that references are more likely to be used to resolve issues related to constitutional jurisdiction and the division of powers. The rate at which governments use the reference power parallels periods in Canadian political history marked by great contestation. We also know that the practice of seeking judicial advice through a reference question is not limited to any one particular party, nor is it exclusive to governments that have difficulties in commanding the legislature. Moreover, we know that reference cases are not limited to obscure legal questions but have been used to address highly salient matters, a feature that is well understood by third-party intervener groups. We also have an understanding of how courts respond to reference cases, in that courts do not act in a restrained manner when responding to reference questions, as they are quite willing to invalidate government action. Finally, we also know that references are more likely to elicit divided decisions, with more dissenting opinions, compared to routine cases.

Yet none of this explains why governments resort to asking the courts reference questions, nor does it address the possible political and strategic advantages in seeking judicial review. Of course, in some specific reference cases, there are convincing explanations for why a reference opinion was sought. For example, in the case of the *Same-Sex Marriage Reference,* Hennigar (2009) demonstrates that seeking a reference case, rather than engaging in the appeal of a live case or simply legislating to allow nonheterosexual marriage, was the most advantageous choice for Jean Chrétien's government. One could also consider the Alberta government's use of a reference to challenge the federal government's National Energy Program as a means to protect provincial jurisdiction over natural resources in *Reference re Exported Natural Gas Tax* (Riddell and Morton 2004).[5]

The goal of this chapter is to take a step back from the fine-grained explanations provided in individual reference cases and attempt to understand more generally why governments have used the reference power across multiple cases. In particular, this chapter highlights some of the strategic advantages that governments can obtain from the reference power, beyond gaining an answer to a legal question. In short, now that we have a good understanding of *how* the reference power has been used, it is possible to address *why* governments have sought judicial advice through reference cases.

Other scholars have also tried to understand the circumstances that might motivate a government to use the reference power. In his discussion of Canadian reference cases, Strayer (1988) finds that one advantage to the reference power is that it allows politicians to gain judicial opinion and review when it might not ordinarily be accessible. More specifically, he argues that since the restrictions related to standing, mootness, and applications for leave do not apply, reference cases provide a low threshold for governments to obtain judicial review. The access provided by the reference power provides the means to challenge the constitutional validity of actions of other governments, allowing for a flexible approach to interjurisdictional relations. Strayer also explains that governments can be motivated to use the reference power to seek legal clarification before proceeding with a desired policy in order to limit uncertainty that would be undesirable once the policy was in place (320).

Focusing exclusively on federalism, Persaud (1998) provides a taxonomy to classify the possible explanations for why governments use the reference power in intergovernmental disputes. He argues that reference questions can be asked either proactively or reactively. To explain the former, Persaud argues (similar to Strayer) that governments ask reference questions in a strategic attempt to affirm their legal jurisdiction to enact a preferred policy (52). In explaining the latter, he finds that governments will seek a reference opinion to circumvent challenges to legal authority posed by other governments or obstacles that prevent the implementation of a policy. Finally, Persaud explains that reference cases will be initiated by governments for the symbolic purpose of asserting autonomy within the division of powers. Although Persaud's explanations for the utility of the reference power concern three federalism-related reference cases, his explanations complement those of Strayer, but with a greater acknowledgment of the political strategy that can influence a government's decision to use the reference power.

Hausegger, Hennigar, and Riddell (2015) also consider why governments initiate reference cases. After outlining the legal explanations provided by Strayer, Hausegger, Hennigar, and Riddell discuss some of the political motivations for a government's use of the reference power (250). Focusing largely on the *Same-Sex Marriage Reference*, the authors explain that references can provide governments a form of "agenda management" or the opportunity to avoid taking action on a divisive issue, like the recognition of same-sex marriage. They explain that references can also act as a powerful form of position legitimization; because courts often have greater public support compared to elected officials, a court decision that endorses or approves a particular government policy can be quite valuable to governments. Finally, the authors explain that references provide governments the ability to "pass the buck" to another decision-making body, which can be an effective political strategy.

Strayer, Persaud, and Hausgegger, Hennigar, and Riddell provide important insights into why governments use the reference power to deal with a variety of political issues, laying an essential foundation for this chapter's analysis. Importantly, this previous work demonstrates that a reference case can be employed by governments for multiple reasons – both legal and political. Like the scholars discussed above, I am interested in trying to explain some of the reasons why a government would use the reference power. Rather than providing an explanation of the motivations behind a single reference episode, this chapter relies on data from individuals involved in multiple reference cases to explain more generally why governments have used the reference power across reference cases. My objective is to create a framework for governments' use of the reference power that can be applied and tested against future reference cases. However, the nature of this analysis is subject to important limitations. Given that there are an unknown number of instances where a government *could* have used the reference power, it is not possible to engage in a more sophisticated methodology of theory testing. As discussed below, because a single reference case can be the product of multiple strategic considerations, it is difficult to quantify the number of times a government relied on the reference power to benefit from any one particular strategy. The motivations behind each reference case are difficult to verify empirically without access to internal decision-making documents, most of which are protected by Cabinet confidence and/or solicitor-client privilege. As a result, interviews with individuals involved in past reference cases are essential to providing some insight into the motivations behind the use of the reference power, even if this work cannot be directly linked back to each reference case in this study's database. In the discussion that follows, my goal is to provide a structure to help guide our understanding of the reference power and the political strategies that it makes possible.

Context and Scope

As established in Chapter 1, the ministers of justice/attorneys general play a key role in advising Cabinet when it decides to engage in a reference question, and they are the primary source of data for the analysis presented in this chapter.[6] That being said, to expand the number of interview subjects, the study involved individuals who had participated in reference cases, including former counsel who are constitutional experts and a former first minister. The inclusion of constitutional experts provides the perspective of reference case insiders who are not influenced by the same constraints and incentives faced by elected officials, which helps to verify generally the motivations and claims made by the attorneys general. The analysis that follows is based on eight in-depth, semi-structured, not-for-attribution interviews. Included in this sample are five former attorneys general, one former first minister, and two former counsel who are constitutional experts.[7] The attorneys general interviewed for this study had served in both provincial and federal Cabinets. The reference case counsel who participated had served as high-level legal advisors to several different governments (across political parties and levels of government) and as either a high-ranking public servant or an outside expert consultant. Although the counsel interview subjects may not have held the power to initiate a reference case, both advised governments during the decision-making process.

Interview responses largely relied on the subject's first-hand knowledge of specific reference episodes; however, some respondents were able to provide insight into other reference episodes that had taken place during their time in office but outside of their time as attorney general. Moreover, some subjects had directly participated in more than one reference case. Importantly, in the discussion that follows, the various thematic explanations for using the reference power are not mutually exclusive, and a government's decision to initiate a reference case was likely the product of a combination of several of these explanations. Indeed, every subject interviewed made it clear that there were multiple motivating factors that had led each government to begin a reference case.

Why Governments Ask Reference Questions

Politics, Controversy, and Hot Potatoes

Perhaps the most commonly assumed reason why governments ask reference questions is to avoid dealing with a controversial issue, or what is often referred to as the "hot potato" effect (Hennigar 2009; Hausegger, Hennigar, and Riddell 2015). For example, Hennigar (2009) argues that this was the impetus behind the Chrétien government's reference to the Supreme Court regarding the constitutionality of same-sex marriage. Hennigar contends that issues such as same-sex marriage may be understood as requiring a no-win decision and that politicians transfer decision-making power to the courts to avoid taking responsibility for making a no-win decision. Indeed, the *Same-Sex Marriage Reference* is perhaps the strongest example of this type of political strategy, as the caucus of the governing party was divided on this issue and there was not an overwhelming majority of support for same-sex marriage among Canadians (Hennigar 2009). However, due to several lower court decisions that supported the notion of same-sex marriage, as well as a Supreme Court decision that found sexual orientation to be a ground protected from discrimination under section 15 of the Charter,[8] the government could not ignore the issue. With these factors under consideration, delegating the decision on same-sex marriage to the Supreme Court became politically advantageous (Hennigar 2009).

It is important to note that the use of references in this manner has not escaped the notice of justices, who are saddled with finding answers to these political controversies. Through interviews with justices of the Supreme Court of Canada, Macfarlane (2013, 89) documents that the justices are conscious of the "political opportunism that arises in the context of the reference procedure." This awareness has caused courts to refuse to answer reference questions that were too political or that would have jeopardized the role of the judiciary in the Canadian constitutional framework. Given that the refusal of reference questions for political reasons is rare, it is puzzling that the courts are so willing to deal with these difficult questions.[9]

This explanation speaks to the strategy of blame avoidance, which occurs when a government passes decision-making power to the courts in an attempt to diffuse responsibility for deciding a politically divisive issue that could alienate both caucus members and voters. In throwing the hot potato to the courts, governments can blame the court for an unpopular decision, or conversely if the court's decision is well received by the public, the referring government can take credit for bringing the issue to the court in the first place. This explanation for why governments ask reference questions is the most overt example of political strategy as a motivation.

Almost all interviewees (except for one former attorney general and one counsel) mentioned politics, or dealing with political controversy, as the motivation for using the reference power. Some of the subjects relying on this explanation expressed the view that any important decision made by a government will have some form of political consideration. For example, commenting on a specific case in which they were involved, former Attorney General C frankly stated that there was "a political aspect, a political evaluation in the decision to go to court like we did."[10] When discussing the use of references in general, the same respondent continued with this premise: "It's a mix between the legal and political ... If you look at every reference and the reason for it, maybe not 100 percent, but a large part of it is politics." In a similar sentiment, former Attorney General D explained, "These are important questions ... Therefore, they are always going to have a political dimension to them, small *p*. It goes without saying."[11]

Other interviewees echoed that the reference power is a valuable tool for governments to deal with political controversies. Respondents who spoke to this theme explained that when dealing with a particularly controversial piece of legislation, it was prudent to seek assurance and to have the courts pronounce on the issue either before the passage of the bill or shortly following the adoption of the new law. A government may face criticism levelled at the constitutionality of a policy – recently enacted or proposed – from multiple sources, such as parliamentarians, opposition parties in the legislature, and other concerned private citizens, like academics. Former Attorney General A explained, "Not surprisingly, in these cases there is a political controversy following the passage of the legislation, and the legitimacy of the constitutional legal question resulted in the reference."[12] A reference decision before the adoption of a new policy can help to protect or insulate a government initiative that may cause political controversy. Former Attorney General B demonstrated this reasoning when stating, "The simple answer is that it was going to be controversial, so why go out on a limb and do something that is possibly illegal without going to the court and having the determination made beforehand."[13] Using a reference case to deal with a political controversy based on the constitutionality or legality of a government initiative was also apparent to counsel who had appeared in previous reference cases. Counsel B explained, "it was obviously politically controversial. There were serious questions about the legal validity and whether it was going to be a violation of the Constitution."[14]

When governments are faced with political controversy based on the constitutionality of a new policy or legislative project, referring the matter to the courts is just one of many options available. Instead of a reference, a government could request study by a parliamentary committee with the aid of external experts, or strike an external commission to conduct an investigation, or rely on the legal expertise available within the public service. Yet there are distinct benefits from delegating the political or constitutional controversy to the courts. Attorney General D spoke at length about the benefits of sending a controversial matter to the courts and thereby placing it outside of the routine parliamentary domain: "These are political hot potatoes usually, and what you're doing is taking it out of the political realm, at least for a period of time, and sending it to the court, where in fact you actually freeze the political discussion."[15] Attorney General D's comments refer to the norm of sub judice, a parliamentary convention and common law principle that prevents public officials from commenting on matters that may prejudice an ongoing judicial proceeding.[16] In other words, by sending the matter to the courts, the governing party can rely on sub judice to essentially mute parliamentary debate and criticism. Indeed, according to Attorney General D, this ability to halt a political debate over a proposed policy or a government action through a reference is one of the benefits unique to the reference power: "When a reference is referred, it's the government deciding that this is a political hot potato and that [it's] better to send it up to the court, better to give us some time, some breathing room."[17] As a result, the reference-initiating government can respond to critics by explaining that it is seeking the advice of the courts.

As indicated in the previous chapter, majority governments have initiated an overwhelming majority of reference cases. As a result, the use of a reference to provide "breathing room" for a government is an interesting finding given that majority governments have greater autonomy in terms of time and are not usually concerned with survival in the legislature compared to minority governments. For majority governments, reference cases are less likely to be driven by electoral pressures, and the desire to obtain "breathing room" implies that a government might be facing pressures within its caucus and party rather than solely from opposition parties within the legislature.

A reference can have the effect of limiting debate and effectively silencing legislative opposition and criticism, at least until the court decides the case. In his analysis of the *Same-Sex Marriage Reference*, Huscroft (2004) hypothesizes that using a reference in this manner was precisely the government's political strategy in this case. Huscroft argues that the Chrétien government embarked on a reference to deal with the issue of same-sex marriage as "crass partisan advantage ... to fend off political criticism and buy time" (258). The comments provided by individuals with direct involvement in reference cases appear to largely confirm Huscroft's assumptions, showing that a reference can be a valuable tool that can effectively silence criticism and allow a government to distance itself from a particular controversy while it waits for the courts to weigh in.

References are a tool that can be used not only to impede or pause a debate in the legislature but also to appeal to voters. A government can signal its disagreement with the actions of another government and engage in position taking through a reference case. Attorney General D discussed an episode where another government had referred a proposed policy of their government. In this example, along with the legitimate constitutional concerns that the reference-initiating government may have had, the proposed legislative scheme received vocal opposition by members of the public and other governments in the federation. As a result, by submitting the legislation for review through a reference case, the referring government was provided with a national platform to express its opposition to the legislation-enacting government. This purpose of the reference was not lost on the interviewee and their government: "I can't speak to their motivations. I don't know what they were, other than the fact that I can assume that it was a dose of politics involved, playing to their base."[18] In this particular episode, the reference allowed the referring government to insert itself into a policy-making process that would otherwise have been closed off. This is a benefit that exists regardless of the outcome of the specific reference case.

Of course, every decision made by an elected official could be interpreted as having some political motivation. As a result, we should not expect it to be otherwise when considering the decision to pursue a reference case by political actors. The practice of blame avoidance through a reference case demonstrates one of the most basic assumptions regarding the motivations of political actors according to rationality-based perspectives, namely that there is a central desire to take credit and to avoid blame (Weaver 1986). It is interesting to note that in deciding to use a reference to deal with a hot potato issue, governments appear to be more concerned with delegating decision making and less concerned with the case outcome. It does not appear that decision makers are overly concerned with how the court will decide; instead, the judicial outcome is secondary to the benefits that are achieved through referring a politically controversial issue. That being said, we can conclude from the findings above that the reference power is not merely a legal tool available to governments but also provides a viable means to deal with political controversies; as First Minister A explained, "It's always a little bit of politics."[19]

Federalism

The quantitative data make it clear that references are routinely employed to deal with issues related to federalism, a finding that is further substantiated when contextualized with qualitative data and interview responses. In his assessment of the reference power and its various benefits to governments, Strayer (1988) argues that like the powers of reservation and disallowance, references are a useful tool for governments to challenge the actions of other governments. Governments are quite willing to challenge the legislation or action of another government through a reference case, with provincial governments using references in this manner more often than federal governments. Furthermore, as demonstrated in Chapters 2 and 3, the vast majority of reference cases have considered federalism-based questions, more than half of which have focused on the *Constitution Act, 1867* as the primary subject, with a majority of these cases considering issues centred on the division of powers. The dominance of federalism disputes remained constant following the introduction of the *Constitution Act, 1982* and the *Canadian Charter of Rights and Freedoms*.

References can be a means to deal with federal relations between governments by mounting a jurisdictional challenge. Governments using a reference in this manner submit the action and/or legislation of another government for review by an appellate court on the basis that the other government has acted outside its legislative jurisdiction. These cases focus on the constitutional division of powers and provide governments a means to protect constitutional jurisdiction. An example of a reference used in such a manner is the *Firearms Reference*, where the attorney general of Alberta challenged the Government of Canada's gun registry legislation on the basis that it infringed on civil and property rights, a matter of provincial constitutional jurisdiction. Similarly, in *Reference re Quebec Sales Tax*, the attorney general of Canada challenged the constitutional validity of amendments to the Quebec sales tax on the grounds that it was too similar to the federal sales tax. In each instance, a government used a reference to solicit judicial review as a means to challenge the actions of another government. The use of references in this manner should be unsurprising given that it largely reflects the original intent behind the creation of the reference power, as discussed in Chapter 1.

Referring the legislation of another government has other benefits aside from protecting constitutional jurisdiction. According to interview subjects, the reference power can be a valuable tool of federalism in several ways, and the referral of another government's legislative project does not necessarily indicate opposition to the legislative goal by the referring government. Instead, as Attorney General C explained, going to court through a reference case can be a tool to force the other government to listen: "It was clear what [they] were doing ... but it was clear that to have our position considered, we had to go directly to court to speak to them." In this example, Attorney General C's government believed that the only way to gain the attention of the legislation-enacting government was to bring the courts in and ask for judicial review. Attorney General C explained that their government did not necessarily disagree with the ultimate goal of the legislation-enacting government but found that a reference case was a means to force the other government to negotiate with it. Attorney General C elaborated on their government's logic: "We are forced to listen to you because we are partners in federalism, and it's our mutual advantage to be respectful of one another and do the same for us, listen to us."[20]

Using a reference to force negotiation between federal partners is what Russell (1987) and Mandel (1994) point to as the impetus for the *Patriation Reference*. The Supreme Court's decision in this case found merit in both the position of the federal government (i.e., provincial approval is not required for constitutional amendment) and the argument of provincial governments (i.e., provincial involvement is essential for constitutional amendment), holding that provincial participation in the amendment process is conventionally, but not legally, required. According to both Russell and Mandel, the reference was the linchpin in bringing the parties back to the negotiation table, moving the constitutional amendment process forward. In his analysis of the *Patriation Reference,* Brandt (1982) takes the logic of negotiation one step further by contending that this case put the Supreme Court in the role of mediator rather than adjudicator, noting the highly political rather than legal nature of the dispute. Using a reference to promote negotiation can provide a government with the means to force itself into the policy debates of another government, gaining media attention in the process – a benefit for the excluded government regardless of the case outcome. To be sure, if the reference-initiating government is successful in its reference case, it will have a greater degree of influence on the policy debate, but the benefits to be gained solely from taking another government's legislation to court cannot be discounted.

If the routine political channels of negotiation are not available or have not been successful, a reference may be the final measure to force the involvement of another interested government in the policy-making process. This explanation is similar to the argument put forward by political disadvantage theory, which explains why some interest groups turn to the courts after exhausting routine political channels (see Cortner 1968). When a government refers proposed legislation of another government, it can pause the policy-making process, and it can ensure that external parties have a role in the process. If a government refers an existing policy to the courts, doing so could impede or stop the implementation of the policy. Using a reference as a means to open up the policy debate to include more groups was one of the explanations Attorney General E gave for their government's decision to initiate a reference case:

> In my view, it was better to facilitate that process by the reference question, which had a number of advantages in this regard ... [such as] allowing a whole group of interveners to come before the court, and that was something that I thought was very important given the fact that it was a matter of national importance.[21]

A reference case can help to address a reality of the Canadian federal system, namely that with multiple governments operating across territorial, provincial, and federal jurisdictions, there could be as many as fourteen different approaches to one public policy issue. Similarly, with regard to the role that courts play in shaping the law and thus public policy, until an issue receives a ruling from the Supreme Court, provincial courts can issue different rulings that create dissimilar access to public policy or an uneven application of rights across provincial boundaries. Accordingly, a reference can be a valuable tool for producing a national ruling or standard in a relatively timely manner, without having to wait for the issue to make its way through the juridical hierarchy. This differential access or treatment across jurisdictions was a concern that led some governments to submit reference questions to a court. According to Attorney General D, the differences between provinces can mean that a particular group has access to a right that is denied to similarly situated individuals in a different jurisdiction.[22] In such a circumstance, obtaining a ruling from the Supreme Court ensures an equality of access across the country, adding clarity to the situation. Attorney General E made a similar argument in explaining that a reference case can create policy convergence across jurisdictions: "[The reference] allowed for a national appreciation of the issue, so it all converged from the disparate hearings in the courts in the provinces; it all converged at the Supreme Court."[23] According to this perspective, references can be a valuable tool to enforce national standards in a federal jurisdiction in a timelier manner than is possible with the organic development of concrete review through the provinces.

Institutional Authority and Protection of the Courts

As discussed in this chapter's introduction, Hausegger, Hennigar, and Riddell (2015) list position legitimization as one of the benefits of the reference power for governments. The authors explain that courts can be an attractive venue for dealing with issues because they generally enjoy a greater level of support by the public compared to the other, more political, branches of government. Hausegger, Hennigar, and Riddell argue that a reference case not only provides elected officials with legitimization of a position but can also do so at the expense of political opponents (250). This logic is quite compelling, as there is convincing scholarship that documents both the popularity of the Supreme Court of Canada and the powerful nature of the court's decisions (Fletcher and Howe 2000; Hausegger and Riddell 2004; Radmilovic 2010). Indeed, the rich debate on the existence of a dialogue between the Supreme Court and policy makers demonstrates the inability or unwillingness of policy makers to overrule the court's decisions (Manfredi and Kelly 1999, 2001; Manfredi 2004, 2007). The persuasiveness of this explanation is clear, for if judicial decisions were not respected and considered authoritative, political actors would not use a reference case as a means to seek assurances from the court. However, it is important to note that there is a long-term tension between using references to acquire the judiciary's institutional authority and using them to avoid political hot potatoes. If governments increasingly rely on the courts to deal with hot potato issues, the institutional authority and legitimacy of the courts will likely suffer over time. Of course, a reciprocal effect could be that the authority and legitimacy of governments as the primary decision maker for salient political issues could also diminish as a result. The incongruence between the use of the reference power by political actors and the effect of the reference power is a conflict examined in the analysis that follows, with a focus on the implications for courts.

The former attorneys general, counsel, and first minister largely validated this legitimization hypothesis. However, the motivations behind using a reference in this manner are slightly more nuanced than simply using the reference power to attempt to legitimize a particular position. Instead, the explanations varied in terms of the following subthemes: using a reference to seek assurance for a controversial decision, the power of an authoritative opinion from a court, and protection for public policies that would be difficult to unravel once implemented. To be sure, these themes are interrelated and virtually impossible to disentangle in practice. It is important to note that this explanation differs from those previously examined, as the benefits are more contingent on a favourable decision from the courts. That being said, an authoritative decision from a high court may still be beneficial to a government, even if it invalidates government legislation, as it can provide the government certainty regarding its legislative program. Moreover, the court's decision may also detail how to amend the legislation to make it more legally or constitutionally permissible.

A government may want to seek assurance that a new policy or program is constitutional prior to implementation, as a finding of unconstitutionality after implementation could create policy instability, disorder, and confusion. To appreciate how seeking a reference can provide assurance when governments are concerned about policy reversal after implementation, it is useful to consider an example. In the 1980s the Ontario government wanted to fund Roman Catholic secondary schools, a program that once in operation would be quite difficult to unwind, as it would create an entirely separate Catholic high school board and school system. However, this proposal was quite controversial in terms of its compliance with the right to freedom of religion under section 2(b) of the Charter and with the right to equality under section 15. The controversy of this case is demonstrated in part by the very high rate of participation by third-party intervening groups, as this case had the highest rate of intervener participation among all reference cases after 1949, with twenty-six intervening groups (as discussed in Chapter 3). As a result, to seek assurance and protect this program from almost certain future challenges under the Charter, the government referred the enabling legislation to the Ontario Court of Appeal.

The decision of the Ontario Court of Appeal was subsequently appealed to the Supreme Court in *Reference re Bill 30, An Act to Amend the Education Act (Ont)*. In this reference, the Supreme Court found Ontario's legislation to be a valid exercise of provincial constitutional jurisdiction over separate schools. The Supreme Court's decision provided the Ontario government with an authoritative opinion that the new separate Catholic school system was constitutionally valid. The decision by the Supreme Court on Bill 30 undermined any future challenges on the basis of the Charter. Although referring Bill 30 made the Ontario government's legislative program vulnerable to invalidation by the courts, it was quite clear that the legislation would have been challenged once in place by the groups that opposed the government's policy. Submitting the legislation in a reference allowed the government to circumvent the likely future challenge and also to maintain a degree of control over the case, as it was able to create the reference questions and frame the terms of the debate.

Four of the participants interviewed made specific comments regarding the authority of the courts and the respect that a judicial decision is afforded in the partisan and political sphere. These attributes of authority and respect mean that policy makers are unlikely to ignore or reject a reference decision, regardless of their technically advisory nature. For example, Attorney General E commented, "I think the authoritative power of the courts is such that governments would seek to reject it at their peril."[24] Most interview subjects, when commenting on the authority of the courts, spoke specifically in relation to the Supreme Court and its position within the Canadian legal and political system. For Counsel A, the court's position within the legal system affords its decisions a higher level of authority compared to decisions made by appellate or lower courts: "The government wants to get a ruling, and it wants to get a ruling by the Supreme

Court because lower courts may be reversed. It's not fully authoritative unless it comes from the Supreme Court."[25] A reference decision can provide a government clout when making decisions regarding policy in a more powerful manner than is possible when obtaining an opinion from experts or commissioning a study from policy experts. Attorney General B explained, "An opinion is an opinion. It's not a court ruling. A court ruling is concrete. [If] you've got a court ruling, then you're on safe grounds. If you don't, you're taking chances."[26] Furthermore, a reference opinion may simply provide a government clarity on a complicated area of law, which could help to resolve the issue through the authority of the court.[27]

Although none of the interview subjects spoke directly about the *Nadon Reference,* their comments can provide some insight into the attorney general of Canada's decision to initiate a reference in this case. The *Nadon Reference* concerned the validity of the appointment of a judge from the Federal Court of Canada to fill one of the three "Quebec seats" on the Supreme Court of Canada. In this reference episode, the government had commissioned an opinion from a former justice of the Supreme Court regarding the legality of Nadon's appointment under the *Supreme Court Act.* This opinion, which was supported by constitutional scholar Peter Hogg and another retired Supreme Court justice, found Nadon's appointment to be valid. However, even with the support of expert opinion, the government still faced public criticism and, subsequently, a legal challenge in the Federal Court by a lawyer from Ontario. Although the Supreme Court's decision in the *Nadon Reference* did not agree with the government's experts, it provided clarity in an authoritative manner and effectively circumvented any future challenges regarding the appointment of a justice from the Federal Court to the Supreme Court. If the federal government had gone forward with the appointment of Justice Marc Nadon without the reference opinion and Nadon had been found ineligible at a later time, it could have jeopardized any decision made by the Supreme Court in which Nadon had participated.

With the high level of authority attributed to decisions by Canadian courts and the Supreme Court in particular, it should be unsurprising that elected officials will rely on such decisions to seek assurances for legislative projects and to gain insulation from future legal challenges. Indeed, this line of reasoning speaks to the explanation offered by Hausegger, Hennigar, and Riddell (2015) regarding political actors' use of references as legitimization. Six of the interview participants specifically commented on the benefits of obtaining a reference opinion that clarified the legality of a policy or validated the proposed policy scheme. For example, Counsel B explained, "We are generally going to use a reference to gain clarity on a measure that might be subject to challenge."[28] Even though there is always a possibility that the courts could find a legislative initiative invalid in a reference, the assurance that results from submitting a policy for review can outweigh the risk of invalidation. In the words of Attorney General B,

> From my point of view, it is a pretty simple issue – controversial proposed scheme. We could have gone ahead and done it without the reference, but then you're really placing yourself at jeopardy, and we knew that someone was going to challenge us if we went ahead and did it ... The reference determines if, for once and for all, you get the red light or the green light.[29]

Governments will initiate references when they know their proposed legislative scheme is controversial and likely to be challenged. If the referring government is successful in its reference case, it can continue with its legislative project with a great deal of confidence, knowing that future legal challenges have been largely pre-empted by the reference case. Indeed, Attorneys General E and C and First Minister A explicitly stated that in their experience a reference case had provided each of their governments a means of protecting itself in going forward with a proposed legislative project. Although a reference does not completely insulate a government from future challenges, according to Attorney General E, "it makes it very difficult for a challenge to be effectively mounted."[30]

As mentioned above, seeking legal assurances from courts through a reference case is arguably more important to governments seeking to implement new policies that will have significant repercussions if they are found invalid once in effect, like Ontario's creation of the separate

Catholic high school system. Speaking about a case in which they were involved, Counsel B explained,

> In a situation where if you go ahead and implement a change that is then very difficult to unwind, it is probably prudent before the fact, and if you think there is a plausible case to be made that the initiative would be, could be, found unconstitutional, that you get legal authority to get the matter cleared up by the courts beforehand.[31]

Certainly, using a reference in this manner requires a government that is willing to slow down or pause the legislative process until it has the court's decision. Additionally, a government in this position should be willing to accept an unfavourable ruling from the court, which could negate its ability to pursue the policy altogether.

These findings largely validate the arguments made by Russell (1977) about *Reference re Anti-Inflation Act*.[32] In his assessment of this case, Russell explains that the Ontario government pushed the federal Cabinet to refer the *Anti-Inflation Act* to the Supreme Court.[33] According to Russell, the attorney general of Ontario was concerned with the uncertainty that would result from protracted litigation challenging the *Anti-Inflation Act* across the country. Furthermore, Ontario wanted assurance from the Supreme Court regarding the constitutionality of the *Anti-Inflation Act*, which it supported. During this time, Ontario was led by Premier Bill Davis's minority government, which wished to avoid dealing with the matter through the legislature, as it faced strong opposition from the other parties. In *Reference re Anti-Inflation Act*, the Supreme Court held that the *Anti-Inflation Act* was a valid exercise of federal constitutional jurisdiction under the "Peace, order, and good government" clause. This reference case not only assured Ontario that passing the legislation was indeed a valid action of the Parliament of Canada but also gave the federal government (the referring party) the authority to move forward with its anti-inflation policy.

Expedited Justice and Pausing the Debate

Looking at the internal workings of the Department of Justice and the political calculations that can shape a government's decision, Hennigar

(2007) has demonstrated that time and resources are important considerations during this process. Not only are governments concerned with the financial costs that can be incurred through litigation, but they also consider other resource-related issues, such as policy costs. Policy costs include issues such as loss of control over a policy and loss of political capital (233). We should expect to see similar considerations made by governments in reference cases. Although participation in a reference differs from appealing a lower court decision, it still impacts these resources. Arguably, in situations where governments refer legislation that is proposed and not yet in force, the impact of policy costs, such as the loss of control over policy making, can be more obvious and direct, as a negative reference decision could cause a government to cancel its policy plans.

Aside from resources, governments also consider the impact of time. Strayer (1988, 321) argues that one of the most significant benefits given to governments by a reference is the ability to obtain judicial review from a high court in a relatively timely manner. Routine or concrete cases can take several years before reaching a provincial appellate court and even longer still to reach the Supreme Court of Canada, whereas in a reference case a government can submit a question and obtain a decision from an appellate court or the Supreme Court in a matter of months. For example, in the *Nadon Reference*, the Supreme Court returned a decision five months after reference questions were submitted via an order in council. The *Nadon Reference* is possibly one of the speediest references, considering the time-sensitive nature of the dispute and the fact that the court was not operating with a full bench. A point of comparison can be provided by looking at other recent references. For example, the Saskatchewan Court of Appeal reached a decision in *Reference re Marriage Commissioners Appointed under the Marriage Act, 1995, SS 1995, c M-4.1,* approximately seventeen months after the questions were first submitted by the Saskatchewan Cabinet.[34] Similarly, only fourteen months elapsed between the Cabinet order and the Supreme Court's decision in the *Senate Reform Reference*.

The ability to obtain a ruling from an appellate court in under two years is an important benefit of the reference power for governments. If a government wishes to implement a wide-ranging program but would like to seek assurance that the proposal is constitutionally valid before proceeding, it can obtain judicial advice in a timely manner. Counsel A provided this reasoning as one of the central motivations behind the use of the reference power by governments: "They usually want to get a timely ruling and if you wait for a case to follow the normal course, you might wait several years before it reaches the Supreme Court."[35] A reference provides a government direct access to an appellate court without requiring that it wait for a concrete dispute or a set of facts to pursue a case. Attorney General A agreed that one of the central benefits of the reference power is that it addresses the "need for a government to obtain a constitutional decision from the courts in a relatively timely manner rather than have disputes drag through the courts in a number of actions."[36] It is interesting to note the juxtaposition between using a reference to obtain a timely ruling from a high court and using a reference to give a government more time (or to pause a debate) in relation to the legislature, as discussed above. A government can seek a reference to gain time and "breathing room" in relation to the legislature but not as much time as routine litigation might require.

The advantages of the expeditious reference process are not only that it allows the referring government to bypass a generally slow-moving judicial system but also that it circumvents the initiation of a slow-moving legislative process and opposition parties. If a government attempts to pursue a legislative program that spurs a great deal of opposition within Parliament, it can be faced with an uphill battle, even if the government holds a majority in the legislature. In such circumstances, those who oppose the governing party's policy proposal can use a variety of parliamentary rules and procedures to attempt to prevent or delay the passage of the government's bill. Understandably, these delaying tactics are even more powerful when the governing party holds only a minority in the legislature. In such situations, a reference case may not only save the governing party time but can also help it to avoid the expenditure of other resources, such as political capital, in an effort to secure the passage of the proposed legislation. Attorney General D found that this aspect of the reference power makes it quite valuable to governments: "You get a clear indication what your power is more quickly than if it was legislated and gone through Parliament with what an undoubtedly controversial legislation held up with all the parliamentary procedural rules that opposition can use ... I think a reference short-circuits that."[37]

A reference decision that confirms the constitutionality of legislation can lend a great deal of authority to a government's objective without requiring the government to expend a potentially great deal of political resources in attempting to marshal the bill through the legislature. A reference requires far fewer resources compared to routine review. As there is only one legal proceeding (or two in situations where a provincial reference case is appealed to the Supreme Court), the costs required have the potential to be significantly outweighed by the benefits that may result. According to Attorney General B, this was certainly one of the central factors that drove their government to submit its proposed policy to the courts in a reference: "If you go and get the opinion right or the decision, then you don't go and waste a lot resources or a lot of time with something that could be eventually overturned later on, and there could be a lot of costs as well, legal costs and political costs too."[38] A government can thus limit the expenditure of future resources by submitting legislation to the courts earlier on in the process.

Although not a benefit mentioned by the individuals interviewed, a reference may be useful for governments dealing with emergency situations in which quick assurance that actions are legal and/or constitutional is essential. Such exigent circumstances would include the use of the reference power during wartime, when governments must respond to multiple crises with confidence in the legitimacy of their policies (Strayer 1988). For example, in *Reference re Regulations in Relation to Chemicals* [*Chemicals Reference*],[39] the Supreme Court validated actions taken by the Parliament of Canada under the *War Measures Act* as a domestic aspect of Canada's war effort in the Second World War.[40] This case provided the basis for the decision of the Judicial Committee of the Privy Council in *Reference re Persons of Japanese Race,* which infamously and shamefully found the Government of Canada's deportation after the war of individuals of Japanese descent to be valid.[41] The *Chemicals Reference* also provided the basis for the decision in *Reference re Wartime Leasehold Regulations,* which held that the federal Parliament's incursion into provincial jurisdiction during the war was legitimate given the emergency circumstances.[42] The data demonstrate that the reference power was used 19 times during the years of the Second World War, 1939 to 1945, a somewhat higher rate compared to most other periods in the twentieth century. However, this number is overshadowed by the flurries of reference activity in the 1930s and 1980s, suggesting that although the reference power was used relatively frequently during the war, it was not used so frequently as to make this period notably distinct from others during the twentieth century.

The relatively quick process and the limited number of required resources are both practical and significant benefits of the reference power for governments. Obtaining judicial advice in a reference decision can help a government to silence critics concerned with the legal and constitutional implications of a new piece of legislation, enabling it to push its policy agenda forward. Furthermore, if a government suspects that it will be challenged on a piece of legislation in the future, it can conserve future resources by pre-empting the challenge and submitting the legislation to the courts itself in a reference case. Again, as mentioned above, unlike some of the other explanations for use of the reference power, in some cases these specific benefits cannot be truly realized by a government unless it receives a favourable ruling. Furthermore, although a reference can be an attractive choice for a government concerned with a timely response to an issue, it is important to note that using the reference power also requires a degree of restraint, as the referring government must be willing to pause its agenda while it waits for a ruling from the courts. As a result, with regard to the motivation for pursuing a reference case, the concept of time can cut both ways. A reference can save a government time in the present by silencing criticism and in the future by limiting the possibility that it will be challenged. However, using a reference requires a government to slow down its agenda and seek the advice of a court before moving forward. As Counsel B explained, a reference "actually requires a measure of restraint from the executive branch ... because typically governments want to proceed. They want to go ahead and act now, as they are elected to. They aren't elected to go to the courts."[43]

Abstract Review and the Structure of the Reference Power

References allow governments to obtain judicial review without a live dispute or a set of concrete facts. Without having to respond to a set of facts, participants in reference cases can construct their arguments in a manner that is most beneficial to their case, unencumbered by the inconvenience of a particular situation or conflict. Given the weight that is placed on the questions submitted in a reference, the party that has the ability to craft the questions can wield a great deal of control and influence over the proceedings. This unique aspect of the reference power has been established by earlier discussions in this book; the intention of this section is to demonstrate that reference case participants recognize and confirm these theoretical benefits of the reference power.

Both former attorneys general and former counsel noted that the abstract nature of reference cases provides two distinct advantages: the ability to frame arguments in a broad fashion and the power to try to craft questions in a manner that is most likely to elicit the desired response from the court. Although governments can exercise a great deal of control in reference cases compared to routine litigation, they can never be certain about how the court will decide. As a result, governments considering a reference case place great emphasis on the creation of the reference questions, with the hopes of ensuring the best possible outcome. Attorney General B explained this situation: "The danger is the answer ... You have to be careful to frame the questions in the way you want, to get the answers that you want."[44]

Due largely to the abstract nature of reference cases, a reference can allow a government a degree of manipulation that is simply not possible in routine litigation. Indeed, Riddell and Morton (2004) demonstrate the lengths to which the Alberta government went to oppose the federal government's imposition of a gas tax. Instead of simply challenging the legality of the federal law, in the *Alberta Gas Tax Reference,* the Government of Alberta went to the trouble of manufacturing a hypothetical situation in an attempt to demonstrate how the gas tax would function in practice. Undoubtedly, the actions of the Manitoba government in the *Egg Reference* provide another classic example of the high level of control that a government can wield over the reference process. The actions of the Manitoba government arguably made a charade of respecting the legislative process with the goal of constructing an ideal reference scenario. In these examples, the level of manoeuvring by the government went even further than simply the creation of reference questions in a particular manner, as it also involved the manufacturing of facts.

The latitude that comes with participating in judicial review without a set of facts was also recognized as a benefit by counsel who had held the responsibility of presenting arguments for governments in past reference cases. Counsel B explained that the preparation for a routine appeal proceeding requires the study and analysis of all prior trial records and an awareness of the possible questions that could be raised by the appellate court justices based on the trial record. A reference case requires a much different style of preparation, as Counsel B described: "You don't have a defined record, you don't have a trial, you don't have parties, and you don't have a bunch of facts that are inconvenient or difficult to explain. It's a pure law case ... It's a more defined, narrow scope."[45] This scope allows counsel to craft the most convincing argument, untethered to any facts or evidence, creating a great source of control for reference case counsel.

The abstract style of reference cases allows governments and its counsel a great deal of liberty when crafting the questions, presenting arguments, and in some circumstances, even manufacturing situations of hypothetical fact. These characteristics of abstract review can also result in reference decisions from courts that are quite broad and wide-ranging. For example, in the *Secession Reference,* a unanimous Supreme Court offered four underlying principles of the Canadian Constitution: federalism, constitutionalism and the rule of law, respect for minorities, and democracy. These constitutional principles are expansive and do not speak solely to the issue of the unilateral secession of a province but rather provide context for all constitutional interpretation. Furthermore, the constitutional principles articulated by the court in the *Secession Reference* were not mentioned in the proceedings, nor were they argued by counsel in the facts submitted to the court. In this case, the court was unconstrained by a specific dispute or a set of facts, permitting it to engage in a broad and wide-ranging analysis.

According to some of the interview participants, the possibility of such broad review in a reference case can be viewed as a benefit by governments. Attorney General E spoke at length regarding the benefits of the abstract nature of a reference when compared to routine litigation: "It has the freedom that it was not structured within an appellate review that would have narrowly framed the question, and this is what would have given a court ... the opportunity to address the issue in an open-ended way ... and to pronounce in an authoritative way."[46] In this particular case, Attorney General E's government could have pursued routine litigation instead of a reference case, but the possibility of broad review by a court through a reference was more appealing. In this example, Attorney General E's government wanted to introduce legislation on the particular issue and valued a decision by the court that would address as many issues and arguments as possible regarding its preferred policy. As a result, for this government, it was more advantageous and a better political strategy to seek a broad decision from a court rather than be constrained by a particular dispute or set of facts. A wide-ranging reference decision can address many of the issues that may be connected to a particular matter rather than just the specific issues resulting from a concrete dispute. This possibility of an expansive answer on a reference question can provide significant assurance for a government when moving forward with corresponding legislation.

On the Reference Power in General

Along with discussing their views on specific reference cases, interview participants reflected on the reference power in general, providing some insight into how they understood the reference power and its place within the Canadian political framework. Attorney General D explained that there should be a high threshold for deciding to invoke the reference power: "It has to be an important question ... You shouldn't refer less than major questions that are considered to be important in some way or dimension to the Canadian public."[47] Attorney General E agreed with the need to be cautious in deciding to use the reference power but felt that the reference power had not been abused by governments in the past.[48]

Both Attorneys General C and D explained that in using the reference power, governments should be conscious of the proper role of the courts and should ensure that judicial independence is not sacrificed through overuse or abuse of the reference power. Indeed, if courts are increasingly understood as the venue for highly contested political questions, the independence of the courts from the more overtly political branches of government could suffer, regardless of how the courts decide reference cases. In discussing the role of the reference power, Attorney General C explained that the courts and governments "are certainly aware of the politics of the reference ... and of course the link between the judicial and the executive branch and the way it can be interfered [with]."[49] Attorney General D was concerned that political actors will avoid deciding contentious issues and rely on references instead: "I think references [should] not become simply a device by which governments attempt to dump difficult political questions on the courts."[50] Even though both of these individuals were aware of the issues that the reference power can have for the proper role of the executive, legislature, and the courts, they each decided that on at least one occasion a reference had been the best possible solution to a particular political problem. Counsel A also commented on the unique role of the reference power within the Canadian institutional framework, explaining that it required the courts to engage in an extra-judicial function: "There is something different about giving advice to a government – that is not a judicial function."[51]

Five of the individuals interviewed explicitly stated that there are no real shortcomings to references, including the individuals who explained the need for caution when using the reference power, such as Attorneys General C and D. Indeed, when asked to consider whether there were negative aspects to the reference power, Attorney General C responded, "No – well, the only thing that I can say is the possibility that you could lose."[52] Attorney General C's candid comment may be startling; however, given that the quantitative data demonstrate that the courts are quite willing to invalidate government action or legislation in reference cases, it is perhaps more surprising that no other interviewee mentioned the possibility that a government could lose a reference case. Courts do not act as a "rubber stamp" in reference cases. As a result, governments should employ references with caution, as it is quite likely that the court could invalidate either proposed or enacted government legislation. Indeed, the possibility that a government could lose self-initiated reference cases is quite evident when examining the reference case success record of Stephen Harper's government. During the era of the Harper government (2006–15), the attorney general of Canada launched a total of three reference cases – the *Securities Reference*, the *Senate Reform Reference*, and the *Nadon Reference* – and the Supreme Court found government action to be invalid in all three instances, save for a minor legislative proposal to amend property qualifications in the *Senate Reform Reference*. As the Harper government was likely keenly aware, each decision to seek a reference introduces a level of risk and the uncertainty of judicial review.

All interview participants found the reference power to be a unique tool that benefits governments, and none of the participants suggested that the power be eliminated. Interestingly, even though some participants recognized that the power can be open to abuse by governments, it was not suggested that the power be amended or reformed in any manner.

Conclusion

Clearly, there are both legal and political benefits to the reference power for governments. A reference can be used by a government to avoid dealing with a highly controversial issue, allowing it to toss the hot potato to the courts to sort out. Governments can initiate a reference case as part of a political strategy to address a particularly controversial issue. The majority of interview participants explicitly stated that the decision to use the reference power by their government was either a political consideration or a means to deal with a political controversy. In speaking about the reference case or cases in which they had participated, none of the interview subjects mentioned any hesitation in involving a court in the political controversy faced by their government.

Governments have also found that references are a useful mechanism for dealing with some of the problems associated with federalism. References have been used to sort out conflicts related to constitutional jurisdiction between governments, and they have been used as a way to influence a decision of another government. In a federal system, a reference can help to ensure the national uniformity of standards or access to a particular benefit, and it avoids the possibility of different rulings across provincial jurisdictions. Governments that have used the reference power recognize the political utility of an authoritative opinion from an appellate court or the Supreme Court. An authoritative opinion can help to clarify a controversial or complicated legal issue, creating a level of legislative assurance for the government. In the same manner, a reference decision that essentially approves a government's legislation, either proposed or enacted, can help to insulate the government from future challenges or at least make a legal challenge difficult to mount in the future. This assurance may be even more important to governments that are considering adopting a new policy that would have significant repercussions if found invalid once in operation.

The structure and abstract nature of the reference power can have distinct advantages for governments. With the reference power at their disposal, governments do not need to wait for a real dispute to manifest before obtaining the advice of a court. Instead, by bringing the matter to a court itself, a government can short-circuit a process that could take years. At the same time, references can pause political debates, giving governments the ability to avoid confrontation with critics or to avoid publicly commenting on the issue while the matter is under consideration by the courts. A reference allows a government to obtain judicial review on virtually any topic or issue without the typical barriers to judicial review, such as justiciability and standing. The range of matters that could be subject to a reference is only limited by the willingness of a government to refer questions to an appellate court.

To be sure, governments are likely aware that for the reference power to function properly, courts must be willing to cooperate in the reference process. As a result, referring governments should be conscious of how a court could respond to a particular reference case. Although courts have refused to answer specific questions in some reference cases, they have yet to refuse to hear a reference altogether.

Notwithstanding the debate surrounding the ability of courts to refuse to answer reference questions and the corresponding government power to resubmit references, the reference power provides the executive a great deal of control within the reference case process. Given the abstract nature of reference cases and the resulting importance placed on the reference questions, the ability to frame the questions becomes an important source of power for governments. The significance of this power becomes more impressive when compared to routine litigation. Unencumbered by a set of facts, a referring government can present the best possible argument for its case. In some instances, such as with the *Alberta Gas Tax Reference*, the reference power has allowed governments not simply to construct the most beneficial questions and legal arguments but also to create a favourable hypothetical-fact scenario. Such examples demonstrate the degree of control and manipulation that can be exercised by governments in reference cases.

The two most common explanations provided by interview subjects for why their governments initiated reference cases were avoidance of political controversy or blame and a desire for the institutional authority or protection of the courts. Yet these two benefits of the reference process for governments are ultimately in conflict with one another in the long term. If governments increasingly rely on the courts to deal with political hot potatoes, embroiling the courts in political controversies, the independence of the judiciary could ultimately suffer. If the courts are not fully independent and, more importantly, *perceived* to be independent, the power of the courts to enhance the legitimacy of government action through a reference case will be reduced. Thus, although governments stand to benefit from the independence of the courts in gaining judicial institutional authority and legitimacy through a reference case, an overuse of the reference process (especially for highly controversial and normative issues) stands to eventually diminish the ability of references to grant this legitimacy.[53] Based on the information provided by interview subjects, it appears that using a reference to legitimize a position occurs more often than using a reference to pass a hot potato, thus alleviating some concerns regarding overuse of references to deal with political controversies. That being said, a government could initiate a single reference case both to avoid making a difficult political decision and to have that decision benefit from the institutional legitimacy of the courts. This disjuncture between the goals of political actors using the reference power and the ultimate effectiveness of the reference power is examined in greater detail in the analysis that follows.

Even with all of the above-mentioned advantages of the reference power for governments, there must be some drawbacks to using the reference power, as reference cases are not a routine aspect of Canadian politics, with only 209 occurring since the first creation of the reference power by the federal government in 1875. The following chapter considers two examples of rejected references with such drawbacks.

Why Not Refer Everything? The *Padlock Act* and Blasphemy

5

With all the advantages of the reference power, one might assume that governments will rely on references whenever faced with a difficult or divisive matter that can be turned into a reference question. However, it is important to remember that compared to *all* litigation in Canadian appellate courts, references comprise only a small fraction of litigation in Canada. Clearly, not all issues or political hot potatoes become reference cases. Indeed, there are some drawbacks to relying on the reference power. In this chapter, I address the limitations of the reference power for governments and examine two cases – Quebec's *Act to Protect the Province against Communistic Propaganda* [*Padlock Act*] and its anti-blasphemy *Act Respecting Freedom of Worship and Maintenance of Good Order* – where a government considered initiating a reference case but ultimately abandoned this strategy. The *Padlock Act* episode, which took place during the tenure of Mackenzie King's government, is contrasted with the confrontational approach taken by King in clashing with the Social Credit government in Alberta. This comparison helps to highlight both the advantages and disadvantages of using the reference power, as the political actors and environment of the two examples were partially constant. Understanding why governments decide not to initiate a reference and the potential pitfalls of a reference case helps to present a more complete picture of the value of the reference power for governments.

Although there can be tangible benefits for governments that initiate reference cases, there are disadvantages to relying on the courts to referee partisan debates or matters of public policy.

Given that the decision to initiate a reference case is a decision of Cabinet, any discussion of a reference case should appear in the record provided by Cabinet conclusions.[1] That being said, the analysis that follows does not examine *all* instances where references were considered; rather, these data are subject to the restrictions imposed by the availability of Government of Canada Cabinet conclusions, and this analysis does not examine instances where provincial governments considered a reference and did not pursue the reference option. Information gained from Cabinet conclusions is supplemented through biographical literature available on the actors involved in the episodes, political writings, such as King's diaries,[2] legislative debates available through Hansard, and secondary scholarly literature.

Both of the two *almost* reference cases, concerning the *Padlock Act* in 1937 and Quebec's anti-blasphemy law in 1955, involved policies that were relatively popular in Quebec but drew criticism from the rest of Canada. In each case, one of the central factors that caused governments to pause before referring the offending legislation to the Supreme Court was concern about how this action would be received within Quebec. The *Padlock Act* was a statute passed by the government of Premier Maurice Duplessis that drew concern about the restrictions it placed on civil liberties in Quebec and about the possibility that the law invaded the federal law jurisdiction over criminal law. The refusal to meddle in the affairs of Quebec and the lack of action on the *Padlock Act* by the King government are interesting when juxtaposed with the King government's confrontation with Alberta over Social Credit legislation, which took place at the same time. This differential treatment of Quebec and Alberta by King and Minister of Justice Ernest Lapointe is analyzed below, as it provides insight into government decision making regarding references while highlighting that many of the factors that ordinarily motivate a government to seek a reference were present in this case but did not result in a reference. The blasphemy episode concerns the existence of a prohibition on blasphemy, a law that was largely considered out of touch with modern secular values in Canada.[3] The lack of governmental action in challenging the blasphemy law through a reference helps to provide further insight into some of the drawbacks of the reference power.

The *Padlock Act*

During the 1930s, communist ideas and sentiment gained popularity in Canada as a direct response to the Great Depression and the ineffectiveness of the governmental response to the financial disaster. Whereas some Canadians embraced communism and the Communist Party of Canada, many political leaders responded by vilifying the movement. This vilification was most prevalent in Quebec through the actions of the Duplessis government. In 1937 Duplessis introduced *An Act to Protect the Province against Communistic Propaganda*, colloquially known as the *Padlock Act*. The *Padlock Act* empowered the attorney general of Quebec, a post filled by Duplessis himself, to direct the police to lock any residence or building that was used to disseminate bolshevism or communism through any means. Although the powers provided by the Act were wide-ranging, their broad application was encouraged by the fact that the law did not define communism or bolshevism. When observers criticized this aspect of the Act, Duplessis responded that communism could simply be "felt" and that the attorney general could employ his own understanding and definition (Betcherman 2002). The *Padlock Act* allowed the attorney general to seize private property for a period of one year without judicial review or oversight. Shifting the burden of proof to the accused, the Act required that the property owner convince a judge that the law had not been broken or that the property would no longer be used for illegal purposes (Neatby 1976). The *Padlock Act* not only appeared to invade the criminal law jurisdiction of the federal government but also raised significant questions for the protection of civil liberties.

The *Padlock Act* was a legislative response to the growing fear of communism in Quebec. This fear was fostered through the dominance of the Roman Catholic Church and the strength of rural values within the province. Communism quickly became a catchall for everything that Catholic rural French society opposed and was easily applied to anything that appeared to threaten this identity (Neatby 1976). Additionally, communism became a scapegoat for all the problems faced by Quebec, such as the Depression and the crippling provincial debt. Given this environment, the *Padlock Act* did not receive strong opposition in Quebec. Quebecers and the Quebec media either ignored the Act and the various police raids that took place or did not speak out in opposition for fear of being labelled a communist (Mills 2005). Indeed, with the extreme fear of communism in the province, those who opposed the actions of the Duplessis government were placed in a no-win situation: opposition to the Act could be read as aiding communism, and support for the Act allowed the violation of civil liberties to continue.[4]

Although the *Padlock Act* did not meet significant opposition in Quebec, it did not go unnoticed by the federal government and the rest of Canada. Parliamentarians in Ottawa were quick to criticize the Act, demanding a response from the federal government. J.S. Woodsworth, leader of the Co-operative Commonwealth Federation, was the *Padlock Act*'s loudest critic in the House of Commons. Within weeks of the passage of the Act, Woodsworth noted several problems with this law, including the argument that the legislation had been enacted ultra vires the constitutional jurisdiction of the Quebec National Assembly. Although Woodsworth did not support the federal power of disallowance in general, he argued that here the federal government must step in as the protector of civil liberties, and he demanded a response from Minister of Justice and Attorney General Ernest Lapointe. Failing the use of the federal disallowance power, which at this point had not been employed by the federal government in several years, Woodsworth suggested that the governor in council refer the Quebec legislation to the Supreme Court of Canada (House of Commons Debates 1937, 2290). Responding for the government, Lapointe accepted Woodsworth's suggestions but avoided committing his government to action, explaining that he had not received an official copy of the Act (2294).

Woodsworth's criticisms of the *Padlock Act* continued in the House and were echoed by other members of the Co-operative Commonwealth Federation, such as E.J. Poole and A.A. Heaps (House of Commons Debates 1938b, 126–28). However, criticism of the Act was met with opposition from Quebec parliamentarians, who argued that it was not the place of the federal government to meddle in the affairs of the province, noting that the people of Quebec had not voiced strong opposition to the Act. Vital Mallette, the Liberal member of Parliament for Jacques-Cartier, opposed Woodsworth's demands for disallowance or a reference case. Mallette argued that the *Padlock Act* represented the views of the people of Quebec and that repealing the law should be left to the population of Quebec (House of Commons Debates 1938a, 114). Outside Parliament, many groups voiced their opposition to the *Padlock Act,* labelling it "one of the most oppressive pieces of legislation in Canadian history" (Mills 2005, 9). Lapointe and the King government received letters from all over Canada criticizing the Act and demanding government action, which included calls for a reference to the Supreme Court. Citizens' groups concerned with the protection of civil liberties mobilized in opposition to the Act, among them the League for Social Reconstruction, whose membership included leading scholars such as F.R. Scott and Eugene Forsey (Mills 2005). Opposition to the *Padlock Act* was instrumental in the creation of the Canadian Civil Liberties Union (Clément 2008).

Although some parliamentarians from Quebec, like Mallette, spoke out against federal government intervention in the *Padlock Act,* Minister Lapointe remained relatively tight-lipped on the subject in the House. However, in Cabinet and in private conversation with Prime Minister Mackenzie King, Lapointe voiced his concern over the Act and struggled with the dilemma he faced as a federal Cabinet minister and as a Quebecer (Betcherman 2002). According to King's personal diary, Lapointe was extremely conscious of how any federal action would be perceived in Quebec, as he was concerned about creating another division between Quebec and the rest of Canada (King 1938a).

The public positioning of the King government and inaction on the *Padlock Act* became more precarious in light of the federal government's feud with the Social Credit government in Alberta and the reference and disallowance of that province's legislation. Lapointe and the King government were accused of giving Quebec special treatment and were perceived as protecting the rights of banks in Alberta over the civil liberties of the citizens of Quebec (Mallory 1976).

In Cabinet meetings, the ministers from Quebec struggled with what action the government should take on the Quebec law. In the summer of 1938, after the *Padlock Act* had been in effect for approximately a year and a half, Cabinet met to discuss options and select a government response. Lapointe argued that the Act could not be viewed as an incursion into the federal criminal law power because communism itself was not made a crime by the Act (King 1938a). Lapointe believed that the federal government should show deference to the preferences of Quebecers, who largely supported the law (Betcherman 2002). Furthermore, according to Lapointe, disallowance by the federal government might provoke an election in Quebec, which would provide an almost certain win for Duplessis. Ultimately, for Lapointe, surrounding the *Padlock Act* was the issue of the French versus the English, and any federal action could threaten national unity (Betcherman 2002). Lapointe believed that the law should be tested by individuals with a specific case in the courts and that it should not be disallowed or be the subject of reference questions (King 1938a). Lapointe clearly recognized that the *Padlock Act* was a political hot potato, but because it was provincial and did not directly implicate the King government, there was no obligation to address the Act's controversy.

Prime Minister King and other ministers from Quebec did not share Lapointe's position on the *Padlock Act;* instead, all preferred a Supreme Court reference case on the Act (King 1938b). However, that being said, King had a great deal of respect for Lapointe and would not overrule him on matters pertaining to Quebec. Moreover, King prioritized federal unity above all other matters when dealing with Quebec (King 1938b; Betcherman 2002). As a result, regardless of the pressure to pursue a reference from parliamentarians, Cabinet ministers, the public, and interest groups, the King government allowed the *Padlock Act* to stand.

To address the *Padlock Act,* the King government had several options, including inaction, the power of disallowance, and of course the reference power. Given the benefits that governments can receive from using a reference to deal with a highly divisive issue, it initially appeared that referring the Quebec legislation to the Supreme Court would be the most advantageous strategy. A reference would remove the decision-making power from the King government and provide the option of blaming the Supreme Court for the outcome, regardless of how the court decided. If the court found the legislation to be ultra vires, the King government could portray itself as a defender of civil liberties to observers outside of Quebec, and within Quebec it could deflect blame to the Supreme Court for the invalidation. Using a reference in this manner would not have been peculiar for the King government given that it had employed essentially the same tactic to deal with R.B. Bennett's New Deal legislation. However, a closer look at the issues in this episode provides good insight into instances where a reference case is not always an advantageous political strategy.

In dealing with the *Padlock Act,* Lapointe believed that turning over the matter to the Supreme Court through a reference case would aggravate tensions between French and English Canada. Lapointe's reservations about a *Padlock Act* reference highlight the problems and restrictions associated with judicial review and relying on the courts to deal with political controversies through reference cases. One of the explanations that Lapointe provided for being hesitant to refer the *Padlock Act* to the Supreme Court was that the law was fairly popular within Quebec, a position that was supported by some Quebec parliamentarians in the House of Commons. Lapointe explained to King and Cabinet that this issue would be best decided by the people of Quebec out of respect for the fact that aside from being relatively popular, the law had been passed by a democratically elected legislature (Betcherman 2002). Sending the law to the Supreme Court for review through a reference could result in a nonmajoritarian institution overruling the generally popular and legitimate actions of a democratic institution.

Although Lapointe was hesitant to refer the *Padlock Act* to the Supreme Court due to the court's weak democratic legitimacy, his reasons for refusing to refer were likely more strategic. According to King's diaries, Lapointe was concerned that devising a reference on the *Padlock Act* would turn the matter into an election issue in Quebec and would aid the re-election of Duplessis, something that the federal Liberal Party strongly opposed (King 1938b). Indeed, throughout his political career, King considered Duplessis to be a political foe, and at the same time, Duplessis was not timid in expressing his disdain for Ottawa (Neatby 1976). King and Lapointe were sensitive to the fact that Duplessis was very capable of vilifying the federal government in the eyes of Quebecers and that doing so was a powerful and successful political tactic for Duplessis (King 1938a). For Lapointe (and eventually King), it was a better political strategy to ignore the issue of the *Padlock Act* and to avoid providing a political opponent with fuel. Referring the matter to the Supreme

Court would undoubtedly draw attention to the issue and would allow Duplessis to position himself as the protector of the interests of Quebec against the interfering federal government and federally appointed Supreme Court. That Lapointe and the King government wanted to avoid giving any ammunition to Duplessis provided a significant motivation for avoiding the *Padlock Act* debate.

Lapointe was likely also concerned with the framing that would result from involving the courts in the debate over the *Padlock Act*. As argued by Morton and Knopff (2000), the structure of judicial review can lead to a framing of issues in terms of pro versus con and winner versus loser. Inserting this type of framing into the *Padlock Act* matter would exacerbate the already narrow debate surrounding communism in Quebec. As mentioned previously, those who opposed the *Padlock Act* or in general the anti-communist actions of the Duplessis government were labelled either communist sympathizers or communists. This debate already lacked nuance and would likely not benefit from the structuring process that can take place as a debate is moved into the judicial arena. Referring this matter to the courts would only intensify this framing, and Lapointe was conscious of the polarizing and narrow debate surrounding the anti-communist legislation in Quebec.

Finally, Lapointe decided that inaction rather than a reference case was the best political strategy for dealing with the *Padlock Act* due to the great amount of tension surrounding communism in Canada, particularly in Quebec. As Howitt and Wintrobe (1995) demonstrate, the more divided the public is on an issue, the more likely it is that political decision makers will prefer the status quo or inaction on the issue, regardless of whether the status quo satisfies their genuine preferences. Political actors are motivated more by a desire to avoid blame and less by a desire to claim credit, making inaction on highly controversial issues an attractive political strategy (Weaver 1986). Thus, even though Lapointe, King, and the Liberal Party were concerned about the curbing of civil liberties within Quebec, this unsatisfactory status quo was preferable, as it allowed for avoidance of blame. Fear of communism was prevalent in Quebec, and it was a force that united Quebecers, fostering French Canadian nationalism. The opposition to and fear of communism became part of the French Catholic identity. As Neatby

(1976, 234–35) explains, "the result was that most responsible or respectable French Canadians had no interest in and no sympathy for left-wing views ... In French Canada the strength of rural values and the official denunciation of communism by the Roman Catholic Church intensified this fear. Communism seems to be the antithesis of everything which French Canada stood for." With such heightened public concern over communism, the most politically attractive option for dealing with the *Padlock Act* was inaction. As a result, as King noted in his diary, although it was not the most courageous decision in terms of the protection of civil liberties, the federal government's refusal to act was the best option politically (King 1938b).

The refusal by Lapointe and King to use the reference power for Quebec's *Padlock Act* demonstrates some of the negative aspects of relying on the courts through the reference mechanism and helps to explain why governments do not refer all political hot potatoes to the courts. First, in this case, since the offending law was quite popular within its enacting province, referring the matter to the courts could have resulted in circumventing the popular will. Second, the refusal to refer the *Padlock Act* served strategic political purposes. Lapointe and King knew that if the federal government stepped into the debate over the *Padlock Act,* it could easily be used by Duplessis as a wedge to help divide French and English Canada, strengthening his power in the province. Lapointe was deeply concerned about exacerbating any French-English tensions. Moreover, King viewed Duplessis as a political opponent and was hesitant to take any action that would benefit Duplessis and aid his re-election in a future provincial election. Third, the discourse concerning communism in Quebec was extremely polarizing, and opening the issue of the *Padlock Act* to the courts would likely have intensified this polarization and further structured the debate in terms of communist sympathizers and opponents of the *Padlock Act* versus anti-communists, leaving little room for subtlety. With such heated debates over communism in Canada in general and in Quebec in particular, inaction on the *Padlock Act* became the best political strategy for dealing with the matter. Simply put, it was better for the King government to be criticized for not protecting civil liberties within one province than to be labelled a sympathizer of communism. The *Padlock Act* did eventually make its way to the Supreme Court of Canada in 1957 in a case that concerned the cancellation of a lease by a landlord who believed that the sublessee had allowed the residence to be used for the dissemination of communist doctrine. In *Switzman v Elbling*, the Supreme Court found that the *Padlock Act* was ultra vires the jurisdiction of Quebec and fell within the federal constitutional jurisdiction over criminal law.[5]

This episode over the drastic *Padlock Act* is telling when compared to how the King government dealt with radical legislation of Premier William Aberhart's Social Credit government in Alberta at the same time. As discussed in Chapter 2, the King government confronted the Alberta government about several policies that were aimed at fulfilling the Social Credit government's attempt to deal with the Depression. First, King and Lapointe (via the governor general) disallowed three of the Aberhart government's policies: the *Credit of Alberta Regulation Act*, which transferred the licensing of banks to the provincial government; the *Bank Employee Civil Rights Act*, which prevented bank employees from accessing judicial review; and the *Judicature Act Amendment Act*, which prohibited courts from reviewing provincial legislation. After disallowing the three Alberta Acts, Lapointe was subject to a great deal of criticism for continuing to refuse to refer the *Padlock Act*, as he was accused of permitting one type of justice for Quebec and a different type for Alberta (Mallory 1976).

Disallowance did not stop Aberhart from pursuing his agenda, and his government responded with three additional constitutionally dubious pieces of legislation. It introduced the *Bank Taxation Bill* and the *Accurate News and Information Bill*, and it reintroduced the *Credit Act* but changed the focus from banks to credit institutions. Again, the federal government took notice and referred the legislation to the Supreme Court of Canada for review in *Reference re Alberta Statutes*.[6] The Supreme Court found the legislation to be ultra vires the jurisdiction of Alberta, with Justices Sir Lyman Duff, Henry Hague Davis, and Lawrence Arthur Dumoulin Cannon finding that the press-related legislation violated the implied bill of rights within the Canadian Constitution. This decision was later upheld by the Judicial Committee of the Privy Council on the grounds that the laws were enacted ultra vires the jurisdiction of the Alberta legislature.

King and Lapointe were criticized for wading into provincial affairs in Alberta but at the same time allowing Quebec to exercise a great deal of latitude with the *Padlock Act*. Comparing the treatment of these two provinces provides important insight into political strategy as it relates to the reference power. First, the events took place within the same time period, and there was no variation in the central players at the federal level, with the refusal to disallow the *Padlock Act* taking place just weeks after the disallowance of the Alberta legislation (Wilson 1975). Second, both provinces passed legislation that gained national attention and was met with opposition from interest groups. Third, in both instances, the legislation was controversial and was criticized for limiting the rights of individual citizens and businesses. Fourth, both instances demonstrate the impact that the reference power can have on jurisdictional disputes between provincial and federal governments. Finally, the similarities between the two situations were not lost on the parliamentarians who pressured the King government to intervene by employing the reference power (Betcherman 2002).

Yet the King government's response to Alberta was markedly different from its response to Quebec. In both instances, the King government could have avoided dealing with the divisive issue of the provincial legislation by asking the courts to intervene. However, the need to deal with a political controversy is not the only reason why governments use the reference power. Although delegating both controversies to the courts would have prevented the federal government from having to deal with the provinces directly, the King government could not be certain about how the court would rule and faced the possibility that the Supreme Court would uphold the provincial legislation. Although a level of uncertainty is present in every reference episode, there are instances where, based on legal advice and previous jurisprudence, governments can be more certain about how a court will decide. With regard to the *Padlock Act,* Lapointe was uncertain that the Act infringed on federal constitutional jurisdiction, whereas the Social Credit legislation was a clear invasion of federal jurisdiction over banking, as Aberhart's legislation sought to explicitly regulate banking within the province (Mallory 1976; Bletcherman 2002).

Although in both cases the King government faced pressure in Parliament to use the reference power, the pressure outside of Parliament for intervention was comparatively quite different. As mentioned above, there was strong criticism of the *Padlock Act* from left-wing civil liberties groups both within Quebec and across the rest of Canada. Indeed, the Canadian Civil Liberties Union formally requested that Minister Lapointe either refer the *Padlock Act* to the Supreme Court or ask the governor general to disallow the legislation. Similarly, both within Alberta and across Canada, nongovernmental groups came out in opposition to the Social Credit legislation; however, these groups included the powerful banking industry and business community, which had the ability to exert a great deal of influence over government.[7] The opposition to the *Padlock Act* came primarily from "poor people or organizations of poor people," whereas supporters of the Act were powerful members of Quebec society, such as the Roman Catholic Church and the Montreal business community (Wilson 1975, 177). The King government was more willing to intervene in Alberta compared to Quebec because, according to Mallory (1976, 176), "property and civil rights are less valuable in monetary terms ... the Padlock Act failed to signally arouse the Department of Justice to the pitch of indignation it might have reached if the property padlocked had been a branch of a chartered bank."

Not only did the opposition to the Social Credit legislation have more influence over government than the opposition to the *Padlock Act,* but the area of constitutional concern (i.e., banking and business compared to civil rights) was of more importance to the King government. The greater importance placed on the Social Credit legislation also reflects that this legislation had more obvious implications for federal constitutional jurisdiction. In considering the Social Credit legislation, not only was the King government subject to more powerful lobbying efforts, but it was also more receptive to external pressure on this issue compared to the *Padlock Act.* As for the thematic reasons why governments ask reference questions, although both provinces had enacted controversial legislation, the King government could simply afford to ignore the situation in Quebec, whereas it faced more pressure to intervene in Alberta.

More generally, Alberta and Quebec were differently situated in respect to negotiation positions vis-à-vis the federal government. During this time, Quebec was much more politically important to the King government, as it was an economic and manufacturing centre and was essential to securing a majority government in national elections (Mallory 1976). Indeed, King's diaries detail the concerns that both he and Lapointe had about making enemies with Quebec and Premier Duplessis. King and Lapointe were concerned that disallowing or referencing the *Padlock Act* would secure re-election for Duplessis and would make future electoral success for the Liberal Party of Canada challenging in Quebec. Simply put, Alberta did not have the ability to bargain with the federal government in the same manner as Quebec. Alberta was not a centre of economic power, nor was it essential to winning a majority government; indeed, at this time, the Liberals held only one seat in Alberta. This inferior relationship with the federal government meant that the King government was much more willing to intervene in Alberta's affairs, regardless of whether it received a negative response from the provincial government.

The dissimilar response by the federal government speaks to one of the reasons why the reference power was created, namely to provide the federal government another means of challenging provincial legislation aside from the power of disallowance. *Reference re Alberta Statues* allowed the federal government to effectively challenge Alberta's legislation and to protect its constitutional jurisdiction over banking. The *Padlock Act,* in contrast, did not pose a direct and clear threat to federal constitutional power, and according to Lapointe, the Act did not fulfil the accepted requirements for disallowance.[8] Lastly, the *Padlock Act* did not impact any individual outside of Quebec, whereas the Social Credit legislation and its implications for national banking and credit agencies would have affected individuals and businesses that operated on a national basis beyond the provincial boundaries of Alberta. Thus the decision to refer the Social Credit legislation to ensure that national banking regulation operated the same way regardless of provincial jurisdiction reflects one of the arguments for using the reference power provided by the attorneys general in Chapter 4, namely that a reference can be a means of ensuring national standards.

Finally, the King government's decision to refer the Alberta legislation demonstrates the institutional authority and protection of the courts, insofar as a reference provides a means for a government to seek protection or judicial approval for new policies that would be difficult to unwind after implementation. If the Social Credit legislation had been implemented, it would have effectively terminated all banks currently operating within the province and created a provincial banking system. If this system had been put into place and then found to be unconstitutional at a later date, it could have created a great deal of chaos for both the provincial and national economies. Instead, referring the legislation before enactment prevented the implementation of unconstitutional legislation and the creation of an entirely new banking system. Comparatively, the implementation of the *Padlock Act* did not pose the wide ramifications that the Social Credit legislation would likely have produced. The *Padlock Act* did not create a new policy scheme or program; instead, it was simply a new law to be enforced by the police. Indeed, the subsequent challenge and invalidation of the *Padlock Act* in *Switzman v Elbling* was relatively unremarkable and had little to no impact on government. The King government's decision to refer the Social Credit legislation helped to prevent the future disorder that could have occurred if the legislation had been implemented and subsequently struck down by the courts.

Blasphemy

Section 296 of the *Criminal Code of Canada* criminalizes blasphemous libel and states that those found guilty of this indictable offence can be subject to a prison sentence not exceeding two years.[9] Patrick (2008) notes that although blasphemy has not been the subject of a reported case since 1935, Canada is one of the few countries in the Western world with a law against blasphemy, a fact that is arguably an affront to modern secularism in society. Blasphemy most often refers to blasphemous libel, which refers to written statements, and although blasphemy simply concerns spoken statements, all Canadian blasphemy cases have concerned only written words (Patrick 2008). Although the Criminal Code does not provide a definition of "blasphemy," it generally involves the disparagement or mockery of a religion and historically was concerned primarily with denominations of Christianity.[10] According to Patrick (2010), although the criminalization of blasphemy predates Confederation, there have been only five prosecutions under the law, four of which have taken place in Quebec. Indeed, before the Quiet Revolution, the law against blasphemy was quite popular in Quebec, indicative of the prevalence of Catholicism within the province (Seljak 2000).

Prior to the consideration of a reference case on blasphemy, there was one significant attempt to repeal the blasphemy law. The move to repeal the prohibition on blasphemy was a response to the conviction of Victor Sterry for the crime of blasphemous libel in 1927.[11] Interestingly, the *Sterry* case was the only blasphemy case to take place outside of Quebec, and it marks the last time an individual was prosecuted in Canada under this section of the Criminal Code. Sterry had published several stories in the *Christian Enquirer* in which he criticized Catholicism, the Bible, and the Judeo-Christian God. Sterry was convicted for blasphemous libel and was sentenced to sixty days in jail at trial. The Ontario Court of Appeal denied Sterry's appeal. As Patrick (2010) documents, the *Sterry* case received a great deal of national media attention and also gained the attention of J.S. Woodsworth, the same parliamentarian who would later speak out against the *Padlock Act*.

Shortly following the conviction of Sterry, Woodsworth introduced Bill C-5, *An Act to Amend the Criminal Code (Blasphemous Libels)*, which would repeal section 296 of the Criminal Code (House of Commons Debates 1928). Woodsworth's bill was straightforward, as it simply repealed the Criminal Code section on blasphemous libel. However, this simplicity would be the bill's downfall, as it did not address the common law crime of blasphemous libel. Although it is no longer the case, in 1938 common law crimes still existed in Canada. As a result, if a section of the Criminal Code was repealed, like section 296, the common law crime would simply be reactivated, making the repeal of no real force or effect (Patrick 2010). Woodsworth's mistake did not go unnoticed by Minister of Justice Ernest Lapointe, who supported the prohibition on blasphemy and exploited the bill's flaw to defeat it in the House of Commons (House of Commons Debates 1928, 364). Several other parliamentarians supported Lapointe's opposition to the blasphemy repeal bill, and Woodsworth's motion was defeated.

The next significant movement toward repealing the criminal prohibition on blasphemous libel in Canada was the consideration of a reference case by Louis St. Laurent's government in 1955. Blasphemy returned to the public debate following the passage of *An Act Respecting Freedom of Worship and Maintenance of Good Order* by the Quebec National Assembly. The Act, which prohibited anyone in Quebec from taking actions that insulted religious practices, beliefs, and/or members of the religious profession, was indicative of the public Catholicism favoured by the Duplessis government prior to the Quiet Revolution, which often violated the lines of state secularism (Seljak 2000). St. Laurent's minister of justice, Stuart Garson, brought the Quebec blasphemy law before Cabinet for discussion not because he opposed the Act but because it appeared to overlap with the Criminal Code provision on blasphemy, creating confusion in the law (Clerk of the Privy Council 1955).

In his report to Cabinet, Garson suggested that a reference could be sent to the Supreme Court of Canada for an opinion on the validity of the Quebec law. As the Cabinet members discussed this possibility, it was argued that if the federal government submitted the Quebec legislation to the court, it "would be criticized in many quarters in the province of Quebec," regardless of the fact that it was the federal responsibility to ensure the compatibility of laws in Canada (Clerk of the Privy Council 1955). Cabinet believed that if the law was ultra vires the constitutional jurisdiction of Quebec, it would likely be subject to challenge by a private citizen, making it unnecessary for the federal government to pre-emptively challenge the law at the Supreme Court. Furthermore, Cabinet believed that a reference would likely make the federal government unpopular in Quebec, which would be unwise prior to an upcoming federal—provincial conference. The Cabinet meeting concluded by deferring the decision on whether to refer the compatibility of the Quebec blasphemy law and the Criminal Code blasphemy provisions to the Supreme Court.

This Cabinet discussion marks the first and last instance in which the St. Laurent Cabinet considered blasphemy and a reference regarding the Quebec law. According to the extensive study of Canadian blasphemy laws by Patrick (2013), there were no other attempts at reference cases concerning the Criminal Code provision regarding blasphemy, nor have there been any significant attempts to repeal the law. The lack of government interest in repealing the blasphemy law arguably is reflective of the fact that no charges have been pursued under the law since 1935. However, the blasphemy law was indirectly engaged in two more recent, yet still dated, cases. The first involved a temporary injunction placed against Denise Boucher's feminist play *Les fées ont soif* (1978) after a negative response from religious groups. In this case, the judge who approved the injunction cited the Criminal Code provision on blasphemous libel as a deciding factor. The second example is from 1980, when the Canadian distributor of the Monty Python film *Life of Brian* (1979) was charged with blasphemous libel; however, the charges were later dropped (see Bowal and Horvat 2011). That being said, the 2015 terrorist attack on the satirical magazine *Charlie Hebdo* in France brought public attention to the Canadian blasphemy law, with opponents reviving calls for Parliament to repeal it (Nasser 2015). Furthermore, recent legal analysis finds it unlikely that the blasphemy law would survive a legal challenge made under the protections of the freedom of expression provided by the Charter (Bowal and Horvat 2011; Ross 2012).

Little is known regarding the St. Laurent government's consideration of the Quebec blasphemy law beyond what was made available in a Cabinet conclusion.[12] However, what was discussed regarding the law does speak to the government's considerations and motivations behind debating a reference case. The Cabinet discussion did not consider the merits of laws against blasphemy in relation to the restriction of civil liberties. Furthermore, the discussion did not prioritize either the Parliament of Canada's responsibility for ensuring the national clarity of laws or the potential problems that could arise with overlapping federal and provincial laws. Interestingly, at no point did the Cabinet discussion consider that the provincial law likely invades the federal jurisdiction over criminal law, unlike the discussions of the King Cabinet regarding the *Padlock Act*. Instead, in this instance, the central considerations by the government were political. The government was primarily concerned with how a federal reference would be received in Quebec and with how it would impact upcoming intergovernmental discussions.

The decision to avoid referring the Quebec blasphemy law demonstrates that inaction is not only a conscious decision made by governments but can also be a viable political strategy. Indeed, this episode demonstrates Weaver's (1986) claim that political actors have a greater propensity to be motivated by blame avoidance than by praise. This motivation often results in the conscious selection of inaction as a policy response to a problem. In the case of the Quebec blasphemy law, the St. Laurent government was not under pressure to address the law or to clarify the jurisdictional issues that could arise from competing provincial and federal laws. There was no concrete problem with the application of the blasphemy law for the government to address, nor was there any imminent threat posed by the Quebec law that required the St. Laurent Cabinet to respond. Those involved in the discussion in Cabinet understood that bringing the blasphemy issue to the Supreme Court would certainly draw a negative response from the Duplessis government and unwanted attention from the public and media. The St. Laurent Cabinet was more concerned with an upcoming federal-provincial meeting than with the relative nonissue of dual blasphemy laws. As a result, in this episode, the St. Laurent Cabinet demonstrated the adage "let sleeping dogs lie." It is important to note that with both the *Padlock Act* and the blasphemy law, there was a strong possibility that a private citizen would challenge the Acts through routine litigation. Indeed, in the *Padlock Act* episode, Lapointe was aware that citizens and interest groups, such as the Canadian Civil Liberties Union, were likely to challenge the Act, making government intervention unnecessary.

The second example of a rejected reference parallels the first in many ways. As with the *Padlock Act,* the blasphemy episode concerned federal government intervention against a Quebec law. In both instances, the laws, although perhaps controversial elsewhere in Canada, were relatively well received and popular in Quebec. In both cases, decision makers were acutely aware that federal government intervention in Quebec could sour relations between Ottawa and the province. A decision by the federal government to refer the Acts could pit it as an aggressor against Quebec, as the reference would be seen as a deliberate attack against the provincial legislation, not simply a reaction to a real conflict or live case. Instead, with the possibility of private citizen litigation despite government inaction, it was a better political strategy to wait for a concrete case to materialize.

It is important to note that these two political episodes are connected by the fact that they concern Quebec laws instituted under the political leadership of Premier Maurice Duplessis and the Union Nationale party. Duplessis's reign over Quebec politics was characterized by policies that were aimed at protecting Quebec culture and advancing Quebec nationalism and autonomy (Leslie 1988). With these goals, Duplessis opted for a style of governance that either isolated Quebec from the rest of Canada or brought the province into direct conflict with the federal government. Through the avoidance of reference cases regarding the *Padlock Act* and the Quebec blasphemy law, the federal governments of King and St. Laurent successfully managed to avoid confrontation with Duplessis and Quebec in one area over which they could exercise complete control: the initiation of a reference case.

Finally, although the position of Quebec vis-à-vis the federal government steered the King and St. Laurent governments away from using the reference power, this has not always been the case with other federal governments. The *Secession Reference* is an important example of a federal government using the reference power to intervene in or respond to actions taken in Quebec. Indeed, the *Secession Reference* was initiated by Jean Chrétien's government in response to Quebec's unilateral declaration of independence, which followed the incredibly close 1995 referendum on sovereignty association. Because of the high stakes of provincial secession and the lack of legal clarity on this issue, the Chrétien government simply could not ignore the actions of the Quebec government, as King and St. Laurent had done previously. At the time of the reference, the legal parameters for secession in both Canadian and international law were unclear, and with the continued movement toward unilateral secession by the Quebec government, an advisory opinion from the Supreme Court was essential (Puddister 2016).

Explaining the Decision to Avoid Judicial Review and the Reference Option

An overview of some of the limitations and disadvantages of judicial review helps to provide a better understanding of some of the pitfalls of relying on the reference procedure and why governments may avoid the reference route. Reconciling judicial review with democracy is a concern that has consumed American constitutional thought at least since the work of Thayer (1893). Scholars have long grappled with what has been regarded as the counter-majoritarian difficulty that arises when unelected judicial actors invalidate or strike down the legislative actions of democratically elected (i.e., majoritarian) individuals (Bickel 1962; Graber 1993). Not only does counter-majoritarianism lack mechanisms of democratic accountability, but it also can require that courts make value decisions and choose between rival policy preferences. Engaging in this role places the courts in the position to encroach on the domain of the legislature. As a result, a great deal of American constitutional thought is focused on setting out the proper boundaries of judicial review and assessing the various degrees of incursion into the responsibilities of the legislature that are acceptable in a representative democracy (see Wechsler 1959; and Ely 1980). Other scholars are less concerned with drawing boundaries for the acceptable types of judicial review and are more critical of the very existence of a process that allows counter-majoritarian institutions to usurp the decisions of democratically accountable legislators. Critics of judicial review, such as Waldron (2006), argue that it is a misconception to view the judiciary as the protector of minority rights against those who oppose minority rights. Instead, judicial review is simply the "confrontation between one view of rights and another," in which courts adjudicate between different conceptions of rights and competing policy choices (1366).

Turning to the specific issue of reference cases, some political actors may reject the reference case route when dealing with complicated or controversial matters of public policy out of respect for the ideal of democratic policy making and a desire to avoid judicial review. In essence, a reference case asks an appellate court to select between rival policy preferences. This is most apparent in references when a court is asked to rule on the legality of legislation in the abstract. In such reference cases, a court is not assessing the application of a law to a set of facts or the alleged violation of rights by one party against another. Instead, in abstract review, the court is tasked with assessing motivations behind the law and how it could be applied, actions that are also the function of policy makers. "Abstract review harnesses the (virtually continuous) struggle between parliamentary majority and opposition over policy outcomes to a particular end" because it asks courts to assess the law without the application to a specific individual or situation

(Stone Sweet 2000, 51). As a result, policy makers concerned about democratic accountability could reject a reference case on the grounds that debates regarding public policy are more legitimate when handled by duly elected legislators.

The argument that political actors refrain from asking reference questions out of respect for democratic legitimacy and the parliamentary process is arguably based on an ideal conception of elected actors. Many scholars have demonstrated that elected officials do not always act with the noble goal of upholding and strengthening legislative representation, sometimes engaging in practices like gerrymandering (see Manfredi and Rush 2008). Alternatively, the decisions of political actors concerning public policy may be motivated by the pursuit of credit claiming or blame avoidance rather than by the goal of crafting the most ideal public policy (Weaver 1986). Decisions regarding public policy can reflect strategic motivations more than a desire to serve the public and a respect for democratic accountability. A "rational choice" perspective views policy makers as goal-oriented actors who make decisions to maximize goal attainment and preferences; however, the individual actor defines or understands his or her preferences (Tsebelis 1990; Hall and Taylor 1996). According to this perspective, elected individuals will make decisions with the immediate goal of protecting their power and interests and the longer-term goal of ensuring re-election (Voigt and Salzberger 2002).

With this understanding of decision making, one can assume that rational actors will make strategic decisions regarding public policy as a means to safeguard power and to avoid judicial review and the expansion of judicial power (Tushnet 1996). Hennigar (2002, 2007) demonstrates that through the weighing of pros and cons, the Canadian federal government will participate in strategic decision making about whether to litigate or appeal in Charter cases rather than rigorously engaging in all opportunities to defend its policies or further its preferences. According to Hennigar (2007), governments will consider several factors that are external to the merits of the specific case, such as time and resources, but one of the most significant factors that influences a government's decision regarding litigation is the constraint on policy-making power that could result from the court's decision. Upon weighing the costs of initiating a reference case, a government may conclude that the loss of control over an issue may be too high. A reference could prevent a government from engaging in credit claiming and could result in the creation of a constraint on future policy making. That being said, these factors can cut both ways, as the very same considerations that may draw a government to a reference case could repel another government away from the reference option.

Regardless of the motivations behind a government's decision making regarding a reference case, it remains that if a government initiates a reference case, it is ceding the power to decide to the courts. Although there are certain benefits from delegating decision making to the courts, as outlined above, the benefits do not negate the fact that the referring government cannot be certain about how the court will decide. Scholtz (2009) documents that a government is more likely to negotiate than to seek judicial review when faced with judicial uncertainty. Therefore, it is reasonable to assume that when a government has a significant stake in the outcome of a policy dispute, it is unlikely to allow the courts to decide in the face of judicial uncertainty. A self-interested rational government that has a serious concern about the outcome of a public policy debate is unlikely to initiate a reference case, regardless of whether the issue is a political hot potato.

Reference case opinions have been used to clarify complex constitutional law, the legality of a legislative enactment, and the constitutional jurisdictions of governments. However, the clear articulation that can result from a reference opinion is not always an advantage for a government. First, like all litigation, a reference decision can create the appearance of clear winners and losers of a dispute.[13] As Morton and Knopff (2000) note, both the general public's interpretation and the media coverage often frame a court case in terms of pro versus con and winner versus loser, regardless of whether the decision by the court actually provides such clear lines between successful and unsuccessful litigants. Furthermore, that a court can determine winners and losers can make the outcome of litigation rigid and inflexible to compromise. When dealing with some types of political disputes, governments may prefer the greater flexibility of routine legislative routes that allow for negotiation and cooperation. For example, with respect to the dispute between the provincial and federal governments concerning rights to offshore resources, relying on judicial review through a reference may have caused more problems than it solved. According to Taylor (1970, 392), provinces resented the federal government's reliance on a reference for this dispute, so "adjudication may have done more harm than good; it may have added salt to an open constitutional wound." Taylor finds that the reference likely hardened the opposing positions of the governments, making the dispute more difficult to negotiate through traditional political means.

In a similar vein, taking an issue to court requires clear articulation of an issue and related arguments, resulting in a framing of the terms of debate. Litigation can create structured conflicts that are often much more inflexible than routine public policy debates (Scheppele and Walker Jr. 1991). Although not all reference cases have a party that expresses clear opposition to the reference-initiating government, the submission of reference questions can still foster a structured conflict. Questions referred in these cases generally ask for the court's opinion regarding the legality of a piece of legislation or action of a government. Typically, questions are framed in a manner that allows the court to answer in either the affirmative or negative, which in many cases causes courts to say either "yes" or "no" to a government's action.

For example, in the *Firearms Reference,* Alberta referred four questions to the Alberta Court of Appeal, which were subsequently appealed to the Supreme Court of Canada. The first question asked the court, "Do the licensing provisions, insofar as they relate to an ordinary firearm, constitute an infringement of the jurisdiction of the Legislature of Alberta with respect to the regulation of property and civil rights pursuant to subsection 92(13) of the *Constitution Act, 1867*?"[14] This question clearly articulated the argument of the attorney general of Alberta that the *Firearms Act* violated the provincial jurisdiction over property and civil rights,[15] and it structured the conflict between the province and the federal government. After providing the reasons for its decision, the Supreme Court responded to this question with a simple "No."[16] In this case, the articulation of a reference question structured the conflict over the firearms policy and focused the debate on the provincial power over property and civil rights. The Supreme Court's answer created a clear winner in the dispute and did so in a manner that did not leave the question open to further negotiation.

Finally, a government may avoid initiating a reference case if it believes that the issue may resolve itself or fade from public concern without government action. In other words, a government may decide that the best political strategy for dealing with an issue is inaction. As Weaver (1986) argues, inaction on a file allows a strategic decision maker to avoid articulating a position on a controversy while also allowing for blame avoidance. Inaction and the status quo may be more preferable to a government than the risks associated with raising a particular issue, especially when the issue is highly divisive among the public, such as abortion (Howitt and Wintrobe 1995). If a government chooses to initiate a reference case, it can no longer avoid blame through ambiguity. Instead, the creation of reference questions forces a government to articulate a position and to formulate arguments surrounding the legality or constitutionality of the issue. Moreover, a reference case could increase media attention and scrutiny. For example, discussions regarding the Senate reform proposals of Stephen Harper's government largely faded from public debate until Quebec referred Bill C-7 to the Quebec Court of Appeal, bringing media and public focus back to the issue (Wells 2013). In contrast, inaction may result in criticism of a government in the short term, but if the issue falls off the public's or opposition parties' radar, a government may benefit from a lack of action.

There are several reasons why a government will reject the choice of a reference case, even when it might be considered an easy solution to a political problem. First, if a government is concerned about the lack of democratic legitimacy that can be attributed to judicial decisions, it will likely not seek a reference case. Instead, such a government will determine that democratically elected parliamentarians should make decisions regarding public policy rather than proactively seeking to turn over decision making to the courts. Additionally, a court decision can create winners and losers in a policy debate, which may not allow for nuance in position or negotiation between the parties involved. Governments may avoid reference cases because the costs associated with the possibility of having policy-making options limited by an unfavourable decision in court are greater than the benefits that may result from passing a hot potato issue to the courts through a reference. Finally, a reference case requires the clear articulation of the terms of a debate over public policy, and it requires the referring government to formulate arguments regarding the legality or constitutionality of that policy. Thus, in some cases, perhaps the best strategy for dealing with a divisive issue is inaction and avoidance.

Seeking the Court's Advice and the Delegation of Decision Making 6

This chapter takes what we have learned about how the reference power is used and analyzes the findings through the lens of delegation. There are three main objectives of this analysis. First, delegation theory provides a structure and organization for understanding the relationship between the executive and the courts as the principal and delegated power holders in relation to the reference power. Second, it links the Canadian case to a larger literature that is typically associated with the European and American cases, doing so in a way that reveals differences and similarities between these cases that have been underexplored in previous Canadian scholarship.[1] Third, a delegation framework helps to articulate some of the potential problems of the reference power for democratic governance. This chapter engages in an analysis of the incentives for political actors to empower the courts as a means of strategy. More specifically, it highlights the use of the reference power as a way for political actors to avoid blame or to engage in position taking or credit claiming, highlighting the unique structural and institutional advantages of reference cases for governments. The final contribution of the chapter is an examination of the implications of the strategic use of the reference power for the protection of judicial independence and its contributions to the centralization of power in the Canadian political executive.

Delegation to the Courts and Strategic Litigation

The act of delegation is the transfer of authority and power to make decisions from a principal to an agent. According to Salzberger (1993), this transfer of authority can be formal and positive, such as a legislature delegating or transferring specific policy-making powers to a local government or administrative body as codified in statute. However, delegation can also be informal and negative. Negative delegation describes a situation where the institution empowered to make laws, such as a parliament, is inactive in making such laws or where this institution creates laws but allows the application to be determined by another institution. This negative and informal delegation essentially depicts the function of common law (Salzberger 1993, 359–60). A negative delegation does not necessarily depict a situation where the agent is either absorbing decision-making power at the expense of the principal or simply filling a void. Instead, this form of delegation can also describe institutional relationships wherein the principal consciously involves an agent to handle a situation or controversy that it cannot or would rather not address itself (Graber 1993, 36). This arrangement aptly describes instances where elected officials rely on judicial review to resolve issues that it lacks the ability or will to address through regular parliamentary or political channels.

When political executives in Canada exercise the reference power, they engage in positive and informal delegation. This is an act of delegation because the executive and legislative branches are the primary sites of policy making, or in other words, they hold the principal decision-making power in matters of public policy. Decision-making power in a particular policy sphere can be effectively ceded to the courts when a government submits reference questions that invite the courts to review the legitimacy of a policy proposal. A reference case empowers a court to decide matters of public policy – a fact that is most pronounced in reference cases where a government asks for a court's advice on legislation that is only proposed rather than enacted. In such a scenario, a court could invalidate a government's legislative proposal by finding it ultra vires or unconstitutional, marginalizing the role of legislators, especially members of the parliamentary opposition. This marginalization of the legislature can in some instances effectively remove a debate from the purview of legislators. Moreover, a reference decision can create winners and losers, vindicating a particular position with the added legitimacy provided by the institutional authority of the courts.

Submitting reference questions is an act of positive delegation by a government. Courts do not invite or solicit reference cases; instead, Cabinet must proactively adopt an order in council to initiate a reference case. This positive delegation is what makes references fundamentally different from routine judicial review. Indeed, in routine or concrete review, the parties involved must react to a live dispute or wrong that has occurred. This dispute exists externally to the court proceedings and likely has a protracted history prior to entering a courtroom. Comparatively, when a reference originates with abstract questions and there is no live external dispute, the case manifests entirely from the carefully crafted reference questions. Without the reference questions, there is no reference case, and there is no dispute. Importantly, reference cases exist solely because a government has made the decision to seek judicial advice.

Asking for the court's advice through a reference is also a form of informal delegation because political actors choose to be bound by reference decisions. A plain reading of the federal reference power makes it clear that it empowers the governor in council to obtain an *advisory* opinion from a court on important legal and constitutional questions. Yet political actors generally abide by the decisions made by courts in reference cases, regardless of whether they run counter to their preferences. Presumably, in any instance where a government is dissatisfied with a decision rendered in a reference, the government could take the court's decision as advisory only and proceed with its desired policy choice. Moreover, a government determined to pursue a particular policy could argue that the abstract reference ruling is not binding on any and all fact scenarios that arise from a concrete dispute.[2] To be sure, ignoring judicial advice delivered in a reference decision and pursing legislation that a court has found to be invalid would not be a wise political choice for several reasons. First, the Supreme Court has explained that in a routine case if it is confronted with the same issues as those that have arisen in a reference, it will follow its previous decision in the reference case.[3] Second, if a government continues to pursue legislation that has been found invalid in a reference case, groups opposed to the policy will have the strength of the court's reasoning on their side, forcing the government to confront the court's reasons for the invalidation. Although it may be imprudent for governments to ignore a reference decision, this situation does not change the reality that deference to reference decisions by governments is entirely self-imposed, with no statutory basis, making it informal.

To review, when dealing with some normative and political controversies, governments will delegate decision making to the courts through reference questions to take advantage of the unique benefits of the reference power. Reasons for using the reference power include a desire to deal with a political controversy by passing the hot potato, to respond to other governments and to address issues of federalism, to benefit or receive protection from the authority of the court, to overcome the limits imposed by time and resources, and to capitalize on the unique structure of the reference power. Of course, these explanations for using the reference power are by no means mutually exclusive, as a single reference case may allow a government to capitalize on the multiple benefits of delegation. The benefits of delegation to the courts can be placed into two broad categories. First, delegating to the courts provides opportunities to avoid blame and to engage in position taking. Explanations that flow from this category are agency- and actor-focused and consider the strategy and motivations that may influence an elected individual to eschew decision-making responsibility in favour of empowering the courts. The second category of delegation focuses less on the individual agency and motivations of actors and more on the incentives provided and limitations imposed on decision makers by structural and institutional considerations, such as governmental resources and federalism. Each of these explanations for the political attractiveness of the reference power is considered below.

Blame Avoidance and Position Taking

Delegation is based on the traditional view of legislators as rational actors primarily concerned with maintaining power and ensuring re-election (Downs 1957). These goals are pursued through three central activities: advertising, position taking, and credit claiming (Mayhew 1974). Political actors who are motivated by credit claiming will also engage in the corresponding behaviour of blame avoidance (Weaver 1986). If political actors seek to avoid blame, they may also attempt to avoid making difficult and controversial decisions altogether. This motivation can result in shifting decision making to another agency, such as a court or administrative tribunal, in an effort to avoid both the decision-making costs and the political costs in dealing with a difficult issue or file (Fiorina 1982).

Courts are valuable sites for delegation by elected political actors. The independence of the judiciary increases the legitimacy of the decisions made by the courts, and the separation of the judicial branch from the executive and legislative branches helps to "maximize the responsibility shift" away from political actors (Salzberger 1993, 363). Judicial independence provides a high level of authority to judicial decision making because the courts are understood to be separate and not easily influenced by elected officials. As a result, courts can provide a valuable means to deflect blame for controversial policy decisions. Using the courts to engage in blame avoidance can also be understood as the "hot potato effect," which is evident when elected officials who are faced with a decision that they would rather not address for a variety of reasons decide to toss the metaphorical hot potato to the courts, more or less stating, "Here, you deal with this!" By forcing another institution to make a difficult decision, a political actor can avoid being blamed by the public and, more importantly, by the voters if that decision is ultimately unpopular. Indeed, several scholars have included blame avoidance or deflection among the central reasons why political actors empower the judiciary (see Lovell 2003; Vanberg 2005, 2015; and Fox and Stephenson 2011).

Although avoiding blame for making decisions can motivate political actors, this cannot be the sole determinant of their decision making. To gain and maintain support from the public, elected officials must engage in some aspect of position taking. In position taking, elected officials or individuals seeking election must attempt to align their positions on salient issues with those of potential voters or constituents (Mayhew 1974). As a result, elected officials experience a tension between the desire to avoid blame for unpopular decisions and, at the same time, the desire to take credit for decisions that are well received. It is an attempt to address this tension that makes courts appealing to political actors as sites for delegation, as courts are traditionally conceived as law interpreters rather than law producers.

This understanding of courts as interpreters of law provides a strategic benefit to actors who delegate to the courts. More specifically, if the courts uphold or approve a policy that is popular with the general public, the tendency will be to give credit to the legislators rather than the court. However, if the courts make an unpopular decision, political actors can make public their dissatisfaction and blame the courts (Salzberger 1993). Delegating to the courts transplants the political problem from the legislature to a forum that is portrayed as rational and nonpolitical (Aranson, Gellhorn, and Robinson 1982). Indeed, several of the interview subjects explained that a reference was a means to remove the controversy from the political-legislative arena for a period of time, placing it in the realm of the judiciary. Not only was this strategy used in an attempt to solve the constitutional controversy, but it also allowed Cabinet some "breathing room," in the words of former Attorney General D.[4]

That a government can prompt judicial review on its own accord through a reference opens up this power to greater use as a tool for blame avoidance or credit claiming than is the case with routine judicial review. For example, a government can signal its dissatisfaction with another government's policy by referring that government's policy to a provincial appellate court or the Supreme Court of Canada. The reference of another government's policy can be either lateral, which occurs when one province refers another province's legislation, or cross-governmental, which occurs when a province makes the federal government's policy the subject of a reference or, the reverse, when the federal attorney general refers a provincial government's legislation. This act can allow a government to play to a particular base of voters and to achieve national coverage of its opposition to the policy-enacting government. In such an instance, a government can take credit for opposing another government's policy, which might be especially appealing to a government seeking re-election.[5]

For example, Quebec was able to stall the Senate reform plans of Stephen Harper's government by referring Bill C-7, a bill aimed at reforming the upper house, to the Quebec Court of Appeal in a provincial reference case. Bill C-7 proposed to introduce nine-year term limits for newly appointed senators and to allow provincial governments to hold elections to determine the selection of new senators. The attorney general of Quebec's referral of Bill C-7 to the Quebec Court of Appeal not only interrupted Ottawa's reform plans but also prompted the federal Cabinet to initiate its own reference regarding Senate reform to the Supreme Court of Canada. The provincial reference made Quebec the central opponent of the federal government, to the approval of Quebecers (Wells 2013). This pragmatic use of the reference power allowed the Government of Quebec to stand up to the federal government and to claim credit with voters as the defender of Quebec interests.

The possibility that a reference can be employed to appease or claim credit with a particular constituency or base of voters is understood as a political benefit by individuals involved in past references. Indeed, during Attorney General D's tenure, their government's legislation was referred to an appellate court by another government. Although Attorney General D was not able to comment with certainty as to the motivations of the referring government, they explained that the referring government was likely motivated by the opportunity to play to its supporters.[6] The ability to invite the courts into a political conflict, including disagreements between governments, makes the reference power amenable to the goal of credit claiming in a manner different from (but perhaps greater than) that originally contemplated by delegation theory. In a reference, the option of attempting to avoid blame or to claim credit is more readily at the disposal of a government, as it does not need to wait for a live dispute to challenge the actions of another government or its own policy.

In a similar vein, judicial review can provide elected officials a "bailout effect" (Fox and Stephenson 2011). Connected to the goal of blame avoidance, the bailout effect holds that political actors can seek judicial review with the goal of being liberated from imprudent or ill-advised policies. The misguided policies could be the result of political posturing of the current government or could be the remnants of a previous government. In other words, courts can provide the opportunity for governments to rid themselves of the policies of predecessors in a way that is less direct and confrontational than simply repealing the legislation of the previous government. The decision of Mackenzie King's government to refer R.B. Bennett's New Deal legislation to the Supreme Court and, ultimately, to the Judicial Committee of the Privy Council (JCPC) demonstrates this bailout effect. As documented in Chapter 2, while in Opposition, King and members of the Liberal Party opposed the New Deal legislation but needed to be conscious of the possibility that their opposition could be perceived or framed as being out of touch or anti-worker. Thus, following an election and the King government's return to power, the New Deal legislation was promptly sent to the court for review via the reference power. Using a reference in this manner provided King with a bailout: his government did not have to worry about implementing legislation that was questionable in terms of constitutionality and that it did not support, and it was able to avoid the backlash that would likely have arisen if King had simply repealed the legislation through the legislature.

Relying on judicial review in this manner also allows legislators to engage in other behaviour aimed at increasing public support. Whittington (2007) explains that legislators can benefit from delegating to the courts to avoid blame when drafting and debating new legislation. The "judicial backstop" allows policy makers to publicize their support of legislation that might be popular with voters but might be constitutionally questionable: "They may vote in favor of a bill that they personally dislike secure in the knowledge that it will never be implemented" (137). If a court invalidates such a law, legislators can distance themselves from attempting to implement the controversial law and rally in opposition to the court for striking it down. This analysis centres on the fact that relying on judicial review may encourage legislators to behave irresponsibly, an effect that Tushnet (1999) refers to as "judicial overhang" – the sentiment that policy makers may act without being mindful of the constitutionality of proposed policies because they know that the courts can sort out the legalities afterward.

Using judicial review in this manner may encourage policy makers to write legislation with ambiguous language or to pass bills without seeking proper parliamentary or bureaucratic review because their ultimate goal is to rely on the courts to sort out the application of the law. Legislating with this approach creates a role for the judiciary in resolving difficult questions of public policy, as it attempts to apply the dubiously drafted legislation to a specific case (Lovell 2003; Stephenson 2006). Similarly, political actors can use the courts as a safety valve for policies that may be good politics but are perhaps ill-advised in other ways, such as when they lack compliance with the Constitution. Delegating to the judiciary in this manner allows elected officials to pass legislation to appease voters or a specific public sentiment, regardless of whether policy makers are certain that such legislation is constitutional. If the legislation is struck down, policy makers can then blame the courts irrespective of whether the legislation was drafted with a genuine belief in its constitutionality.

Political actors can also use the reference power to delegate decision-making power to the courts when faced with a decision that may be "no-win." Yet, unlike routine judicial review, a reference case allows for a unique form of political opportunism regarding blame avoidance. A government can seek a reference opinion on a controversial subject, removing the burden of making a decision about a controversial policy matter. If the court makes a decision that is unpopular, the referring government can shift blame for the decision to the court. Comparatively, if the decision is well received, the referring government also has the ability to claim credit for referring the matter to the courts in the first place and can simply follow the court's guidance. Using the reference power in this manner can also free political actors from the responsibility of ensuring that a proposed policy is legal and constitutional since they know that a court can provide a "judicial backstop" by sorting out the constitutionality or legality of a policy through a reference. Thus a reference can serve two of the most rudimentary goals of political actors – to avoid blame and to engage in position taking – in a unique way that generally cannot be achieved in routine litigation.[7]

Structural and Institutional Considerations

One of the earliest explanations for the delegation of decision making to the judiciary by political actors is simple and instrumental: the division of labour. This explanation holds that political actors will delegate powers that are not important to them or that concern issues of low political salience. Elected officials simply cannot deal with every issue related to governing. If the issue is not important or pressing, offloading the issue to another agency becomes a valuable option. This situation helps us to understand the offloading of mundane and routine issues to the courts, and it also explains why elected officials create administrative or regulatory agencies to deal with issues of low political salience, such as the regulation of telecommunications or trade (Fiorina 1982; Whittington 2007). If elected officials are motivated primarily by a desire to maintain power and to secure future re-election and if they are faced with a finite amount of time and resources, delegation will become a necessity. Issues that are unlikely to aid an elected official in power maintenance and vote winning are not "politically profitable" and are more likely to be delegated to another decision-making body (Whittington 2007, 121).

Perhaps the most functional explanation for why governments submit reference questions to appellate courts concerns the benefits related to time and resources. Compared to routine litigation, a reference allows a government to obtain a ruling from a penultimate appellate court or the Supreme Court in a relatively short amount of time. In a reference, unlike other parties who may wish to challenge a government action, a government does not need to wait for a concrete dispute with an ideal fact scenario in order to obtain judicial review. Furthermore, in a reference, a government can reduce expenditures, such as on financial and personnel resources, that would be required for routine judicial review.

When elected officials delegate to the courts, they can also overcome issues related to gridlock within a legislature. Judicial decision making is a relatively streamlined process, as the judiciary does not have to deal with complex rules and the stalling tactics that may take place within a legislature.[8] When faced with legislating on a highly divisive topic without a strong governing majority, a parliament may be unable to reach a consensus to take effective action. Instead, although a judicial decision may produce dissenting opinions, it will ultimately result in a decisive action, and when made by a final court of appeal, this decision will be definitive and final. Furthermore, because judicial actors are electorally unaccountable, they are able to make decisions when there is a lack of consensus on an issue both among the public and among legislators (Graber 1993).

Understood in this way, a reference can help a government to circumvent delay and opposition in the legislature. Indeed, Hennigar (2009) argues that the lack of consensus regarding same-sex marriage both within Parliament and among the Canadian public made delegating to the courts through a reference a viable option for the government of Jean Chrétien, despite its majority in the House of Commons. The Chrétien Cabinet was aware that simply introducing a bill to extend marriage to same-sex couples would have been met with strong opposition from within its caucus and from the other parties in the House of Commons. Although the Chrétien government held a majority, it could not be guaranteed that a bill permitting same-sex marriage would not be subjected to institutional and procedural delay. Thus seeking a reference to allow the Supreme Court to make a pronouncement on the legal parameters of same-sex marriage helped to avoid this gridlock. Many of those interviewed recalled that the reference power had been used in this manner and explained that one of the benefits of inviting the courts to decide controversial matters was that it overcame the slow-moving nature of Parliament and the procedural stalling tactics of the Opposition. In short, courts, unlike legislatures, have the ability to engage in unilateral action unencumbered by the same constraints as policy makers, making them attractive options for political actors in dealing with issues that lack a majority consensus.

Similarly, if a government is facing an uphill battle over a legislative project, a favourable reference decision will provide the government a great deal of momentum to move forward, sparing it the unnecessary expenditure of political capital. As a result, a government can help to conserve future resources by pre-empting challenges that may be mounted in response to a legislative program. The reason for using the reference power most cited by interview participants was the political assurance that can be gained through an authoritative decision of the court – or what some scholars refer to as "position legitimization" (Hausegger, Hennigar, and Riddell 2015). Governments that are unsure of the constitutionality or legality of a proposed policy can have the courts decide on the matter through a reference case, allowing governments to legislate with assurance. This assurance may be more important for a government attempting legislative change that would be problematic to unwind once in place. A reference can provide a government with an authoritative opinion, which if favourable will legitimize a government's policy preference and can help to circumvent future legal challenges. Although submitting the proposed policy to the courts opens up a government to the possibility of invalidation, the assurance that can be achieved through an authoritative court ruling can outweigh concern about this potential negative outcome.

Several interviewees explained that a reference opinion is a valuable tool in dealing with a constitutional controversy. A reference decision in such a case helps to assure a government that it is operating on a valid interpretation of the Constitution before moving forward. This assurance has been vital to obtain in situations where the proposed legislative scheme would have been problematic to disentangle if found unconstitutional or illegal at a later date. Other interviewees explained that obtaining a reference opinion prior to enacting a particularly controversial piece of legislation had "short-circuited" litigation that was likely to occur once the legislation was in place. In such circumstances, a reference opinion in support of a government's proposed legislative scheme helps to eliminate future challenges, both political and legal. When employed in this manner, references, and incidentally the courts, can act as a shield for a government that must address a controversial political issue. Such references highlight that delegation to the courts can provide a form of political insurance by reducing policy uncertainty and helping to prevent future reversal (Salzberger and Voigt 2002; Tridimas 2009).

The benefits regarding time and resources that can be gained by a government in a reference case speak to the structure of the reference power; however, this is not the only structure-related benefit that can prompt a government to engage the reference power. Governments will also initiate references to profit from the abstract nature of reference cases. Unencumbered by a set of facts, a government can manufacture the ideal hypothetical-fact scenario to test a policy in court through a reference case. Indeed, a reference provides a government unparalleled power to frame the terms of a case. Since the reference question determines the central terms of the case, a government can frame the question in a manner that best suits its goal in an attempt to elicit a particular decision from the court. Furthermore, without a set of facts, a government can rely on a reference to achieve a broad ruling from a court instead of a narrow decision that applies only to a particular dispute. A reference allows a government to control aspects of a case in a way that is simply not possible when dealing with a concrete case bound by a set of facts.

Finally, perhaps the defining reason of Canadian governments for delegating decision making is that the reference power can help them to navigate the implications of federalism. First, a reference can enable the federal government to eliminate differences in public policy across provincial jurisdictions, thus ensuring national standards. When faced with different judicial interpretations at the provincial level, a reference can allow the federal government to quickly obtain an authoritative decision from the Supreme Court that will have national implications. When a government relies on the reference process instead of appealing a lower court ruling, the reference is not limited to the facts of a specific case in a particular province. Clearly, this explanation pertains more to the federal than to the provincial reference power. Second, a reference enables governments to challenge the public policy of another government, as discussed above. The referral of another government's legislative project can be a means for the referring government not only to stall that project but also to make its opinion on the legislation heard. Finally, a government can use a reference as a powerful way to protect its constitutional jurisdiction if it believes that the legislation of another government is infringing on its constitutionally prescribed powers. Indeed, in the early twentieth century, through a series of provincially empowering JCPC decisions, provincial governments were able to effectively use the reference power to combat the expansion of federal government jurisdiction (Cairns 1971).

Implications of Delegation

Whether governments use the reference power to delegate to the courts as a means to avoid blame or claim credit or as a means to respond to institutional and structural limitations imposed by the legal or federal system, governments have found references to be a viable political strategy. Indeed, the use of the reference power over the almost 150 years since its creation clearly shows that political actors have strategically chosen to empower courts in order to serve their own political ends by asking the courts to answer difficult and controversial questions through reference cases. Instances when governments considered using the reference power to respond to a political controversy but ultimately abandoned the reference option further demonstrate the political-strategic calculations that can influence a government to engage in reference litigation. This practice of empowering the courts to sort out divisive questions that are political and often abstract has several implications for the relationship between the executive, legislature, and judiciary. The following section addresses these implications by discussing the normative significance of democratically elected actors relying on nondemocratic institutions for advisory opinions to address political conflicts. Additionally, this section examines two specific implications of the reference power: first, the consequences raised for the independence of the judiciary when judicial advice is requested though the submission of reference questions to the courts; and second, the reference power's contribution to the centralization of policy-making power in the Canadian executive.

Empowering the Courts

Addressing the implications of delegation for the judiciary requires a consideration of the counter-majoritarian difficulty that arises when the unelected and democratically unaccountable judiciary overrides the will of elected and democratically legitimate individuals such as legislators (Graber 1993; Salzberger 1993; Martens 2007). The nonmajoritarian difficulty arguably becomes more problematic in circumstances where political actors actively delegate their decision-making responsibility to the courts. If political actors make a conscious decision to delegate decision making over particular issues to the courts, thus inviting the courts to wade into political controversies, these actors are either tacitly supporting or actively encouraging judicial power, which has implications for policy making. With this relationship in mind, the argument that judicial policy making is illegitimate within a democracy overlooks the nuanced relationship between elected policy makers and the judicial branch (Graber 1993). As a result, in some cases, a rise in judicial power is not necessarily at odds with the goals of elected officials.

For this relationship between elected policy makers and the judiciary to exist and, more importantly, for it to effectively benefit policy makers, two institutional features must be present. First, political actors must view the courts as "relatively friendly," meaning that judicial review must not be understood as solely antagonistic and adversarial (Hirschl 2004, 11; Whittington 2007, 87). Of course, for policy makers to delegate decision making to the courts, they must be willing to allow the courts to decide and generally willing to respect the outcome of judicial decisions. Second, and more importantly, there must be an appreciation of and respect for judicial independence. The independence of the judiciary not only increases the legitimacy of the decisions made by the courts in delegated situations but also means that those decisions are more likely to be respected by all parties involved. Furthermore, the separation of the judicial branch from the executive and legislative branches fostered by judicial independence helps to "maximize the responsibility shift" away from political actors (Salzberger 1993, 363). In other words, when decisions are made by the courts, elected officials are less likely to be held accountable or to be blamed for such decisions. Judicial independence imparts a high level of authority to decisions rendered by the judiciary because the courts are understood to be separate, nonpartisan, and not easily influenced by elected officials.

Empowering the judiciary to make authoritative decisions on political and/or constitutional controversies appears to be at odds with the central motivations of political actors when we consider the Downsian goals of elected officials: power preservation and re-election. Indeed, on the surface, pivoting toward courts to make decisions on policy appears counterintuitive for elected officials. Relying on judicial review creates the possibility that political actors will have their powers limited and their ability to make decisions over public policy restrained or in some cases restricted altogether. For example, if a government submits reference questions to a court asking it to consider whether a new policy is intra vires or ultra vires its constitutional jurisdiction, it opens itself up to the possibility that the court could find the policy outside of its legal authority. Such a decision has the immediate effect of limiting the government's ability to enact its desired policy, while also creating the possibility that the court's decisions could limit future policy making in similar or related policy spheres. Judicial review has the power to create clear winners and losers and can essentially provide the judiciary a veto over the public policy objectives of elected officials (Whittington 2007). A precedent set in a reference case can create conditions favourable to further limitation in the future. Yet, regardless of the possibility of being limited by the courts both immediately and in the future, political actors consistently defer to the judiciary and delegate to the courts the power to make decisions regarding politically salient issues. As a result, scholars have sought to understand why elected officials will delegate to the courts and how judicial review can be considered "friendly."[9]

Expanding on the concept of "friendly" judicial review, Hirschl (2004) explains that judicial review can be affable toward political actors because the judicial and political elite hold similar interests, experiences, and preferences. Political actors who face uncertainty regarding their future in power are wise to empower a like-minded judiciary that can ensure the enforcement of the political elite's core values in the future due to the virtually guaranteed tenure of the judiciary. When faced with uncertainty over the continuation of power, elected officials will seek to empower the judiciary as a form of regime maintenance, or what Hirschl describes as "hegemonic preservation." This preservation can be a valuable political strategy because the courts can insulate policy making from the volatility of democratic politics and, at the same time, produce judicial decisions that are often compatible with the interests of political elites (12). Strategically oriented political actors will seek to empower the courts as a means of preserving or constitutionalizing policy preferences, which can lead to circumstances where political actors will adopt a bill of rights that constitutionalizes a particular vision of rights and empowers a judiciary to interpret those rights. Hirschl uses this understanding of delegation to explain the preservation of large-scale regime values rather than routine policy choices. When used toward this goal of regime enforcement, delegation helps threatened political actors to ensure that their legacy and rights preferences are preserved in the future through favourable judicial decision making.

Hirschl's (2004) explanation for hegemonic preservation is concerned with the maintenance of fundamental regime values like liberalism in the face of threats from competing ideologies like socialism. This explanation can be contrasted with the arguments of political insurance theory put forward by Ginsburg (2003) and Finkel (2008), which maintain that elected officials will empower the courts to ensure a possible venue for policy influence in the event they lose power in a future election. Thus, as Ginsburg (2003, 32) explains, "judicial review, like insurance, is a risk-reduction device" that is attractive not only to those in power (as Hirschl explains) but also to minorities or those vying for power. Empowering the courts to exercise judicial review provides another venue where groups can attempt to influence policy if they cannot be certain about electoral success. As a result, including avenues for judicial review helps to appease more parties during the process of Constitution drafting in a manner that helps to secure a constitutional agreement.

The explanations for judicial empowerment offered by political insurance theory and by Hirschl's thesis of hegemonic preservation are useful for understanding political delegation in large projects, such as the adoption of a bill of rights, the design of a new Constitution, and the macro effects of an empowered judiciary. The same features that make the delegation and empowerment of the judiciary attractive to political actors in the context considered by this literature can also provide insight into smaller-scale decision making, such as deciding to use the reference power. When using a reference to seek assurances or to take advantage of the institutional legitimacy of the courts, a government is anticipating that an authoritative judicial decision will help to insulate its policy making from future challenges – both political and legal. It would be difficult to mount a legal challenge that asked a court to consider legal questions that did not vary greatly from those previously addressed in a reference case. Similarly, if a government obtains a ruling from a high court confirming the legal and/or constitutional validity of a policy, it becomes difficult for the opposition to mount a challenge along similar lines. Although using the reference power requires a much smaller-scale decision than envisioned by hegemonic preservation or political insurance theory, the relationship in both examples is the same: elected political actors rely on counter-majoritarian actors to preserve and protect their interests from political opposition through judicial review.

With this better understanding of the relationship between the courts and elected policy makers, it is now possible to consider the implications of this relationship in a broader institutional sense. First, the following discussion looks at the implications for the courts in terms of the reference power's consequences for judicial independence. Second, it looks at the corresponding effects on the political process in terms of the reference power's contribution to the centralization of policy-making power in the executive at the expense of the legislature. This examination is complemented by a comparison of the reference power to abstract review in several European constitutional courts, which provides insight into the possible institutional arrangements that can facilitate advisory opinions in a manner less centralized than in the Canadian reference system.

References as Confounding Judicial Independence

In *Reference re References,* Chief Justice Sir Charles Fitzpatrick recognized that when providing advisory opinions in a reference case, a court engages in an extrajudicial role that is ordinarily filled by Cabinet, particularly by the attorney general. As discussed in Chapter 1, in *Reference re References,* the Supreme Court did not find this intrusion into a routine function of Cabinet to be an issue because in a reference a court does not make decisions that bind the other branches of government but merely provides advice. The court found that this advice is still a legal function and therefore respects the constitutional role of the judiciary. In *Reference re References,* the court's reasoning was contingent on the fact that a reference opinion is advisory only: "The answers do not bind the Governor in Council. He may act in accordance with them or not, as he pleases, giving them just such weight as he pleases. They are advisory only."[10] The court found that because the executive is not bound or constrained by anything decided in a reference, the judiciary cannot be understood as directing the executive in its reference decisions, and therefore concerns over the separation of the executive from the judiciary – or judicial independence – are not realized.

In *Reference re References,* the Supreme Court and the JCPC were asked to confront arguments that criticized the reference power from the perspective of judicial independence. The provincial attorneys general who participated in the case argued that the reference power requires courts to provide advice to the executive and to fulfil a responsibility of Cabinet. Indeed, as this study has argued, if courts engage in a function that is a routine responsibility of Cabinet, they become implicated in the political arena, which transgresses the separation of the judiciary from the other, more political, branches of government. The fulfillment of a political function can erode the independence of the judiciary, as it requires that the judiciary be answerable to the executive in providing advice. This issue is a pressing concern because the courts do not hold any formal power to reject reference cases and because the executive can force the courts to answer reference questions if it so desires. For judicial independence to be effective, there must be a degree of institutional separation of the judiciary from the more political branches of government, facilitating the responsibility of the courts to "check" the actions of the other branches of government.

Judicial independence, as distinct from judicial impartiality, is both a relational and behavioural concept.[11] Judicial independence, when understood in a relational sense, considers whether the courts are protected from undue interference and influence by the political branches in the system. In contrast, when judicial independence is considered from a behavioural perspective, the focus is on the very decisions rendered by the courts, with a concern for autonomy and objectivity (Russell 2001; Hausegger, Hennigar, and Riddell 2015). Centred on the relational aspect of judicial independence, the autonomy of the judiciary is maintained by allowing the courts to exert a great deal of control over their docket and administration, as well as by protecting judicial tenure and salaries. Without the formal power to reject reference questions or grant leave to reference cases, references can be understood to violate the judiciary's administrative control and thus its independence. However, for both the Supreme Court and the JCPC in *Reference re References*, the questions related to judicial independence that arise with the reference power were easily solved through the safety valve of the "advisory only" nature of reference cases. Indeed, according to this reasoning, if the executive can simply reject the advice of the courts, there is no significant implication for the division of institutions and the separation of the judiciary from the other branches of government.

In the *Secession Reference,* the Supreme Court was asked to revisit the constitutionality of the reference power. The amicus curiae argued that the Supreme Court's role had greatly changed since it had last ruled in *Reference re References* and that the ability of the court to render advisory opinions is not expressly provided for in the Canadian Constitution. The Supreme Court rejected this argument, explaining that there is nothing in the Constitution that bars a court from exercising other legal duties aside from its routine judicial function.[12] The court affirmed the validity of the reference power, explaining that the Constitution does not prescribe a strict separation of powers. Courts are not precluded from engaging in actions that are outside their traditional adjudicative role.[13] It is important to note that the Supreme Court did not rely on the same "advisory only" reasoning as in the earlier challenge to the reference power.

It was prudent of the Supreme Court to avoid relying on the "advisory only" logic of *Reference re References*. As demonstrated throughout this study, reference decisions are advisory in name alone. Among the federal and provincial statutes that provide governments a reference power, all but Prince Edward Island's *Judicature Act* specify that a decision rendered in a reference case is to be considered a judgment or treated like a judgment.[14] Importantly, there are no documented examples of a government flagrantly ignoring the findings of a reference case, and Hausegger, Hennigar, and Riddell (2015) note that reference cases are cited by courts like any other legal precedent. Likewise, all individuals interviewed for this project confirmed that they did not view a reference case to be different from other legal decisions. Even in instances where the courts have served as a roadblock to government actions, governments have abided by the findings in reference cases.

That reference cases are informally binding speaks to the institutional relationship between the judicial branch and the executive and legislative branches in general and has unique implications for judicial independence. In 2014, for example, in *Reference re Senate Reform,* the Supreme Court blocked the federal government's plans to reform the Senate, a longstanding promise of the Conservative Party of Canada that can be traced back to its Reform Party roots. The Harper government observed the court's ruling that unilateral reform was unconstitutional and did not pursue further Senate reform. Under the logic implied by the early decisions affirming the reference power, the Harper Cabinet could have simply disregarded the Supreme Court's advice and proceeded with the reform measures.

Another good example, also from 2014, is the *Nadon Reference*. In this case, the federal government had obtained independent advice that validated the Supreme Court appointment of Justice Marc Nadon, and the chief justice of the Supreme Court had already sworn in Nadon. In this case, instead of complying with the court's decision in the *Nadon Reference* that Nadon was ineligible for the Supreme Court, the government could have respectfully disagreed and followed the independent advice that validated the appointment. To be sure, a rejection of the reference opinion could have created difficulties for the government when a related concrete case, filed by a Toronto lawyer who challenged the appointment of Nadon, materialized at the Supreme Court (see Fine 2014). That being said, in the interim, ignoring the reference opinion would have allowed the government to have Nadon continue to fill the otherwise vacant seat. Furthermore, with Nadon participating in hearings at the Supreme Court, the Supreme Court would have been unlikely to find his appointment invalid at a later date, as doing so would have jeopardized the cases in which he had participated, creating a greater institutional problem.

The acceptance of judicial advice, even when it runs counter to a government goal, should be unsurprising in light of the relationship between political actors and the courts. Political actors are unlikely to override the constitutional interpretation of the courts (Manfredi 2001; Huscroft 2007; Baker 2010). When political actors are unwilling to pursue their *own* constitutional interpretation in the face of a contrary judicial interpretation, they are relegated to a subordinate role in constitutional interpretation. This role not only prevents legislators and the executive from engaging in constitutional interpretation that differs from that of the courts in the short term but also reinforces the superiority of the courts' interpretation going forward. The implication is that political actors are unlikely to override reference case decisions, making references advisory in name alone. This realistic understanding of the reference power and how actors respond to reference decisions heightens the concerns regarding the independence of the judiciary and the separation of the courts from the more political branches of government.

However, the concern that judicial independence is compromised due to the informally binding nature of reference cases is eased in part if courts can refuse to answer reference questions. Indeed, Hausegger, Hennigar, and Riddell (2015) note that the concerns about judicial independence that arise from reference cases are neutralized if courts continue to refuse to answer some reference questions, as the Supreme Court did in the *Same-Sex Marriage Reference*. As discussed in Chapter 3, if the judiciary maintains the power to refuse to answer reference questions, it can safeguard its independence and avoid answering questions that it considers inappropriate. The courts are reactive institutions, as they must respond to the matters that other parties bring before them and cannot seek out matters to adjudicate. As a consequence of their reactive nature, the courts must maintain a great deal of control over deciding what matters are appropriate for judicial determination under the common law rules of justiciability. Justiciability is a gatekeeping power that helps to ensure that the courts will not address matters that involve them in judicial determinations that are contrary to their legitimate constitutional role (Sossin 2012). Nonetheless, due to the mandatory wording in the reference-granting statutes and the lack of a formal leave process, in a plain reading of the reference power legislation, the courts do not hold the power to refuse reference questions.

Given that judicial independence can be threatened by the extrajudicial role that the courts are required to fill in reference cases and given that reference decisions have become effectively binding on political actors, one way to protect the independence of the courts would be to formally apply the parameters of justiciability to reference cases. Providing the courts with the power to explicitly consider the justiciable nature of any question referred and the ability to either grant or refuse leave in reference cases would allow for the safeguarding of judicial independence while working within the current institutional framework for reference cases. Although only the Supreme Court has the wide-ranging power to grant or refuse leave – indeed, most of its cases are appeals by leave (see Hausegger, Hennigar, and Riddell 2015, 60) – all Canadian courts must consider whether the matter before them is justiciable and whether judicial intervention is warranted (Sossin 2012, 6). As discussed in Chapter 3, assessing justiciability ensures that matters heard by courts are not moot, are ripe for judicial determination, and cannot be solved through other means. In agreeing to hear a matter, a court must consider the legitimacy and capability of the judicial process to address the specific matter; the constitutional role of the legislative, executive, and judicial branches; and the specific nature of the dispute (Sossin 2012). The common law requirements of justiciability help to protect the constitutionally prescribed roles of the judiciary and the other branches of government and help to ensure that the disputes heard by the courts do not endanger this institutional framework.

However, reference cases have no leave process and no explicit consideration of justiciability. Instead, the courts are required by statute to answer the reference questions submitted by governments. Doing so would not be a problem if the reference process involved the courts in only an advisory capacity. However, a realistic understanding of how the reference process operates and how governments respond to reference cases makes it clear that viewing references as simple advice overlooks the implications of these cases for judicial independence. Given that references have become effectively binding in practice, it is essential that the courts be allowed to safeguard the proper role of the judiciary and judicial independence by incorporating a leave process for reference cases. To be sure, the threshold for leave in a reference case would be much lower than in routine cases, as standards related to mootness would not be applicable to abstract review. Applying the doctrine of mootness to reference questions presents obvious difficulties since it refers to situations where a dispute that was once live is no longer active and where a judicial determination would have no real effect on the litigating parties (Sossin 2012, 107). As a result, all abstract reference questions where no live dispute exists could be considered moot, and thus there would be little value in applying a strict standard of mootness to references.

The requirement of ripeness can prevent reference questions from materializing into reference cases if courts decide that other venues, such as the legislature, are more appropriate for addressing issues raised by the reference questions. In essence, the doctrine of ripeness is concerned with the factual nature of cases. Ripeness requires that there be a legal controversy for courts to address rather than purely hypothetical matters (Sossin 2012, 33). A court will assess ripeness in light of the constitutional separation of powers, the legitimacy of the judicial process, and the nature of the dispute, with the first factor holding greater importance in reference cases compared to routine litigation. Taken to its logical conclusion, the suggestion of applying ripeness to reference cases would result in the elimination of virtually all abstract reference cases. The strict application of ripeness (as applied to routine cases) is not tenable for the reference power. Instead, a modified doctrine of ripeness could be adopted where a court required that reference questions for abstract review be based on legislation that, at a minimum, had been drafted, thus providing a scope for the terms of the reference. The Supreme Court considered this issue in *Reference re Court of Unified Criminal Jurisdiction,* where it criticized the New Brunswick government for failing to provide a legislative scheme that would help to guide the proposed unified criminal court in its analysis of the reference questions. The lack of materials supporting the reference led the court to reflect on whether it should answer the questions posed in the reference. Although the Supreme Court went on to answer the questions, there is a benefit to the court pausing to reflect on the appropriateness of answering reference questions and on the greater implications for the policy-making process.

The courts should be cognizant of intervening in an emerging political or societal debate, and considering some form of ripeness in reference cases can help to ensure that a reference opinion does not become the means of staving off political deliberation. Creating the minimum requirement of a draft bill for reference cases is merely one suggestion aimed at promoting careful reflection by the courts in reviewing the justiciability of reference questions. A more candid discussion of the appropriateness of the questions in all reference cases would ensure thoughtful reflection by the courts and greater transparency for observers.

It is the consideration of these factors (albeit informally) that has led courts to refuse to answer reference questions in the past, specifically in the *Same-Sex Marriage Reference* and in *Reference re Constitution Act*

1867, ss 26, 27, and 28 (BC).[15] The Supreme Court's refusal to answer a question in the *Same-Sex Marriage Reference* was highly controversial and has been the subject of much scholarly analysis (see McEvoy 2005; and Huscroft 2006). However, this work does not address the role that justiciability could and arguably should play in reference cases. If it is accepted that reference cases are not functionally different from routine review, it should also be accepted that courts, giving consideration to the principles of justiciability, should have some control over entertaining reference questions. To maintain the intended purpose of the reference power, the requirements for hearing or answering reference questions should be liberally interpreted, and the refusals to hear a reference case or to answer specific questions should be rare. However, in cases where the judicial independence or the proper functioning of the constitutional separation of powers could be threatened through a reference case, the courts should maintain the discretion to refuse to answer questions. Given the many nonlegal factors that may prompt a government to ask a reference question, the courts should maintain this mechanism of docket control. This control would ensure that the courts do not become an outlet for the delegation of all difficult political questions through the reference power. The application of justiciability requirements and a leave process for reference cases could provide a valuable safety valve to protect against reference cases that could have negative implications for judicial independence.

Although this study is not the first time that concerns regarding the reference power and its implications for judicial independence have been raised (for similar concerns, see Persaud 1998), readers familiar with the nature of public support for the Supreme Court of Canada may conclude that concerns related to judicial independence are overstated. Indeed, some scholars have found that the public may prefer that the courts, rather than elected officials, decide controversial matters of public policy (Fletcher and Howe 2000). However, it is important to consider the nature and strength of the public's support for the Supreme Court of Canada and what it means for the legitimacy of the court in the future when deciding controversial issues.

In attempting to explain the nature of public support for the Supreme Court of Canada, Hausegger and Riddell (2004) find that public support for the court is outcome-oriented and is dependent more on agreement with specific judicial decisions and less on the nature and importance of the institution itself. Hausegger and Riddell argue that the nature of this support could be problematic if the court made a series of decisions that sparked public disagreement, as doing so would undermine the court's public legitimacy over time. Goodyear-Grant, Matthews, and Hiebert (2013) attempt to further disentangle the nature of public support for the decisions made by the Supreme Court of Canada by examining the relationship relative to support for Parliament. Goodyear-Grant, Matthews, and Hiebert, similar to Hausegger and Riddell, find that although Canadians often prefer the courts to make controversial decisions, this preference is focused on the result of a decision rather than on considerations related to process or on the concerns that would rise from a reflection on the roles of each institution within the Canadian system of government (381). More specifically, because the nature of public support is largely focused on outcome, the public would likely be similarly supportive of the decision if it was made by the legislature rather than the courts.

The findings regarding public support for the courts in making decisions about public policy tell us that public support and the perceived legitimacy of the institution are dependent on results rather than the process. This situation means that public support is not founded on a deeply held respect for the courts as an institution but on a superficial preference for an outcome. Arguably, because the public is outcome-oriented, rather than concerned with process, it is more important *how* the courts answer reference questions than that they are involved in the reference process at all. Any awareness of the public's focus by the courts might help to explain why highly contentious and salient cases like the *Secession Reference* and the *Patriation Reference* resulted in rather balanced decisions that avoided creating clear winners and losers.

Although Canadian courts have often produced decisions that have received the support of the public, this support could erode overtime if the courts began to make a series of decisions that were out of step with the preferences of the public. Given the nature of public support, such decisions would ultimately undermine judicial independence and legitimacy, as well as disregard the responsibility of democratically elected officials to create public policy rather than relying on nonelected courts.

Given the controversial nature of some reference cases, there is value in examining the concerns that arise when the courts are implicated in contentious matters of public policy, and there is value in reflecting on the long-term effects of delegating decision making to the courts on judicial independence.

References as Contributing to the Centralization of Power in the Executive

One of the central findings of this study is that a great deal of autonomy and power are available to the executive in deciding to use the reference power. The power to obtain an advisory opinion and initiate a reference case is the sole prerogative of the executive via the (lieutenant) governor in council. As there are few parameters respecting this power, the ability to launch a reference case is a great source of power for an executive given that a reference has the potential to serve many ends aside from constitutional or legal clarification. A reference case provides the executive with the ability to engage in issue management and a means to delegate politically controversial issues to the courts, making the initiation of references a valuable political strategy.

The reference power, when used to circumvent the legislative process, can marginalize the role of the legislature. When a government decides to use a reference to deal with an issue, it not only pauses legislative debate on the matter but also prevents legislators from engaging in position taking, limiting one of the essential characteristics of the legislative role. Indeed, according to interviewee Attorney General D, this was a valuable aspect of the reference power for governments because submitting a reference takes the issue out of the routine legislative domain and enables political actors to invoke the principle of sub judice to avoid commenting on the matter.[16] When a reference case is used to curtail a debate, the result is the marginalization of the legislature and an increase in the centralization of power in the executive, specifically in the attorney general and the prime minister or premier. A government can capitalize on the abstract nature of a reference and can engage in a great deal of manipulation since a reference gives it the ability to manufacture or propose hypothetical scenarios unencumbered by a live dispute. All of these factors can amount to a great deal of power in the hands of the executive, as there are few impediments to this power and virtually no accountability mechanisms.

Scholars assessing the role of the legislature and the power of the executive have convincingly demonstrated that power has become centralized in the executive to the detriment of the legislature, line departments, and ministers (Savoie 1999, 2010). Focusing solely on the federal government and the power of the prime minister, some scholars have argued that the Canadian system demonstrates elements of "presidentialization" without the powerful checks and balances that are essential aspects of the presidential system (Bakvis and Wolinetz 2005). According to this literature, the only real domestic constraints on executive power during periods of majority government are the courts, the federal division of powers, and the strength of the provinces. Although strong provinces are a valuable counterpoint to the centralization of power in the federal executive, the power invested in provincial first ministers parallels and in some respects exceeds that of the prime minister (Marland 2014).[17] Given these factors, the reference power is another example of the various sources of power available to Canadian first ministers, both federal and provincial.

However, obtaining advisory opinions from the courts or engaging in abstract review does not need to operate in such a centralized manner. Comparatively, the Canadian reference case process is an example of one of the most centralized systems of abstract review given that only the executive can engage in this process. In many European constitutional courts, the power is not limited to the executive alone, and there is more than one access point for this form of review. For example, in Italy, Germany, and Spain, regional governments can access review at the constitutional court without having to go through regional lower courts first. In Spain, France, and Germany, both the executive and the legislature have the power to engage in abstract review. More specifically, in all three countries, a designated number of legislators must group together to seek abstract review. For example, one-third of the Bundestag in Germany can submit matters for abstract review at the constitutional court, the Bundesverfassungsgericht. Thus, when a substantial number of legislators agree that a government policy should be reviewed by a court, the option of abstract review is available. The ability to refer governmental legislative proposals to the constitutional courts has become a valuable tool for opposition parties in the legislature, who use this power at a greater rate than governing parties (Stone Sweet 2000).

Comparing the abstract review process of the constitutional courts in France, Germany, Italy, and Spain with the process in Canada reveals several important points of divergence, all of which highlight the centralization in the Canadian system. Canada is the only country that restricts access to abstract review to the executive alone. All European countries allow at least one other party to access abstract review at the constitutional court. In France, Germany, and Spain, given that oppositional parties or parliamentarians can initiate abstract review, it is believed that review extends parliamentary debates over the law into the constitutional courts (Stone Sweet 2000; Vanberg 2005). Although the Italian framework does not provide ordinary legislators the power to initiate abstract review, it is still not as restrictive as the Canadian system. The Italian abstract review system allows regional governments direct access to the Italian Constitutional Court, whereas Canadian provincial governments must first submit reference questions to provincial appellate courts and do not have direct access to the Supreme Court of Canada. This comparison is interesting given that in the Canadian case interviewees explained that a reference can be an effective means to circumvent the stalling tactics of the parliamentary opposition when dealing with controversial legislation. Conversely, in the European case, where the reference power is open to use by legislators, abstract review has become a valuable tactic for the parliamentary opposition, which has utilized the abstract review power at a greater rate than governing coalitions (see Vanberg 2005). Thus, both in the Canadian and European contexts, the utility of inviting a judicial review of contested policies is recognized, whereas in Canada this benefit is available only to the governing party.

In terms of time restrictions on the referral of legislation to the courts, Canada stands as an outlier again since it has no formal time restrictions on when legislation can be referred to the Supreme Court. This situation means that the period for contesting legislation through a reference is unlimited and ongoing. Indeed, in the *Nadon Reference*, the Supreme Court was asked to interpret sections 5 and 6 of the *Supreme Court Act*, which have been in operation since 1875 and 1974 respectively. Ostensibly, an executive can refer any Canadian law, regardless of how long it has been in force. A government can refer major legislative projects of previous governments as a means to nullify legislation that it opposes if it desires, and the King government's use of references to respond to the Bennett New Deal is a case in point. Comparatively, in the constitutional courts examined above, the referral of laws for abstract review is limited to laws that are not yet in force. More specifically, in France laws that have been adopted by Parliament, but not yet promulgated, can be subject to abstract review, and in Germany, Spain, and Italy, laws that have been promulgated, but are not yet in force, can be referred to the constitutional court. Imposing a limitation on when laws can be referred has three central consequences. First, the examination of laws before they are in force seeks to avoid the criticisms of judicial activism that are often levelled at the American style of review by limiting the possibility that unconstitutional laws will be struck down by courts at a later date (Stone Sweet 2000, 2003). Second, the early examination of laws by constitutional courts helps to amend unconstitutional laws before they can have any effect, which can help to prevent circumstances where an unconstitutional law could be enforced against an individual or group. Third, the limitation period eliminates the potential for the current governing coalition to use abstract review as a strategic tactic to invalidate the laws of a previous government.

Another structural feature that differentiates the Canadian case from the European cases is the selection or appointment mechanism for the justices that sit on the high court. In Canada the appointment of a Supreme Court justice is the sole prerogative of the governor in council (in practice, the prime minister in consultation with the minister of justice), making the appointment of a Supreme Court justice a great source of power for a government. The Canadian system is not only an outlier in relation to European constitutional courts but also stands out compared to all high courts internationally. According to Russell (2004, 17), the Supreme Court of Canada is "the only constitutional democracy in the world in which the leader of government has an unfettered discretion to decide who will sit on the country's highest court." Although beyond the scope of the present study, the vast amount of power and autonomy that are afforded the executive in its appointment of judges to the Supreme Court of Canada, including the power to unilaterally amend some aspects of the selection process,[18] has the potential to raise concerns for judicial independence as well. This power and related concerns are well documented in the Canadian literature (see Russell 2004; Hogg 2006; Crandall 2010; and McCormick 2012).

In the context of Spain, Italy, France, and Germany, one single individual or group does not hold the power to appoint all the justices on the constitutional court. In Germany, Spain, and Italy, which use elections as a selection mechanism, justices selected for the constitutional court must be elected by a majority of legislators, either two-thirds, as in Germany and Italy, or three-fifths, as in Spain. Given that all three of the European cases are multiparty systems, no party will control enough seats to push a desired partisan appointee through, making appointees to the constitutional courts the product of a multiparty negotiation (Stone Sweet 2000). France does not rely on elections; however, no single political actor holds the power to select all members of the Constitutional Council: three are selected by the president, three by the president of the National Assembly, and three by the president of the Senate, and all former presidents receive a lifetime appointment.[19] It is interesting to note that the French system has no formal requirements regarding previous legal experience for appointment to the Constitutional Council, resulting in many political appointments, such as former parliamentarians and ministers, although most appointees do have some legal training (Stone 1992; Stone Sweet 2000).

Finally, the Canadian system of abstract review departs from the European model in terms of structure. In the Kelsen-European model, constitutional courts are detached from the rest of the judicial system and hierarchy and do not hold appellate jurisdiction over any other court. Comparatively, the Canadian Supreme Court is the apex of the Canadian judicial system, meaning that all legal matters have the possibility of being appealed to the Supreme Court, regardless of the court of origin. Moreover, every court in the Canadian judicial system has the ability to apply and interpret the Constitution. In the Kelsen-European model, the constitutional court is the sole interpreter of the Constitution (Sadurski 2005). The divorce of constitutional courts from the judicial system means that any constitutional matter that arises in a lower court must be sent to the constitutional court for review. The separation of constitutional courts is aimed at preserving the formal separation of powers that permeates most European constitutional systems. As a result, constitutional courts exist in a separate legal realm that is "neither clearly judicial nor political" (Stone Sweet 2000, 34). This separation would suggest that most of the problems arising from a court participating in the abstract review of legislation and from the implications of this extrajudicial function could largely be eliminated.

Abstract review in these four European cases is subject to a process that is highly structured and that requires the participation of multiple groups, ensuring that power is not concentrated in any single actor or institution. Compared to European constitutional courts, the Canadian system is an outlier. Canada is the only case where abstract review is the sole power of one institutional body, the governor in council. This power over abstract review becomes even more impressive when we consider that the same actor also has the exclusive power to appoint justices to fill the bench of the court that provides abstract review. This striking concentration of power is simply not possible within the European system of constitutional courts, although this is not to suggest that the exclusive appointment powers of the prime minister will result in sympathetic reference decisions from appointees. Instead, the objective is to highlight the concentration of power that is present in the Canadian reference system and to examine the other possibilities for the institutional structure of abstract review. Finally, it is important to remember that whereas the exercise of abstract review by constitutional courts in Europe is a routine practice, Canadian courts deal with reference cases much less frequently, which can help to explain why the European abstract review system is much more structured than the Canadian one. That being said, the European system does provide important lessons on how to make the reference power less centralized and more democratic.

The abstract review systems in the European countries examined here explicitly recognize the manner in which politics and the strategic motivations of political actors can percolate through abstract review. As a result, they rely on institutional frameworks that seek to segregate abstract review as a means to protect the independence of the regular judicial system and to democratize access to this power. In contrast, the Canadian system operates almost in ignorance of the political strategy that can enter into the reference process and, as a result, arguably opens itself up to straining the independence of the judiciary and contributing to the centralization of power in the executive, largely at the expense of the legislature.

Conclusion

The reference power provides elected actors with the opportunity to delegate decision making over difficult, contentious, or unpopular issues to the courts. Using a reference to engage in blame avoidance or to rely on the authoritative decision-making capacity of the courts can be a viable political strategy. However, the logic that makes this delegation possible relies on a rather nuanced relationship between the public and its understanding of the roles of elected officials and the courts in policy making. For the arguments about blame avoidance to be truly convincing, they require a public that is attentive enough to understand that the courts, rather than elected officials, are responsible for a salient policy decision (Stephenson 2003). At the same time, the public must not be too attentive to realize that elected officials could ignore judicial decisions or manipulate the courts if desired. This appreciation for the public's understanding of the relationship between policy makers and the courts is even more important in the context of the Canadian reference power. The technically advisory nature of reference opinions creates the very real possibility that a government could legitimately ignore a court's advisory opinion in a reference case if it so desired. However, governments are not in the practice of manipulating the courts mostly due to their respect for the principle of judicial independence and because of the public's strong support of judicial independence and the courts. According to Stephenson (2003), the public support of judicial review suggests that voters will penalize elected officials who openly manipulate or ignore the courts. Both the general public's support for the courts and its limited understanding of the relationship between elected officials and judicial review help to create the conditions that make it possible for political actors to rely on the reference power as a political strategy.

The reference power provides a government with a unique set of advantages that cannot be attained through routine judicial review or through the ordinary legislative process. The above analysis demonstrates that the benefits that can be had through a reference can become the primary motivation for submitting reference questions and that the outcome of the case, win or lose, is *almost* secondary. The impetus to delegate to the courts in order to benefit from the effects of judicial review becomes more powerful when political actors are unable or unwilling to override the constitutional interpretation of the courts. In such a system, the public often sees the courts as infallible on any controversy regarding the Constitution, so political actors are wise to avoid confronting the courts on constitutional disputes (Martens 2007).

Following the adoption of the *Charter of Rights and Freedoms* in 1982, the Supreme Court expanded its authority over constitutional and rights interpretation at the expense of political actors. This rise in judicial power in Canada is evident in the marginal use of section 33, the notwithstanding clause, which allows legislatures to override the judicial interpretation of rights. Manfredi (2001) demonstrates that for several reasons, including the wording of the provision itself, Canadian political actors have not made great use of the notwithstanding clause and have essentially rendered it de facto inoperative. The ineffectual status of the notwithstanding clause negates the most powerful tool legislators have for upholding a constitutional interpretation that deviates from that of the courts. Furthermore, aside from the notwithstanding clause, Manfredi and Kelly (1999, 2001) have established that legislators are often subordinate to the courts in constitutional interpretation and likely to simply follow the decisions of the courts rather than adopting their own interpretation or engaging in a true dialogue over the meaning of the Constitution. This situation demonstrates that in the Canadian case political actors are unlikely to override the constitutional interpretations of the courts, regardless of whether they hold a constitutional power to do so.

In looking at why political actors ask reference questions, it has become apparent that when the decision to initiate a reference case is the product of strategic political considerations, it demonstrates a lack of consideration of future consequences for the role of the courts. Indeed, a reference offers a short-term solution to an immediate political problem without taking into account the long-term implications, especially for judicial independence. Judicial independence and, more importantly, respect for judicial independence are essential for delegation. Yet the frequent delegation of political controversies to the courts in reference cases can be a direct threat to this independence.

Conclusion: A Legal Solution to Political Problems

Canadian courts have been relied upon time and again through the reference power to deal with some of the most difficult and complicated issues facing Canadian democracy. A government's reliance on the courts to sort out challenging questions contributes to judicial power, regardless of the reference-initiating government's intent. This book has demonstrated not only that judicial power is the result of activist courts but also that judicial power can be a by-product of the decisions of political actors – in a manner that is not contingent on the *Canadian Charter of Rights and Freedoms*. Indeed, the very purpose of the reference power demonstrates elements of judicialized politics, as elected policy makers will seek an advisory opinion before proceeding with a policy or project. Politics become judicialized when judicial power is expanded at the expense of democratically elected officials, and as a result, debates and decision making regarding public policy are transferred from the legislature and executive to the courts (Tate and Vallinder 1995).

The reasons why governments have used the reference power – whether to examine the constitutionality of same-sex marriage, or to invalidate the policies of an opponent, or to clarify the requirements for secession – indicate that courts are being asked, unequivocally, to determine the validity and wisdom of public policy within the context of the Constitution. The reference power judicializes politics in a manner that is arguably more explicit compared to routine judicial review. With the submission of reference questions to the courts that concern ongoing political or policy debates, the judicialized nature of the process is laid bare, being unobscured by the live disputes and fact scenarios that accompany routine litigation. Furthermore, the judicialization of politics promoted through the reference power is most apparent in scenarios where elected policy makers avoid dealing with particular issues by shipping them off to the courts. Indeed, every reference case exists because a political actor made the conscious decision to delegate decision making and thus involve the courts in a political or constitutional problem.

The reference power can provide elected officials unparalleled power and unique advantages that simply cannot be achieved through routine judicial review or the legislative process. This study demonstrates how the strategic benefits that can be attained through a reference can become the primary motivation for submitting reference questions, whereas the actual outcomes of the case are *almost* secondary. Judicial review can be friendly to elected policy makers, and these actors can use the courts to serve their own ends. With this understanding, there is little doubt that Canadian appellate courts, particularly the Supreme Court, are political institutions. What makes the courts distinct from the political *and* partisan institutions of government is judicial independence and the separation of the judiciary from the partisan branches of government. However, the reference power complicates this relationship.

A reference case raises some difficulties for judicial independence because in a reference a court is asked to provide the executive with advice regarding the legality or constitutionality of an existing or proposed policy. When engaging in this advisory role, courts effectively fulfil a responsibility that would ordinarily be carried out by the attorney general. Furthermore, although providing a reference opinion is certainly a legal function, in principle it is not adjudicative when the reference is abstract and lacks a concrete case or controversy. In *Reference re References*, the Supreme Court found that the legitimacy of the reference power is saved by the simple fact that in responding to reference questions, courts are simply providing advice, and this advice can be either followed or rejected by the reference-initiating government. However, this narrow legal depiction of the reference power does not reflect the reality of how reference cases have been used and how the actors understand them. References are fundamentally different from all other types of litigation in Canadian appellate courts, but they are not distinguished in practice. In practice, political actors have used the reference power to receive judicial opinions on matters both highly controversial and normative. Governments have realized that the reference power is a valuable tool for delegating decision making to the judiciary regarding virtually any issues it desires.

Canadian reference cases are understood in two very different and, in many respects, competing ways that have animated this study's analysis of the reference power: narrow and legalistic or pragmatic and political. As this book has demonstrated, the events that can transpire before a government decides to seek a reference opinion can have elements of political opportunism, strategy, and partisan conflict. This should be unsurprising given that these features are routinely part of legislative politics and the context in which elected governments regularly operate. Furthermore, it has been established in the Canadian literature on law and politics that many of the decisions made by governments regarding litigation, such as the decision to defend a policy against a constitutional challenge or to seek an appeal, are pragmatic and done with an appreciation for a variety of nonlegal factors, such as public opinion, political capital, and government resources (Hennigar 2002, 2007, 2010).

Many of these considerations also shape a government's decision to use the reference power, whether a reference is used to circumvent a resource- and time-intensive litigation process, to respond to uncertainties regarding the validity of legislation, or to negotiate with another government. However, compared to the decision to litigate or appeal, when a government decides to pursue a reference case, the strategy and politics that shape decision making are heightened and more apparent. Unlike with routine litigation, where a government often finds itself on the defensive in responding to challenges to its policy or actions, a reference puts a government in an offensive position because the decision to initiate a reference is one that is both deliberate and voluntary. Thus the decision to refer is an intentional choice to invite the judiciary into a political conflict as a means to obtain a legal solution to a political problem.

The political nature of the events that can lead a government to use the reference power is well demonstrated in many of the reference cases examined in this study. One such example is found in Mackenzie King's promise to refer R.B. Bennett's New Deal during an election campaign, which he did once in office with six different references, resulting in an invalidation of a majority of Bennett's policies, much to King's benefit. Another demonstrative case is Manitoba's use of its reference power to enter the ongoing "chicken and egg war" between Ontario and Quebec with the *Egg Reference*. Similarly, the decision of Jean Chrétien's government to seek a reference on the constitutionality of same-sex marriage with the *Same-Sex Marriage Reference*, rather than appealing the Ontario Court of Appeal's decision in *Halpern v Canada (AG)*, which found that the limitation of marriage to heterosexual couples is a violation of the Charter's section 15 equality rights, serves as another illustrative case of the political gamesmanship made possible through the reference power. Or one could consider the confluence of events that led the Governments of Newfoundland, Manitoba, and Quebec to invoke their respective reference powers to involve the courts in the ongoing dispute between the provinces and Ottawa over constitutional reform, as well as the important role that the Supreme Court's decision in the *Patriation Reference* played in moving forward the constitutional negotiations.

What makes the aforementioned examples different from other high-profile court cases is that the decision to involve judicial scrutiny was an active choice made by the parties involved. Indeed, instead of using the reference power to respond to Bennett's New Deal, King could have used his commanding majority in Parliament to repeal or amend Bennett's legislation. In the *Egg Reference*, Manitoba could have engaged in intergovernmental negotiations with Ontario and Quebec in an attempt to arrive at a mutually agreeable agricultural policy. Similarly, in the episode respecting same-sex marriage, the Chrétien government had several options to respond to demands for same-sex marriage: it could have appealed the decision in *Halpern v Canada (AG)*, or it could have legislated the right to same-sex marriage through Parliament. In the *Patriation Reference*, although there may have been few viable options available to the provinces that opposed Pierre Trudeau's constitutional reform package given that intergovernmental negotiations had reached a standstill, the political impetus behind the decisions of the Governments of Newfoundland, Manitoba, and Quebec is undeniable. Although each of these reference cases is individually unique, they all demonstrate the political considerations and strategy that lead governments to use the reference power.

Regardless of the political calculations that can influence a government's decision to seek a reference opinion, once a reference question is submitted to the courts, the narrow and legalistic conception of the reference power takes over, and the reference process largely follows the same process as routine litigation: a date for an oral hearing is set, involved parties submit factums to the court outlining their legal arguments, and third-party intervener groups may be invited to participate. A reference case hearing is largely indistinguishable from an ordinary case, and a court will issue a written judgment that is not substantially different from any other decision rendered by an appellate court. In a reference case, the process is largely no different from in a routine case, and as this study has demonstrated, the way that courts render reference decisions is virtually the same as in concrete review. The judgments in reference cases are also not distinguished in practice from those in routine review, as they are afforded the same respect and deference as any other decision made by a high appellate court.

Given how reference cases come before the courts, perhaps it is to be expected that the context leading up to the submission of reference questions is one shrouded in politics and that once the courts are part of the reference process, the approach becomes almost entirely legal. Although the courts may be keenly aware of the politics and possible opportunism that can come from use of the reference power (see Macfarlane 2013), the response to reference questions speaks to the strength of judicial independence in Canada. However, this book has made clear that when political actors increasingly divert difficult issues to the courts through the reference power, they run the risk of undermining the authority and independence of the courts in the future and thus the very elements of judicial review that make the reference power a valuable political tool.

One of the central goals of this book is to encourage critical reflection on the use of the Canadian reference power. With this focus, this book makes several important contributions to the study of Canadian politics, the study of courts, and judicial politics. This study has provided insight into how the reference power has been used and how other actors such as courts and third-party interveners have responded to reference cases. This study documents that there have been 209 reference cases since the creation of the power by the federal government in 1875. Although the majority of reference cases have been adjudicated by the Supreme Court of Canada, penultimate provincial appellate courts have heard almost one-third of all cases, meaning that provincial governments will initiate references without always exercising the right to appeal to the Supreme Court. Furthermore, as the history of reference cases shows, decisions rendered by the Judicial Committee of the Privy Council (JCPC) still play an important part in the reference story, as its decisions comprise over 27 percent of all Canadian reference cases, even though the JCPC has not heard a reference case in over half a century.

The analysis of provincial appellate courts in this study has provided several noteworthy insights into the relationship between provincial governments and the reference power. At a basic level, the provincial use of the reference power is interesting in that the federal government originally created the reference power to provide another means of controlling provincial legislation alongside the powers of disallowance and reservation. Provincial governments were quick to notice the many benefits that the reference power provided the federal government, and they followed its lead by enacting parallel legislation that granted provincial governments the power to ask reference questions. Since the 1940s, provincial governments have consistently outpaced the federal government in use of the reference power. Provincial governments have now made it a practice to refer federal government legislation for review in provincial appellate courts at a rate that surpasses the federal government's referral of provincial legislation. Indeed, it appears that successive federal governments have backed away from referring provincial legislation altogether, as one must go back over twenty years to find a case where a federal government referred provincial legislation.[1] Provincial governments have effectively turned the original purpose of the reference power on its head, making it a valuable tool for provincial governments in intergovernmental relations.

Although provincial use of the reference power has converted a tool of federal dominance into an effective strategy for provincial governments, the subject matter of references has changed little since the creation of the reference power. Indeed, the reference power was created with the central goal of determining how the division of powers outlined in the *Constitution Act, 1867* was to be applied to the practical concerns of governance. This study establishes that a majority of reference cases have concerned the division of powers between federal and provincial governments, a trend that has remained constant since the introduction of the Charter. Governments use the reference power to understand the parameters of their own power and that of other governments; the reference power has not become a tool for determining the rights of citizens and groups vis-à-vis government action. This is an interesting finding given that post-1982 constitutional jurisprudence at the Supreme Court overwhelmingly concerns the Charter.

The courts do not appear to view references as distinct from other cases. In references, the courts do not prioritize speaking with one voice, and the rate of unanimity in reference cases is actually lower than the Supreme Court's general unanimity rate. Furthermore, despite the fact that most reference cases are abstract and thus do not concern a live dispute, the courts do not view their power to invalidate government action as limited in any manner.

Although the courts may not treat reference cases as distinct from routine litigation, third-party interest groups do appear to understand references to be different, as demonstrated by the high rate of intervener participation in reference cases. An overwhelming majority of reference cases after 1949 have involved the participation of at least one intervening party – either nongovernmental actors or other governments – with the majority of third-party participation coming from nongovernmental groups. The high rate of intervention speaks to the salient nature of many reference cases, as these cases have attracted the participation of groups that, although not direct parties to the case, have found it important to expend (often limited) resources on participating in these cases. Reference cases present intervening groups with a unique opportunity to influence the policy-making process in a manner different from that of regular legislative channels.

In exploring the unique benefits of delegating decision making to the courts, this study highlights the implications that the reference power can have for the separation of powers and judicial independence. Governments will use the reference power to deal with controversial political issues. In such instances, it can benefit a government not to have to make a decision on a divisive matter or to deflect blame for an unpopular decision. Seeking a reference in such circumstances is a valuable political strategy that can benefit a government, regardless of how the court decides. The reference power is also a valuable means for governments to deal with matters concerning federalism and to police the division of powers between governments. This use of the reference power demonstrates that it can still benefit governments in the way it was originally envisioned when the power was created in the late nineteenth century.

In some of the explanations for why governments use the reference power, the advantage of the reference case is not contingent on a successful case outcome. Instead, by simply involving the courts, a government can realize some political rewards. Case outcome is more important when a reference case is used to attempt to validate a government policy or used as a form of insurance against future challenges. Such insurance may be more important to governments enacting a policy that would be problematic to unwind once in place. A decision from a court that validates a government policy is highly valuable due to the institutional authority of the courts, which rests on the foundation of judicial independence. It is the independence from political actors that makes judicial decisions powerful and delegation to the judiciary more effective than delegation to other agents, such as bureaucratic and administrative bodies.

In assessing why governments ask reference questions, this study has provided two important insights. First, in many instances the case outcome or disposition can be *almost* a secondary concern for governments. The submission of a reference question can be the product of multiple factors aside from a quest for constitutional or legal clarification. Involving the courts through a reference case has many distinct strategic advantages for governments that are not contingent on winning or losing a particular case. Additionally, this study demonstrates that both weak and strong democratic actors will empower the courts through the reference power. The finding that governments ask reference questions from a position of legislative security, such as when they have a majority in the legislature, runs counter to other theses of judicial empowerment, like political insurance theory. References enable those in power to delegate decision making on issues of both high and low political salience to the courts in a manner that cannot be explained by many of the existing accounts of elected actors' empowerment of the judiciary.

Second, the reasoning of government decision makers when involving the courts through a reference case demonstrates a logic that is focused on a short-term solution rather than on the case's long-term implications. In this sense, the decision to use the reference power is similar to most decisions made by governments, being an instance of pragmatic decision making focused on immediate problems rather than on long-term planning. This reality of governing indicates that judicial independence is one of the central reasons why the reference power is useful to governments and why the courts are a valuable agent for delegation. However, reliance on the courts in this manner can harm judicial independence. As a result, there is a direct and real tension between the use of the reference power as a political strategy and the effectiveness of a reference opinion for political actors.

The empowerment of the courts through the reference power ultimately comes at the expense of Parliament and representative democracy. Although Parliament is not the primary focus of this study, it is important to highlight the implications for representative democracy when governments use the reference power to turn political issues into legal questions. References have the effect of preventing Parliament from participating in the contestation of political disputes, with the result that ordinary parliamentarians are no longer part of the deliberative process. Once the court makes a pronouncement on a reference question, it narrows the space for legislators to engage in position taking, especially if a legislator wishes to take a position that runs counter to that of the court. As demonstrated by this study, this effect of a reference case is one factor that can motivate a government to use the reference power. As discussed in Chapter 6, this situation contributes to the centralization of power in the Canadian executive and ultimately provides additional evidence for the thesis of democratic deficit; indeed, the criticism that Canadian executives hold too much power at the expense of representative institutions, thus creating a democratic deficit, is a well documented reality of Canadian politics (Franks 1987; Savoie 1999; White 2012; Lewis 2013). The marginalization of legislators can be seen as even more problematic when power is transferred to a nondemocratic and elite institution such as a court, something that has been noted since the adoption of the Charter (Manfredi and Kelly 1999; Morton and Knopff 2000). An important issue that has not been explored in this study is the impact on and reaction of legislators when highly salient matters are removed from parliamentary debate and sent to the courts through a reference case. This issue is ripe for further investigation, especially from a perspective of legislative studies or democratic theory.

In a larger comparative sense, this book contributes to an understanding of judicial review that moves beyond the simple divide between European civil law constitutional courts and American-style judicial review. The Canadian reference power results in a system that provides for both abstract review and advisory opinions within a common law legal framework. This study defines how Canadian abstract review operates, and it highlights multiple implications of abstract review for governance and judicial power. Scholars who seek to compare American-style judicial review with European constitutional courts should recognize the uniqueness of the Canadian case and its departure from this dichotomy and should seek to incorporate the Canadian case into their analyses. Lastly, in terms of comparative work, this project expands delegation theory to the Canadian case, demonstrating that the Canadian reference power typifies delegation and that criticisms of delegating to the courts, especially in terms of judicial independence, are relevant when assessing the reference power.

It is important to note that the approach of this book marks a movement away from the overwhelming focus on the Supreme Court of Canada in the Canadian literature on judicial politics. Given the important role that the Supreme Court has played in Canadian politics, this focus on the top court in existing literature is understandable. However, provincial appellate courts have a much larger caseload compared to the Supreme Court, serving as the final court of appeal for most legal matters in Canada. As a result, it is imperative that the decisions of these courts and their role within the Canadian judicial framework become the subject of more empirical analysis.[2] It is important to understand how each of these courts operates individually and in comparison with one another. The inclusion of provincial appellate courts in the present analysis aims to encourage more scholars to investigate these important but relatively understudied courts.

Final Thoughts

A reference case provides a government with unparalleled power before the courts. Through the creation and submission of reference questions, a government has the ability to frame the terms of the case, free from a particular conflict or set of facts. In pursuing a reference case, some governments have manufactured elaborate hypothetical-fact scenarios, whereas others have enacted legislation with the sole purpose of referring it to a court. This power becomes even more impressive when we consider that reference decisions have been afforded the same respect as all other judicial decisions, regardless of their advisory status. One of the central goals of this study is to focus attention on how political actors use the courts to serve their own ends, suggesting that the courts alone do not bear responsibility for the increase of judicial power. Instead, this analysis of the reference power demonstrates that courts have a powerful role in normative and public policy debates because political actors have either welcomed or actively encouraged judicial power by seeking a court's advice.

Appendix A
Canadian Reference Legislation

Jurisdiction	*Original Statute*	*Current Statute*	*Current Section*
Federal	*Supreme and Exchequer Court Act*, SC 1875, c 11	*Supreme Court Act*, RSC 1985, c S-26	Section 53(1): "The Governor in Council may refer to the Court for hearing and consideration important questions of law or fact concerning ... [examples]. Section 53(2): "The Governor in Council may refer to the Court for hearing and consideration important questions of law or fact concerning any matter."
Alberta	*An Ordinance for Expediting the Decision of Constitutional and Other Legal Questions*, Ord NWT 1901, c 11	*Judicature Act*, RSA 2000, c J-2	Section 26(1): "The Lieutenant Governor in Council may refer to the Court of Appeal for hearing or consideration any matter the Lieutenant Governor in Council

(*Continued*)

(Continued)

Jurisdiction	*Original Statute*	*Current Statute*	*Current Section*
			thinks fit to refer, and the Court of Appeal shall hear or consider the matter that is referred."
British Columbia	*An Act for Expediting the Decision of Constitutional and Other Provincial Questions,* SBC 1891, c 5	*Constitutional Questions Act,* RSBC 1996, c 68	Section 1: "The Lieutenant Governor in Council may refer any matter to the Court of Appeal or to the Supreme Court for hearing and consideration, and the Court of Appeal or the Supreme Court must then hear and consider it."
Manitoba	*An Act for Expediting the Decision of Constitutional and Other Provincial Questions,* SM 1890, c 16	*Constitutional Questions Act,* CCSM 2014, c C180	Section 1: "The Lieutenant Governor in Council may refer any matter to the Court of Appeal or to the Court of Queen's Bench for hearing or consideration and the Court of Appeal or the Court of Queen's Bench shall hear or consider the matter."
New Brunswick	*An Act to Provide for References by the Governor-in-Council to the Appeal Division of the Supreme Court,* SNB 1928, c 47	*Judicature Act,* RSNB 1973, c J-2	Section 23(1): "Important questions of law or fact ... may be referred by the Lieutenant-Governor in Council to the Court of Appeal for hearing and consideration, and any question touching any of the matters aforesaid, so referred by the

Jurisdiction	*Original Statute*	*Current Statute*	*Current Section*
			Lieutenant-Governor in Council, shall be conclusively deemed to be an important question."
Newfoundland and Labrador	*The Judicature Amendment Act*, SN, 1953, No. 3	*Judicature Act*, RSNL 1990, c J-4	Section 13: "The Lieutenant Governor in Council may refer a matter to the Court of Appeal and upon the reference the Court of Appeal shall hear and determine that matter."
Nova Scotia	*An Act for Expediting the Decision of Constitutional and Other Provincial Questions*, SNS 1890, c 9	*Constitutional Questions Act*, RS 1999, c 89	Section 3: "The Governor in Council may refer to the Court for hearing or consideration, any matter which he thinks fit to refer, and the Court shall thereupon hear and consider the same."
Ontario	*An Act for Expediting the Decision of Constitutional and Other Provincial Questions*, SO 1890, c 13	*Courts of Justice Act*, RSO 1990, c C.43	Section 8(1): "The Lieutenant Governor in Council may refer any question to the Court of Appeal for hearing and consideration."
Prince Edward Island	*An Act to Amend the Judicature Act*, SPEI 1941, c 16	*Judicature Act*, RSPEI 1988, c J-2.1	Section 7(1): "The Lieutenant Governor in Council may refer any question to the Court of Appeal for hearing and consideration."

(*Continued*)

(Continued)

Jurisdiction	*Original Statute*	*Current Statute*	*Current Section*
Quebec	*An Act to Authorize the Reference, by the Lieutenant-Governor in Council, of Certain Questions to the Court of Queen's Bench*, SQ 1898, c 11	*Court of Appeal Reference Act*, RSQ 1975, c R-23	Section 1: "The Government may refer to the Court of Appeal, for hearing and consideration, any question which it deems expedient, and thereupon the court shall hear and consider the same."
Saskatchewan	*An Ordinance for Expediting the Decision of Constitutional and Other Legal Questions*, Ord NWT 1901, c 11	*Constitutional Questions Act*, SS 2012, c C-29.01	Section 2(1): "The Lieutenant Governor in Council may refer any matter to the Court of Appeal for hearing and consideration, and the Court of Appeal shall hear and consider the matter."

Appendix B
Reference Case List

Act Respecting Jurisdiction of Magistrate's Court (Quebec), [1965] SCR 772

Act to Amend the Family Services Act (NB), [1994] 120 DLR (4th) 609, 157 NBR (2d) 241

Administration of Justice, [1892] 21 SCR 446

Adoption Act, Jurisdiction of County and District Courts, [1938] SCR 398

AG Ontario v AG Canada, [1894] AC 189

Agricultural Land Relief Act, [1938] AJ No 54, [1938] 4 DLR 28

Agricultural Products Marketing Act, [1978] 2 SCR 1198

Alberta (Attorney General) v Canada (Attorney General), [1947] JCJ No 50, [1947] AC 503

Alberta Legislation, [1913] 48 SCR 9, [1915] AC 363

Alberta Marketing Choice Program, [1998] AJ No 306, 1998 ABCA 80

Alberta Statutes, 1937, [1938] SCR 100, [1939] AC 117

Amendment to the Canadian Constitution, [1982] 2 SCR 793 [*Quebec Veto Reference*]

Amendments to the Residential Tenancies Act (NS), [1996] 1 SCR 186

Anti-Inflation Act, [1976] 2 SCR 373

Application of Hours of Work Act to Metalliferous Mines, [1947] 1 WWR 841, 2 DLR 737

Assisted Human Reproduction Act, [2010] 3 SCR 457

Authority of Parliament in Relation to the Upper House, [1980] 1 SCR 54 [*Upper House Reference*]

BC Motor Vehicle Act, [1985] 2 SCR 486

Bill 30, An Act to Amend the Education Act (Ont), [1987] 1 SCR 1148

Bill C-7 Concerning the Reform of the Senate (QC), [2013] QJ No 7771, 2013 QCCA 1807 [*Quebec Senate Reform Reference*]

Bill C-7 Respecting the Criminal Justice System for Young Persons (QC), [2003] QJ No. 2850
Board of Commerce, [1920] 60 SCR 456, [1922] 1 AC 191
Bowater's Newfoundland Pulp and Paper Mill, [1950] SCR 608
Bread Sales Act (Ontario), [1911] 18 OWR 251, 23 OLR 238
British Columbia Fisheries, [1912] 47 SCR 493, [1914] AC 153
British North America Act, the Term "Indians," [1939] SCR 104
Broome v Prince Edward Island, [2010] 1 SCR 360
The Brothers of the Christian Schools in Canada, [1874] Cout Cas April 4
Brothers of Christian Schools v Ontario (Minister of Education), [1907] AC 16 at 23, AC 69
Canada Assistance Plan (BC), [1991] 2 SCR 525
Canada Pacific Rail v BC, Hours of Work Act, RSBC, 1936, [1948] SCR 373, [1950] AC 122
Canada Provident Association, [1882] Cout Cas 48
Canada Temperance Act, [1907] Cout Cas SC 204 No 3
Canada Temperance Act, 1927, [1935] SCR 494
The Canadian Temperance Act, [1946] AC 193, 2 DLR 1, 2 WWR 1
Certain Titles to Land in Ontario, [1973] 2 OR 613, 35 DLR (3d) 10
Chief Justice of Alberta, [1922] 64 SCR 135, [1923] JCJ No 1
Combines Investigation Act, [1929] SCR 409, [1931] AC 310
Common School Fund and Lands, [1901] 31 SCR 516, [1903] AC 39
Companies Creditors Arrangement Act, 1933, [1934] SCR 659
Constitution Act 1867, ss 26, 27, and 28 (BC), [1991] 78 DLR (4th) 245,
Constitutional Questions Act (Ontario), [1957] OR 28
Constitutional Questions Act (SK), [1936] SJ No. 65, [1936] 4 DLR 134,
Constitutional Questions Act (SK), [1981] 128 DLR (3d), 13 Sask R 100
Constitutional Questions Determination Act, [1927] 2 WWR 808, 4 DLR 195
Constitutional Questions Determination Act and Vancouver Charter, [1958] 121 CCC 241, 15 DLR (2d) 169
Constitutional Validity of Section 11 of the Judicature Act Amendment Act, [1971] 2 OR 521-531
Corporations Act (Manitoba), [1991] 4 WWR 1993, 80 DLR (4th) 431
Court of Unified Criminal Jurisdiction, [1983] 1 SCR 704
Criminal Code – Bigamy, [1897] 27 SCR 461
Criminal Code – Lord's Day Act, [1910] 43 SCR 434
Criminal Law Amendment Act, [1970] SCR 777
Currie v Niagara Escarpment Commission, [1984] 14 DLR (4th) 651, 48 OR (2d) 609
Debt Adjustment Act, Alberta, 1937, [1942] SCR 31, [1943] AC 356
Deportation and Section 43 Immigration Act, [1933] SCR 269
Dominion Trade and Industry Commission Act, 1935, [1936] SCR 379, [1937] AC 405
Earth Future Lottery (PEI), [2002] 215 DLR (4th) 656, 166 CCC (3d) 373

Education Act of Ontario and Minority Language Education Rights, [1984] OJ No 3260, 47 OR (2d) 1
Education Act (Que), [1993] 2 SCR 511
Education in Montreal, [1926] SCR 246, [1928] AC 200
Elections Act (BC), [2012] BCJ No 2037, 2012 BCCA 394
Electoral Boundaries Commission Act, [1991] AJ No 1065, 86 DLR (4th) 447
Electoral Divisions Statutes, [1994] AJ No 768, 119 DLR (4th) 1
Employment and Social Insurance Act, 1935, [1936] SCR 427, [1937] AC 355
Employment Insurance Act (Can) ss 22 and 23, [2005] 2 SCR 669
Employment of Aliens, [1922] 63 SCR 293, [1923] JCJ No 6, AC 203
Esquimalt and Nanaimo Railway Co Land Grant, [1948] SCR 403, [1950] AC 87
Exported Natural Gas Tax, [1982] 1 SCR 1004 [*Alberta Gas Tax Reference*]
The Family Relations Act SBC 1978, [1982] 1 SCR 62
Farm Products Marketing Act RSO, 1950, [1957] SCR 198
Farm Security Act, 1944, [1947] SCR 394, [1949] AC 110
Farmers' Creditors Arrangement Act, 1934, [1936] SCR 384, [1937] AC 391
Final Report of the Electoral Boundaries Commission, 2017 NSCA 10, 411 DLR (4th) 271
Firearms Act (Can), [2000] 1 SCR 783 [*Firearms Reference*]
Fisheries, [1895] 26 SCR 444
Fisheries Act, [1928] SCR 457, [1930] AC 111
Freedom of Informed Choice (Abortions) Act (SK), [1985] 25 DLR (4th) 751, 44 Sask R 104
Goods and Services Tax, [1992] 2 SCR 445
Grain Marketing Act, 1931 (SK), [1931] 2 WWR 146, 25 Sask LR 273
Grand Bend (Village), [1956] OR 615
Grand Trunk Railway, [1909] 42 SCR 505, [1912] AC 204
Horsefly Mining Co, [1895] BCJ No 37, 4 BCR 165
Hours of Labour, [1925] SCR 505
The Improvement Act and CPR Assessment, [1924] 1 DLR 1005, [1924] 1 WWR 513
Incorporations of Companies, [1912] 48 SCR 331, [1916] 1 AC 598
Industrial Relations and Disputes Investigations Act, [1955] SCR 529
Initiative and Referendum Act (MB), [1919] 3 WWR 1, [1919] AC 935
Insurance Act, 1910, [1912] 48 SCR 260, [1916] 1 AC 588
Insurance Act (Can), [1932] AC 41
International and Provincial Ferries, [1905] 36 SCR 206
Interpretation of Human Rights Act, [1998] 50 DLR (4th) 647, 69 Nfld & PEI R 264
Intoxicated Persons Detention Act (MB), [1981] 116 DLR (3d) 91, 1 WWR 333
Japanese Treaty Act, 1913, [1920] 3 WWR 937
The Jesuits' Estates Act, [1889] 12 LEGAL NEWS 283
Jones v Canada (AG), [1975] 2 SCR 182
Judges Act, [1923] 2 DLR 604
The Judicature Act, [1984] 2 SCR697

Judicature Act, 1924, [1924] OJ No 81, 3 DLR 433
Judicature Act, 1924 (Ontario), [1925] 1 WWR 1131, AC 750, 2 DLR 753
The Jury Act of Alberta, [1947] SCR 213
Labour Relations Act, s 46A (MB), [1962] 40 WWR 354, 36 DLR (2d) 560
Legal Proceedings Suspension Act (ALTA), [1942] AJ No 45, [1942] 3 DLR 318
Legislative Authority over Bypass Pipelines, Indexed as: Reference re Constitution Act 1867, s 92(10)(a) (Ont CA) (1988), [1988] 64 OR (2d) 393, OJ No. 176
Legislative Privilege (1978), [1978] 18 OR (2d) 529
Lord's Day Alliance of Canada v MB (Att-Gen), [1925] 1 WWR 296, AC 384
Manitoba Act, [1924] SCR 317, [1925] AC 561
Manitoba (AG) v Manitoba Egg and Poultry Association, [1971] SCR 689 [*Egg Reference*]
Manitoba Education Act, [1893] 22 SCR 577, [1895] AC 202
Manitoba Language Rights, [1985] 1 SCR 721
Manitoba Language Rights, [1992] 1 SCR 212
Marriage Act, [1912] 46 SCR 132, [1912] AC 880
Marriage Commissioners Appointed under the Marriage Act, 1995, SS 1995, c M-4.1, [2011] 327 DLR (4th) 669, 3 WWR 193
Meaning of the Word "Persons," [1928] SCR 276, [1930] AC 124 [*Persons Case*]
Milgaard (Can), [1992] 1 SCR 866
Militia Act, 1906, [1930] SCR 554
Milk Industry Act (BC), [1960] SCR 346
Mineral and Other Natural Resources of the Continental Shelf, [1983] 145 DLR (3d) 9, 119 APR 27 [*Newfoundland Continental Shelf Reference*]
The Minimum Wage Act, [1948] SCR 248
Minimum Wages Act, Limitation of Hours of Work Act, Weekly Rest in Industrial Undertakings Act, [1936] SCR 461, [1937] AC 326, 1 WWR 299
Mining and Mineral Rights Tax Act, [1982] 2 SCR 260, 138 DLR (3d) 577 [*Mining and Mineral Rights Reference*]
Minority Language Education Rights (PEI), [1988] 69 Nfld & PEI R 236, 49 DLR (4th) 499
Moratorium Legislation Act (SK), [1955] 35 CBR 135
The Municipal Act, [1958] SCR 744
The Natural Gas Utilities Board, [1945] AJ No 43, [1945] 3 WWR 257
Natural Products Marketing Act, 1934, [1936] SCR 398, [1937] AC 377
Natural Products Marketing Act (BC), [1937] 4 DLR 298, [1938] AC 708
Natural Resources Saskatchewan, [1931] SCR 263, [1932] AC 28
New Brunswick Penitentiary, [1880] Count Cas 24
Ng Extradition (Can), [1991] 2 SCR 858
Offshore Mineral Rights, [1967] SCR 792
Ontario (AG) v Canada (AG), [1947] AC 127
Ontario (AG) v Hamilton Street Railway, [1903] AC 524, 7 CCC 326, 2 OWR 672
Ontario Liquor License Case Prohibitory Liquor Laws, [1894] 24 SCR 170, [1896] AC 348

Ontario Medical Act, [1906] 8 OWR 766
Order in Council (MB), [1926] 2 WWR 844, 36 Man R 34
Orderly Payment of Debts Act, Alberta 1959, [1960] SCR 571
Ottawa Special Schools, [1917] OJ 32, 40 DLE 465
Ownership of the Bed of the Strait of Georgia and Related Areas, [1984] 1 SCR 388
Persons of Japanese Race, [1946] SCR 248, [1947] AC 87
The Power of the Governor General in Council to Disallow Provincial Legislation and the Power of the Reservation of a Lieutenant-Governor of a Province, [1938] SCR 71 [*Powers of Disallowance and Reservation Reference*]
Powers of Notaries Public in British Columbia, [1969] BCJ No. 444, 6 DLR (3d) 447
Powers of Ottawa (City), Powers to Levy Rates on Foreign Legations, [1943] SCR 208
Precious Metals, [1927] SCR 458, [1929] AC 285
Prohibition Act (BC), [1919] 2 WWR 27, 44 DLR 584
Proposed Legislation Concerning Leased Premises and Tenancy Agreements, [1978] AJ No 989, 89 DLR (3d) 460
Provincial Electoral Boundaries (Sask), [1991] 2 SCR 158
Provincial Treasurer of Nova Scotia, [1937] SCR 403
Public Schools Act (Man), s 79(3), (4) and (7), [1993] 1 SCR 839
Public Service Employee Relations Act (Alta), [1987] 1 SCR 313
Qualifications for Mayor and Aldermen of the City of Calgary, [1933] AJ No 25, 3 WWR 385
Quebec Sales Tax, [1994] 2 SCR 715 [*Quebec Sales Tax Reference*]
The Quebec Timber Company, [1882] Cout Cas 43
Race-Tracks and Betting, [1921] OJ No 144, 61 DLR 504
Radio Communication, [1931] SCR 541, [1932] AC 304
Rail Act, Exchequer Court Jurisdiction, [1926] SCR 239
Railway Act Amendment, [1905] 36 SCR 136, [1907] AC 65
Railway Act, Canada v Canada Pacific Railway, [1958] SCR 285
Reciprocal Insurance Legislation, [1922] OJ No 35, 53 OLR 195
References, [1910] 43 SCR 536, [1912] AC 571
Refunds under Timber Regulations, [1933] SCR 616, [1935] AC 184
Regina v Coffin, [1956] SCR 191
Regina v Snider, [1954] SCR 479
R v Truscott, [1967] SCR 309 [*Truscott Reference*]
Regulation and Control of Aeronautics in Canada, [1930] SCR 663, [1932] AC 54 [*Aeronautics Reference*]
Regulations in Relation to Chemicals, [1943] SCR 1 [*Chemicals Reference*]
Remuneration of the Judges of the Provincial Court of Prince Edward Island, [1997] 3 SCR 3
Representation of Prince Edward Island in House, [1903] 33 SCR 594, [1905] AC 37
Residential Tenancies Act, [1981] 1 SCR 714
Resolution to Amend the Constitution, [1981] 1 SCR 753 [*Patriation Reference*]

Sale of Shares Act and Municipal and Public Utility Board Act (MB), [1929] 1 WWR 136, [1929] AC 260
Same-Sex Marriage, [2004] 3 SCR 698 [*Same-Sex Marriage Reference*]
Seabed and Subsoil of the Continental Shelf Offshore Newfoundland, [1984] 1 SCR 86 [*Seabed and Subsoil Reference*]
Secession of Quebec, [1998] 2 SCR 217 [*Secession Reference*]
Section 5 of the Family Benefits Act (NS), [1986] 75 NSR (2d) 338, 186 APR 338
Section 16 Special War Revenue Act, 1932, [1942] SCR 429
Section 17 Alberta Act, [1927] SCR 364
Section 31 Municipal District Act, Amendment Act, 1941, [1943] SCR 295
Section 57(2) of the Alberta Labour Act, [1948] AJ No 60, [1948] 2 DLR 428
Section 98 of the Constitution Act, 1867, [2014] QCCA 2365
Section 110 Dominion Act, 1927, [1934] SCR 653
Section 189 Railway Act, [1926] SCR 163, [1926] AC 715
Section 498(a) of the Criminal Code, [1936] SCR 363, [1937] AC 368
Sections 193 and 195.1(1)(C) of the Criminal Code (Man) (Bawdy House and Solicitation), [1990] 1 SCR 1123
Sections 222, 224 and 224A of Criminal Code (CA) (NB), [1971] 18 DLR (3d) 559, 3 NBR (2d) 511
Securities Act, [2011] 3 SCR 837 [*Securities Reference*]
Senate Reform, [2014] 1 SCR 704
Sess Papers No 85a, 1885 (Can) [*McCarthy Act Reference*]
Sessional Allowances under the Ontario Legislative Assembly Act, [1945] OR 336, 2 DLR 631
Sisters of Notre Dame v Ottawa (City), [1912] 21 OWR 394, 1 DLR 329
Stony Plain Indian Reserve, [1981] AJ No 1007, 130 DLR (3d) 636
Sunday Observance Labour, [1905] 35 SCR 581
Supreme Court Act Amendment Act 1964 (BC), [1965] SCR 490
Supreme Court Act, ss 5 and 6, [2014] 1 SCR 433 [*Nadon Reference*]
Tariff Board of Canada, [1934] SCR 538
Taxation of Canadian Pacific Railway, [1953] AC 594, 3 DLR 785
Taxation of University of Manitoba Lands, [1940] 1 WWR 145, 1 WWR 240, 47 Man R 457
The Thrasher Case, [1882] BCR 153
Ultimate Heir Act (AB), [1928] AC 475
United States Military or Naval Forces, [1943] SCR 483
Upper Churchill Water Rights Reversion Act, [1984] 1 SCR 297
Use of French in Criminal Proceedings in the Courts, [1987] 44 DLR (4th) 16, 5 WWR 577
Validity of a By-Law Respecting Taxi Cabs, [1958] 122 CCC 51, 16 DLR (2d) 348
Validity of Section 5(a) of the Dairy Industry Act, [1949] SCR 1, [1951] AC 179
Vehicles Act, 1957, [1958] SCR 608
Wartime Leasehold Regulations, [1950] SCR 124

Water and Water Power, [1929] SCR 200
Workers' Compensation Act, 1983 (Nfld), [1989] 1 SCR 922
Young Offenders Act, Judicature Act (NB) s 23, [1988] 54 DLR (4th) 430, 96 NBR (2d), 243 APR 11
Young Offenders Act (PEI), [1991] 1 SCR 252

Notes

Introduction

1 Ultra vires, or beyond the powers of a legal jurisdiction, which effectively renders the law invalid, can be contrasted with intra vires, or within the powers a legal jurisdiction, which effectively validates the law in question.

2 *Reference re Manitoba (AG) v Manitoba Egg and Poultry Association,* [1971] SCR 689 [*Egg Reference*].

3 The national agricultural-marketing policy was subsequently largely upheld by the Supreme Court in *Reference re Agricultural Products Marketing Act,* [1978] 2 SCR 1198.

4 *Reference re Same-Sex Marriage,* [2004] 3 SCR 698 [*Same-Sex Marriage Reference*]; regarding reform of the Senate, *Reference re Authority of Parliament in Relation to the Upper House,* [1980] 1 SCR 54 [*Upper House Reference*], and *Reference re Senate Reform,* [2014] 1 SCR 704; *Reference re Supreme Court Act, ss 5 and 6,* [2014] 1 SCR 433 [*Nadon Reference*]; *Reference re Resolution to Amend the Constitution,* [1981] 1 SCR 753 [*Patriation Reference*]; *Reference re Secession of Quebec,* [1998] 2 SCR 217 [*Secession Reference*]; *Reference re Amendment to the Canadian Constitution,* [1982] 2 SCR 793 [*Quebec Veto Reference*].

5 *Supreme Court Act,* RSC 1985, c S-26.

6 See Appendix A.

7 Cases appealed "by right" are those that courts have no discretion in hearing. This type of case can be contrasted with cases appealed "by leave," in which courts must first grant access to the parties for the matter to be heard.

8 *Constitution Act, 1982,* being Schedule B to the *Canada Act 1982* (UK), 1982, c 11.

9 Some scholars who have looked at the reference power do not rely on a case study methodology (see Strayer 1988; Holland 1990; Huffman and Saathoff 1990; Persaud

1998; and Hausegger, Hennigar, and Riddell 2015). Although this work is not (and does not claim to be) comprehensive and/or comparative, it nonetheless makes important contributions to our understanding of the Canadian reference power and informs the present study. Importantly for the purposes of the present analysis, only Holland (1990), Persaud (1998), and Hausegger, Hennigar, and Riddell (2015) examine references with an explicit appreciation of the political implications and context of the power.

10 India is a noteworthy exception in the common law world. *Constitution of India* (1950), art 143(1), provides the president the power to request an advisory opinion from the Supreme Court: "If at any time it appears to the President that a question of law or fact has arisen, or is likely to arise, which is of such a nature and of such public importance that it is expedient to obtain the opinion of the Supreme Court upon it, he may refer the question to that Court for consideration." Persaud (1998) notes that the Indian advisory power is modelled after the Canadian reference power.

11 *US Const,* art 3, s 2, cl 1: "The judicial power shall extend *to all cases,* in law and equity, arising under this Constitution, the laws of the United States, and treaties made, or which shall be made, under their Authority, ... *to Controversies* to which the United States shall be a Party; to Controversies between two or more States" (emphasis added).

12 *Ashwander v Tennessee Valley Authority,* 297 US 288 (1936), at 346.

13 See also *Baker v Carr,* 369 US 186 (1962).

14 *Judicial Committee Act,* 1833, 3 & 4 Wm IV, c 41 (UK).

15 *Re Judiciary and Navigation Act,* [1921] 29 CRL 257 (Australia) at 267.

16 Obiter dicta are incidental remarks made by a court that do not contribute to legal precedent.

17 Although it should be noted that reference cases might not be considered litigation in the specific conception involving the settlement of a live legal dispute (as in a lawsuit), the hearing of reference cases largely resembles routine litigation in a general sense, as it involves making claims in the form of a legal action in a court (see "litigation," in Martin and Law 2012). As a result, this book considers references to be a form of litigation.

18 This total includes cases decided before May 1, 2017. For a list of cases, see Appendix B.

19 Notable exceptions are found in Hirschl (2000, 2004) and Hennigar (2009, 2010).

20 *Reference re References,* [1912] AC 571; *Reference re Secession of Quebec,* [1998] 2 SCR 217 [*Secession Reference*].

21 This dataset includes only references to provincial courts of appeal, the Supreme Court of Canada, and the Judicial Committee of the Privy Council. As a result, it does not include the instances of reference cases from lower provincial courts since some provinces, such as British Columbia and Manitoba, have an ability to refer cases to lower courts, being trial courts established under section 96 of the *Constitution Act, 1867.* These cases are excluded as a means to ensure consistency across provinces and a focus exclusively on appellate courts.

22 *An Act to Protect the Province against Communistic Propaganda,* 1 Geo VI, 1937, c 11 [*Padlock Act*]; *An Act Respecting Freedom of Worship and Maintenance of Good Order,* SQ 1953–54, 2–3 Eliz 11, c 15.

23 The tensions that arise for judicial independence have been noted by the Supreme Court in the past, notably in the *Same-Sex Marriage Reference* of 2004, where the court refused to provide an opinion on the constitutionality of the heterosexual definition of marriage. The court's refusal was due in part to the fact that the government had already committed to pursuing same-sex marriage, which meant that answering the question would have served no legal purpose. At this point, addressing the heterosexual definition of marriage would have required the court to step beyond its legal role in rendering an advisory opinion and would have thrust the Supreme Court into a political debate.

24 See, for example, Hausegger and Riddell (2004) and Radmilovic (2010), who examine the changing nature of public support for the Supreme Court of Canada and how its institutional legitimacy is affected following highly salient decisions.

Chapter 1: Origins and Implications of the Reference Power

1 *AG Ont v AG Can,* [1912] AC 571.

2 *Supreme Court Act,* SC 1875, c 11, s 52.

3 The reservation power permits the lieutenant governor general to refrain from either approving or rejecting a provincial law to allow for review by the federal government. The disallowance power permits the federal government to veto provincial legislation, regardless of whether it has received royal assent, as per sections 55 and 56 of the *Constitution Act, 1867* (UK), 30 & 31 Vic, c 3.

4 As Smith (1983) explains, some parliamentarians expressed concern and criticism when debating the merits of the reference power as part of 1875 discussions on adoption of judicial review. For example, Senator Robert Haythorne of Prince Edward Island was concerned that reliance on the reference power and the courts for constitutional advice would undermine ministerial responsibility. Similarly, Thomas Moss, a member of Parliament from Ontario, thought it was "extreme" that the governor general in council would rely on the opinions of others and seek advice from the courts. For additional detail on the debates over the adoption of judicial review, including the reference power, see Smith (1983).

5 *An Act Respecting the Supreme and Exchequer Courts,* SC 1891, c 25, s 4.

6 The provincial power to appeal as a matter of right to the Supreme Court in a reference case is found in section 36 of the *Supreme Court Act,* RSC 1985, c S-26.

7 *Federal Courts Act,* RSC 1985, c F-7, s 18.3.

8 See *Reference re Section 293 of the Criminal Code of Canada,* [2011] BCJ No 2211 (QL), BCSC.

9 To date, there exists no scholarship that details the internal governmental process of engaging in reference cases. As a result, requests under the *Access to Information Act,* RSC 1985, c A-1, were submitted to all provinces and the federal government

with the goal of understanding what actors are involved in the decision to ask a reference question in order to determine whether the process is entirely contained within Cabinet, as the legislation suggests, or whether there is involvement by officials under the minister of justice/attorney general. Additionally, the information requests inquired about each government's process for engaging in a reference case, as well as whether any formal departmental memoranda or directives have been created to structure the reference process.

10 Access was denied on these grounds regardless of the fact that the submitted application specifically requested information that was general rather than case specific.

11 For example, the Department of Justice Canada provided a completely redacted copy of Chapter 12 of the Supreme Court of Canada's Department of Justice deskbook, which suggests that the department does have a process for the submission of reference questions to the Supreme Court. However, the amount of detail and direction provided in the document remains unknown.

12 Senior Department Solicitor A, author interview, February 26, 2013.

13 Senior Department Official A, author interview, March 21, 2013.

14 I must thank a particularly insightful reviewer for drawing my attention to the noteworthy nature of this process.

15 *Access to Information Act,* RSC 1985, c A-1.

16 *Reference re References,* [1910] 43 SCR 536.

17 The provinces were Alberta, Manitoba, Ontario, Nova Scotia, New Brunswick, and Prince Edward Island.

18 *Reference re References,* [1910] 43 SCR 536 at 7.

19 Ibid. at 17.

20 Ibid. at 32.

21 Ibid. at 29.

22 *Reference re References,* [1912] AC 571, para 16.

23 The court appointed counsel from the Quebec law firm Joli-Coeur Lacasse S.E.N.C.R.L. as an amicus curiae to represent the interests of Quebec, as the Government of Quebec refused to officially participate in the reference case.

24 *Constitution Act, 1867* (UK), 30 & 31 Vic, c 3, s 101: "The Parliament of Canada may ... from Time to Time provide for the Constitution, Maintenance and Organization of a General Court of Appeal for Canada."

25 Ibid., s 92: "In each Province the Legislature may exclusively make Laws in relation to ... (14) The Administration of Justice in the Province, including the Constitution, Maintenance, and Organization of Provincial Courts."

26 *Reference re Secession of Quebec,* [1998] 2 SCR 217 [*Secession Reference*], para 10.

27 Specifically, *US Const,* art 3, s 2, cl 2, states, "In all Cases affecting Ambassadors, other public Ministers and Consuls, and those in which a State shall be a party, the supreme court shall have original Jurisdiction." I thank a helpful reviewer for calling my attention to this important fact.

28 *Reference re Secession of Quebec,* [1998] 2 SCR 217, [*Secession Reference*], para 14.
29 Ibid., para 15.
30 *Reference re Same-Sex Marriage,* [2004] 3 SCR 698 [*Same-Sex Marriage Reference*].
31 *Proposal for an Act Respecting Certain Aspects of Legal Capacity for Marriage for Civil Purposes,* Order in Council PC 2003-1055, July 16, 2003.
32 Between 1945 and 1985, constitutional courts were created in Italy, Germany, France, Portugal, Spain, and Belgium. After this first wave, constitutional courts were introduced in the postcommunist world, beginning in 1989 with Hungary, which was followed in 1991 by Russia, Albania, Bulgaria, and Romania. This trend was observed in all other postcommunist states, culminating with Bosnia in 1995 and Latvia in 1996.
33 Judicial activism is neutrally defined in this case and simply involves the judiciary's act of striking down democratically enacted statutes (see Russell, Morton, and Knopff 1989, 19; and Manfredi 2001).
34 *Civil Marriage Act,* SC 2005, c 33.
35 Hennigar (2009) is an exception.
36 *Reference re Exported Natural Gas Tax,* [1982] 1 SCR 1004 [*Alberta Gas Tax Reference*].

Chapter 2: Contestation and Reference Cases

1 *Reference re Resolution to Amend the Constitution,* [1981] 1 SCR 753 [*Patriation Reference*]; *Reference re Authority of Parliament in Relation to the Upper House,* [1980] 1 SCR 54 [*Upper House Reference*]; *Reference re Amendment to the Canadian Constitution,* [1982] 2 SCR 793 [*Quebec Veto Reference*]. For a discussion of the impact of these cases, see Mandel (1994, 27–36), Russell (2004, 118–19; 2011), and Girard (2015).
2 *Reference re Bill C-7 Concerning the Reform of the Senate (QC),* [2013] QJ No 771 [*Quebec Senate Reform Reference*].
3 *Reference re Quebec Sales Tax,* [1994] 2 SCR 715 [*Quebec Sales Tax Reference*]. The order in council that initiated the *Quebec Sales Tax Reference* was passed by the Campbell government on August 26, 1993 (Order in Council PC 1993-1740), and the Campbell government is therefore credited with the initiation of this case. It should be noted that following the order in council, a federal election occurred. When the case was decided by the Supreme Court in 1994, a Liberal government led by Prime Minister Jean Chrétien was in power.
4 *Reference re Manitoba Language Rights,* [1992] 1 SCR 212; *Reference re Manitoba Language Rights,* [1985] 1 SCR 721.
5 *Reference re Farm Products Marketing Act RSO, 1950,* [1957] SCR 198.
6 *Reference re Public Schools Act (Man), s 79(3), (4) and (7),* [1993] 1 SCR 839; *Reference re Assisted Human Reproduction Act,* [2010] 3 SCR 457.
7 Quebec continues to be a clear proponent of using the reference power to challenge the actions of the federal government. In 2017 the Quebec Court of Appeal ruled on a reference initiated by the Quebec government aimed at challenging federal

securities legislation. See *Référence re Renvoi relatif à la réglementation pancanadienne des valuers mobiliéres*, 2017 QCCA 756. Additionally, the Court of Appeal is currently considering reference questions submitted by the Quebec government concerning the recently enacted federal bill on genetic nondiscrimination (see Court of Appeal of Quebec 2017).

8 *Reference re Employment Insurance Act (Can) ss 22 and 23*, [2005] 2 SCR 669; *Reference re Bill C-7 Respecting the Criminal Justice System for Young Persons (QC)*, [2003] QJ No 2850.

9 *Reference re Firearms Act (Can)*, [2000] 1 SCR 783 [*Firearms Reference*].

10 Mackenzie King served as prime minister intermittently for a total of twenty-one years, from December 29, 1921, to June 28, 1926, from September 25, 1926, to August 7, 1930, and from October 23, 1935, to November 15, 1948.

11 During this decade, provincial appellate courts and the Supreme Court of Canada heard 83 cases concerning the division of powers between the federal and provincial governments. The 21 reference decisions regarding the division of powers represent approximately one-quarter of all litigation on the division of powers during the 1930s.

12 *Reference re Meaning of the Word "Persons,"* [1928] SCR 276, [1930] AC 124 [*Persons Case*]; *Reference re the Power of the Governor General in Council to Disallow Provincial Legislation and the Power of the Reservation of a Lieutenant-Governor of a Province*, [1938] SCR 71 [*Powers of Disallowance and Reservation Reference*].

13 *Farmers' Creditors Arrangement Act*, 24–25 Geo V, 1934, c 53.

14 *Natural Products Marketing Act*, 24–25 Geo V, 1934, c 57.

15 *Weekly Rest in Industrial Undertakings Act*, 25–26 Geo V, 1935, c 14; *Employment and Social Insurance Act*, 25–26 Geo V, 1935, c 38; *Minimum Wages Act*, 25–26 Geo V, 1935, c 44; *Limitation of Hours of Work Act*, 25–26 Geo V, 1935, c 63.

16 However, it should be noted that the *Employment and Social Insurance Act* was specifically enacted without reference to articles of the Treaty of Versailles, as Bennett wanted to prevent the Co-operative Commonwealth Federation from demanding that Parliament also adopt relief assistance, which was associated with the corresponding unemployment insurance conventions in the treaty (McConnell 1968).

17 *Criminal Code of Canada*, RSC 1985, c C-46.

18 *Dominion Trade and Industry Commission Act*, 25–26 Geo V, 1935, c 59; *Combines Investigation Act*, RSC 1927, c 26.

19 In both of these cases, there was no consideration of section 95 of the Constitution, which provides shared provincial and federal jurisdiction over agriculture, with federal paramountcy. The federal government could have made an argument that both Acts were primarily concerned with the control of agriculture and therefore not ultra vires. However, it appears that this argument was not put forward by the attorney general of Canada in both cases.

20 *Reference re the Dominion Trade and Industry Commission Act, 1935,* [1936] SCR 379, [1937] AC 405; *Reference re Section 498(a) of the Criminal Code,* [1936] SCR 363, [1937] AC 368; *Reference re Natural Products Marketing Act, 1934,* [1936] SCR 398, [1937] AC 377; *Reference re Farmers' Creditors Arrangement Act, 1934,* [1936] SCR 384, [1937] AC 391; *Reference re Minimum Wages Act, Limitation of Hours of Work Act, Weekly Rest in Industrial Undertakings Act,* [1936] SCR 461, [1937] AC 326, 1 WWR 299 [*Labour Conventions Reference*]; *Reference re Employment and Social Insurance Act, 1935,* [1936] SCR 427, [1937] AC 355.

21 However, the *Labour Conventions Reference* has still had the important and lasting effect of significantly limiting the federal treaty-making power, as the court held that the federal government could not rely on "Peace, Order, and Good Government" in agreeing to international treaties. Instead, if matters of provincial jurisdiction are impugned by an international treaty, provincial governments must be in agreement (see Mallet 2007).

22 King explained in personal correspondence that this appeal to the JCPC "arises in no way from dissatisfaction on the part of the government with the opinions given or the expectation of their being reserved" (quoted in Hart 1991, 60).

23 Indeed, the *British North America Act, 1867* was amended by Westminster in 1940 to transfer jurisdiction over unemployment insurance to the Parliament of Canada from the provinces in response to *Reference re Employment and Social Insurance Act* and to overcome the federal inability to act in this policy sphere in the future.

24 The JCPC was subject to a great deal of criticism for promoting a decentralized version of Canadian federalism in several decisions, especially in response to the New Deal cases (see Laskin 1947; Forsey 1976; and Vaughan 1986).

25 *Credit of Alberta Regulation Act,* SA 1937, c 1, Session II; *Bank Employee Civil Rights Act,* SA 1937, c 2, Session II; *Judicature Act Amendment Act,* SA 1937, c 5, Session II.

26 *Credit Act,* SA 1937, c 8, Session III; *Bank Taxation Bill,* SA 1937, c 1, Session III.

27 *Accurate News and Information Bill,* SA 1937, c 9, Session III.

28 *Reference re Alberta Statutes, 1937,* [1938] SCR 100, [1939] AC 117; *Reference re the Power of the Governor General in Council to Disallow Provincial Legislation and the Power of the Reservation of a Lieutenant-Governor of a Province,* [1938] SCR 71 [*Powers of Disallowance and Reservation Reference*].

29 *Reference re Grain Marketing Act, 1931 (SK),* [1931] 2 WWR 146, 25 Sask LR 273; *Reference re Insurance Act (Can),* [1932] AC 41; *Reference re Qualifications for Mayor and Aldermen of the City of Calgary,* [1933] AJ No 25, 3 WWR 385; *Reference re Provincial Treasurer of Nova Scotia,* [1937] SCR 403; *Constitutional Questions Act (SK),* [1936] SJ No. 65, [1936] 4 DLR 134; *Reference re Natural Products Marketing Act (BC),* [1937] 4 DLR 298, [1938] AC 708; *Reference re Agricultural Land Relief Act,* [1938] AJ No 54, [1938] 4 DLR 28.

30 *Reference re the Regulation and Control of Aeronautics in Canada,* [1930] SCR 663, [1932] AC 54 [*Aeronautics Reference*].

31 The national dimensions doctrine assesses whether the legislation under scrutiny "goes beyond local or provincial concern or interests and must from its inherent nature be the concern of the Dominion as a whole" (Hogg 2012, 17.3(a)). Understandably, the national dimensions doctrine has the ability to greatly increase the powers of the federal government at the expense of the provinces. However, it should be noted that the Supreme Court has not relied on this test to inform much of its jurisprudence regarding the division of powers.

32 *Reference re Minimum Wages Act, Limitation of Hours of Work Act, Weekly Rest in Industrial Undertakings Act,* [1936] SCR 461, [1937] AC 326, 1 WWR 299.

33 *Reference re Meaning of the Word "Persons,"* [1930] AC 124 [*Persons Case*] at para 44.

34 *Act to Give Effect to the Requirement for Clarity as Set Out in the Opinion of the Supreme Court of Canada in the Quebec Secession Reference,* SC 2000, c 26.

35 *Constitution Act, 1982,* s 35(1): "The existing aboriginal and treaty rights of aboriginal peoples of Canada are hereby recognized and affirmed."

36 It should be noted that the Charlottetown Accord and the process that led up to the agreement are not an example of pure executive federalism. Because the Meech Lake Accord was subject to a great deal of criticism for being anti-democratic and not transparent, the Mulroney government took deliberate steps in the Charlottetown process to attempt to make the exercise more open and legitimate in the eyes of Canadians. Among these steps were citizen participation through the Spicer Commission, opening up the consultation process to more groups, including many Indigenous groups, and a public referendum.

37 Appointments to the House of Federation were to take place following a national or provincial election and were to be made in a manner proportional to the election results.

38 Section 91(1) of the *Constitution Act, 1867* permitted the Parliament of Canada "the amendment from time to time of the Constitution of Canada." This section was repealed through the adoption of the *Constitution Act, 1982.*

39 See also *Reference re Resolution to Amend the Constitution,* [1981] 1 SCR 753 [*Patriation Reference*] at 826–31.

40 Mandel (1994) notes that of the thirteen justices who heard the provincial references, six were against the federal government and seven in support, further demonstrating the ambiguous force of these appellate court decisions.

41 Indeed, Quebec expressed significant dissatisfaction with the outcome of the *Patriation Reference* and its influence on the adoption of the 1982 Constitution, subsequently submitting the *Quebec Veto Reference* to ask the courts whether provincial unanimity for constitutional amendment was required.

42 *Reference re Amendment to the Canadian Constitution,* [1982] 2 SCR 793 [*Quebec Veto Reference*] at 798.

43 *Reference re Mining and Mineral Rights Tax Act,* [1982] 2 SCR 260, 138 DLR (3d) 577 [*Mining and Mineral Rights Reference*]; *Reference re Mineral and Other Natural Resources of the Continental Shelf,* [1983] 145 DLR (3d) 9, 119 APR 27 [*Newfoundland*

Continental Shelf Reference]; *Reference re Upper Churchill Water Rights Reversion Act*, [1984] 1 SCR 297; *Reference re Ownership of the Bed of the Strait of Georgia and Related Areas*, [1984] 1 SCR 388; *Reference re Seabed and Subsoil of the Continental Shelf Offshore Newfoundland*, [1984] 1 SCR 86 [*Seabed and Subsoil Reference*]; *Reference re Exported Natural Gas*, [1982] 1 SCR 1004. The *Newfoundland Continental Shelf Reference* and the *Seabed and Subsoil Reference* concerned largely the same matters; however, the provincial decision in the *Newfoundland Continental Shelf Reference* of 1983 was not directly appealed to the Supreme Court in the *Seabed and Subsoil Reference* of 1984, as the first case was a reference from the provincial government, whereas the second was a federal reference.

44 *Reference re Upper Churchill Water Rights Reversion Act*, [1984] 1 SCR 297; *Reference re Mining and Mineral Rights Tax Act*, [1982] 2 SCR 260, 138 DLR (3d) 577 [*Mining and Mineral Rights Reference*].

45 *Reference re Mineral and Other Natural Resources of the Continental Shelf*, [1983] 145 DLR (3d) 9, 119 APR 27 [*Newfoundland Continental Shelf Reference*]; *Reference re Seabed and Subsoil of the Continental Shelf Offshore Newfoundland*, [1984] 1 SCR 86 [*Seabed and Subsoil Reference*]; *Reference re Ownership of the Bed of the Strait of Georgia and Related Areas*, [1984] 1 SCR 388.

46 *Mining and Mineral Rights Tax Act, 1975*, 1975 (Nfld.), c 68.

Chapter 3: Routine Politics and Nonroutine Litigation

1 *Reference re Farm Security Act, 1944*, [1949] AC 110, and *Reference re Validity of Section 5(a) of the Dairy Industry Act*, [1949] SCR 1, [1951] AC 179, are excluded from this analysis.

2 *Reference re Securities Act*, [2011] 3 SCR 837 [*Securities Reference*].

3 *Reference re Education Act (Que)*, [1993] 2 SCR 511.

4 *Reference re Canada Assistance Plan (BC)*, [1991] 2 SCR 525.

5 *Reference re R v Truscott*, [1967] SCR 309 [*Truscott Reference*].

6 Of course, as I was reminded by an astute reviewer, it could also mean that the courts simply agree with the government's interpretation of the division of powers.

7 However, teasing out the difference between these two explanations is quite difficult, as it requires access to the internal decision making of the court (see Epstein and Knight 1998).

8 *Bush v Gore*, 531 US 98 (2000).

9 Sossin (2012) notes that the Supreme Court has not provided parameters for the concept of "ripeness." For the criteria used in assessing "mootness," see *Borowski v Canada (Attorney General)*, [1989] 1 SCR 342.

10 *Reference re Secession of Quebec*, [1998] 2 SCR 217 [*Secession Reference*], para 26.

11 Ibid.

12 *Constitutional Questions Act*, RSBC 1996, c 68.

13 *Reference re Canada Assistance Plan (BC)*, [1991] 2 SCR 525, para 54.

14 Ibid., para 26.

15 Missing data equal 1.1 percent (1 case). In 2 cases, courts refused to answer different questions for different reasons, resulting in 2 cases being counted twice. The PEI Court of Appeal provided reasons concerning both practical matters and a lack of information for refusing to answer all the questions referred to it in *Reference re Interpretation of Human Rights Act*, [1998] 50 DLR (4th) 647, 69 Nfld & PEI R 264. Similarly, in *Reference re Constitution Act 1867, ss 26, 27, and 28 (BC)*, [1991] 78 DLR (4th) 245, the BC Court of Appeal did not answer all the questions referred to it both for practical reasons and due to the inappropriateness of some of the questions referred.

16 In an attempt to increase the consistency and reliability of coding, answer refusals are categorized based on the clear and apparent reasoning provided by the court for declining to answer. However, considering only clear examples of courts declining to answer could not capture *all* refusals, limiting the present analysis. More specifically, instead of a clear refusal to answer, some courts provided "answers" that did not actually address the questions referred to them to the fullest extent possible or to the satisfaction of the parties involved. Nevertheless, verifying such responses (or refusals) would have required too much independent judgment and would ultimately have sacrificed the reliability of coding.

17 *Reference re Earth Future Lottery (PEI)*, [2002] 215 DLR (4th) 656, 166 CCC (3d) 373; *Reference re Interpretation of Human Rights Act*, [1998] 50 DLR (4th) 647; *Reference re Constitution Act 1867, ss 26, 27, and 28 (BC)*, [1991] 78 DLR (4th) 245; *Reference re Workers' Compensation Act, 1983 (Nfld)*, [1989] 1 SCR 922; *Reference re Freedom of Informed Choice (Abortions) Act (SK)*, [1985] 25 DLR (4th) 751, 44 Sask R 104; *Reference re Upper Churchill Water Rights Reversion Act*, [1984] 1 SCR 297; *Reference re Legislative Privilege (1978)*, [1978] 18 OR (2d) 529; *Reference re Jones v Canada (AG)*, [1975] 2 SCR 182; *Reference re Validity of a By-Law Respecting Taxi Cabs*, [1958] 122 CCC 51, 16 DLR (2d) 348; *Reference re Railway Act, Canada v Canada Pacific Railway*, [1958] SCR 285; *Reference re Moratorium Legislation Act (SK)*, [1955] 35 CBR 135.

18 *Reference re Freedom of Informed Choice (Abortions) Act (SK)*, [1985] 25 DLR (4th) 751, 44 Sask R 104.

19 *Reference re Interpretation of Human Rights Act*, [1998] 50 DLR (4th) 647, 69 Nfld & PEI R 264; *Reference re Goods and Services Tax*, [1992] 2 SCR 445; *Reference re Public Service Employee Relations Act (Alta)*, [1987] 1 SCR 313; *Reference re Stony Plain Indian Reserve*, [1981] AJ No 1007, 130 DLR (3d) 636; *Reference re Authority of Parliament in Relation to the Upper House*, [1980] 1 SCR 54 [*Upper House Reference*]; *Reference re Manitoba (AG) v Manitoba Egg and Poultry Association*, [1971] SCR 689 [*Egg Reference*].

20 *Reference re Goods and Services Tax*, [1992] 2 SCR 445, para 71.

21 Ibid.

22 *Reference re Court of Unified Criminal Jurisdiction*, [1983] 1 SCR 704 at 2.

23 Ibid. at 2–3.

24 Ibid. at 7.
25 *Reference re Same-Sex Marriage*, [2004] 3 SCR 698 [*Same-Sex Marriage Reference*]; *Reference re Constitution Act 1867, ss 26, 27, and 28 (BC)*, [1991] 78 DLR (4th) 245.
26 *Reference re Same-Sex Marriage*, [2004] 3 SCR 698 [*Same-Sex Marriage Reference*], para 8.
27 Ibid., para 3.
28 The other questions in the *Same-Sex Marriage Reference* asked the Supreme Court, "(1) Is the annexed Proposal for an Act respecting certain aspects of legal capacity for marriage for civil purposes within the exclusive legislative authority of the Parliament of Canada? If not, in what particular or particulars, and to what extent? (2) If the answer to question 1 is yes, is section 1 of the proposal, which extends capacity to marry to persons of the same sex, consistent with the Canadian Charter of Rights and Freedoms? If not, in what particulars, and to what extent? (3) Does the freedom of religion guaranteed by paragraph 2(a) of the Canadian Charter of Rights and Freedoms protect religious officials from being compelled to perform a marriage between two persons of the same sex that is contrary to their religious beliefs?"
29 *Reference re Same-Sex Marriage*, [2004] 3 SCR 698 [*Same-Sex Marriage Reference*], para 10.
30 Ibid., para 65.
31 Ibid.
32 Ibid., para 67.
33 Ibid., para 68.
34 *Supreme Court Act*, RSC 1985, c S-26, s 53.
35 See also *Arizonans for Official English v Arizona et al*, 520 US 43 (1997); and *Aetna Life Insurance Co v Haworth et al*, 300 US 227 (1937).
36 In reference cases, concrete review contains one or more of the following (but most often all three): an agreed statement of facts; opposed parties named in the title of the case, or headnote, instead of "*Reference re*"; and nongovernmental entities listed as direct parties to the case.
37 It should be noted that categorizing a case as either abstract or concrete is based on the questions referred, not on whether the court made any connections to concrete disputes or to related routine litigation in its decision. Categorizing cases based on the questions referred, rather than on the text of the decision, also allows for greater consistency and reliability in coding.
38 In 2 cases, courts were referred questions that were both abstract and concrete. See *Reference re Milk Industry Act (BC)*, [1960] SCR 346 and *Reference re Railway Act, Canada v Canada Pacific Railway*, [1958] SCR 285. For example, in *Reference re Milk Industry Act (BC)* [1960] SCR 346, Question 1 asked the Supreme Court whether British Columbia's *Milk Industry Act*, 1956 (B.C.), c. 28, was in pith and substance ultra vires the Legislative Assembly of British Columbia, and Question 2 asked the court to consider whether a specific order issued by the Milk Board on January 18,

1957, was intra vires the powers of the Milk Board. In *Reference re Railway Act, Canada v Canada Pacific Railway,* Question 1 asked the Supreme Court, "Is section 198 of the Railway Act *ultra vires* of the Parliament of Canada," an abstract question, whereas Questions 2, 3, and 4 asked specific questions regarding land title.

39 *Reference re R v Truscott,* [1967] SCR 309 [*Truscott Reference*], para 4.

40 It should be noted that Justice Emmett Matthew Hall wrote a rather stinging solo dissent in this case, finding that the original trial "was not conducted according to law ... There were grave errors in the trial brought about principally by Crown Counsel's method in trying to establish guilt" (ibid. at 65). In his conclusion, Justice Hall found that the conviction should have been quashed and a new trial ordered.

41 *Truscott (Re),* 2007 ONCA 575, 225 CCC (3d) 321.

42 To be clear, this should not be understood as an endorsement of the Supreme Court's finding in the Truscott case.

43 *Reference re Milgaard (Can),* [1992] 1 SCR 866.

44 *Reference re Ng Extradition (Can),* [1991] 2 SCR 858.

45 *Reference re Broome v Prince Edward Island,* [2010] 1 SCR 360.

46 *Reference re Provincial Electoral Boundaries (Sask),* [1991] 2 SCR 158.

47 Ibid., para 12.

48 *Legislative Authority over Bypass Pipelines Indexed as: Reference re Constitution Act 1867, s 92(10)(a) (Ont CA) (1988),* [1988] 64 OR (2d) 393, OJ No. 176; *Reference re Minority Language Education Rights (PEI),* [1988] 69 Nfld & PEI R 236, 49 DLR (4th) 499.

49 *Reference re Supreme Court Act, ss 5 and 6,* [2014] 1 SCR 433 [*Nadon Reference*].

50 *Reference re Bill 30, An Act to Amend the Education Act (Ont),* [1987] 1 SCR 1148.

51 *Reference re Court of Unified Criminal Jurisdiction,* [1983] 1 SCR 704 at 2.

52 *EGALE Canada Inc v Canada (AG),* [2003] BCCA 251.

53 *Halpern v Canada (AG),* [2003] OJ No 2268.

54 *Supreme Court Act,* RSC 1985, c S-26, s 53(5): "Where the question relates to the constitutional validity of any Act passed by the legislature of any province, or of any provision in any such Act, or in case, for any reason, the government of any province has any special interest in any such question, the attorney general of the province shall be notified of the hearing in order that the attorney general may be heard if he thinks fit."

55 The cases without intervenors, but with nongovernmental parties appointed as amici curiae, are *Reference re Freedom of Informed Choice (Abortions) Act (SK),* [1985] 25 DLR (4th) 751; *Reference re Constitutional Questions Act (SK),* [1981] 128 DLR (3d), 13 Sask. R. 100; *Reference re Intoxicated Persons Detention Act (MB),* [1981] 116 DLR (3d) 91, 1 WWR 333; and *Reference re Powers of Notaries Public in British Columbia,* [1969] BCJ No. 444, 6 DLR (3d) 447.

56 *Reference re Marriage Commissioners Appointed under the Marriage Act, 1995, SS 1995, c M-4.1,* [2011] 327 DLR (4th) 669, 3 WWR 193; *Reference re Public Service Employee*

Relations Act (Alta), [1987] 1 SCR 313; *Reference re Secession of Quebec*, [1998] 2 SCR 217 [*Secession Reference*]; *Reference re Remuneration of the Judges of the Provincial Court of Prince Edward Island*, [1997] 3 SCR 3; *Reference re Workers' Compensation Act, 1983 (Nfld)*, [1989] 1 SCR 922; *Reference re Provincial Electoral Boundaries (Sask)*, [1991] 2 SCR 158; *Reference re Securities Act*, [2011] 3 SCR 837 [*Securities Reference*]; *Reference re Firearms Act (Can)*, [2000] 1 SCR 783 [*Firearms Reference*]; *Reference re Education Act of Ontario and Minority Language Education Rights*, [1984] OJ No 3260, 47 OR (2d) 1; *Reference re Same-Sex Marriage*, [2004] 3 SCR 698 [*Same-Sex Marriage Reference*]; *Reference re Bill 30, An Act to Amend the Education Act (Ont)*, [1987] 1 SCR 1148; *Reference re Anti-Inflation Act*, [1976] 2 SCR 373; *Reference re Manitoba (AG) v Manitoba Egg and Poultry Association*, [1971] SCR 689 [*Egg Reference*]; *Reference re Residential Tenancies Act*, [1981] 1 SCR 714.

57 Reference cases can be reactionary in some sense when one government refers the legislation of another, as in *Reference re Bill C-7 Concerning the Reform of the Senate (QC)*, [2013] QJ No 771 [*Quebec Senate Reform Reference*], wherein the Government of Quebec referred the federal government's Bill C-7 to the Quebec Court of Appeal. However, this type of reference case still demonstrates the proactive selection of litigation by one party (in this case, the Government of Quebec), even if the case concerns the legislation of another government.

Chapter 4: "It's Always a Little Bit of Politics"

1 The references concerning electoral boundaries are *Reference re Electoral Boundaries Commission Act*, [1991] AJ No 1065, 86 DLR (4th) 447; *Reference re Electoral Divisions Statutes*, [1994] AJ No 768, 119 DLR (4th) 1; and *Reference re Final Report of the Electoral Boundaries Commission*, 2017 NSCA 10, 411 DLR (4th) 271. The references concerning Senate reform are *Reference re Authority of Parliament in Relation to the Upper House*, [1980] 1 SCR 54 [*Upper House Reference*]; *Reference re Senate Reform*, [2014] 1 SCR 704; and *Reference re Bill C-7 Concerning the Reform of the Senate (QC)*, [2013] QJ No 7771, 2013 QCCA 1807 [*Quebec Senate Reform Reference*]. The reference concerning patriation is *Reference re Resolution to Amend the Constitution*, [1981] 1 SCR 753 [*Patriation Reference*].

2 *Reference re Secession of Quebec*, [1998] 2 SCR 217 [*Secession Reference*]; *Reference re Sections 193 and 195.1(1)(C) of the Criminal Code (Man) (Bawdy House and Solicitation)*, [1990] 1 SCR 1123; *Reference re Criminal Code – Bigamy*, [1897] 27 SCR 461; *Reference re Same-Sex Marriage*, [2004] 3 SCR 698 [*Same-Sex Marriage Reference*].

3 A few examples of the several references concerning agriculture or natural resources are *Reference re Natural Products Marketing Act, 1934*, [1936] SCR 398; *Reference re Agricultural Land Relief Act*, [1938] AJ No 54, [1938] 4 DLR 28; *Reference re Agricultural Products Marketing Act*, [1978] 2 SCR 1198; *Reference re Mineral and Other Natural Resources of the Continental Shelf*, [1983] 145 DLR (3d) 9, 119 APR 27 [*Newfoundland Continental Shelf Reference*]; *Reference re Mining and Mineral Rights Tax Act*, [1982] 2 SCR 260, 138 DLR (3d) 577 [*Mining and Mineral Rights Reference*];

Reference re Exported Natural Gas Tax, [1982] 1 SCR 1004 [*Alberta Gas Tax Reference*]; *Reference re Seabed and Subsoil of the Continental Shelf Offshore Newfoundland*, [1984] 1 SCR 86 [*Seabed and Subsoil Reference*]; and *Reference re Upper Churchill Water Rights Reversion Act*, [1984] 1 SCR 297. Human reproduction was considered by the Supreme Court in *Reference re Assisted Human Reproduction Act*, [2010] 3 SCR 457. The regulation of firearms was considered in *Reference re Firearms Act (Can)*, [2000] 1 SCR 783 [*Firearms Reference*]. The constitutionality of a national securities regulator was addressed in *Reference re Securities Act*, [2011] 3 SCR 837 [*Securities Reference*].

4 Examples include *Reference re Section 498(a) of the Criminal Code*, [1936] SCR 363, [1937] AC 368; *Reference re Farmers' Creditors Arrangement Act, 1934*, [1936] SCR 384, [1937] AC 391; and *Reference re Employment and Social Insurance Act, 1935*, [1936] SCR 427, [1937] AC 355. More recent reference cases concerning labour relations or economic regulation are *Reference re Public Service Employee Relations Act (Alta)*, [1987] 1 SCR 313; *Reference re Canada Assistance Plan (BC)*, [1991] 2 SCR 525; and *Reference re Employment Insurance Act (Can) ss 22 and 23*, [2005] 2 SCR 669.

5 *Reference re Exported Natural Gas Tax*, [1982] 1 SCR 1004 [*Alberta Gas Tax Reference*].

6 Interviews are a valuable source of data for the present study for two central reasons. First, as in most contexts, interviewees can provide insight into phenomena that are relatively unknown (see Lilleker 2003). Second, interview data are essential as one of the few means to access the inner workings of Cabinet decision making and the choice to use the reference power by governments. This analysis uses semi-structured interviews, as this method allows for the probing of perceptions and opinions. Although this method requires more preparation by the interviewer, it is valuable because it provides the opportunity for in-depth conversation and the ability for subjects to clarify responses, which maximizes response validity (Aberbach and Rockman 2002).

7 This sample was gathered from 19 of the reference cases heard between 1994 and 2014, and it excluded only 2 cases from this period, which were initiated by a current sitting attorney general. Limiting the reference cases to this period provided fifteen different attorneys general as possible subjects, all of whom were contacted for interviews. Five former attorneys general participated, a response rate of 33 percent. Interviews took place over three months during the spring and summer of 2014. Subjects were questioned about the specific reference case or cases in which they had participated and about the reference case process in general. The analysis that follows is primarily based on direct quotations, with minimal editing (when possible), to maintain the integrity of the interviewee statements. Furthermore, as confidentiality was a condition to gaining access to the participants, all interviewees are referred to using gender-neutral language as well as pseudonyms that identify their previous position as it relates to the project.

8 *Egan v Canada*, [1995] 2 SCR 513.

9 Determining the answer to this puzzle is unfortunately beyond the focus of the present analysis, as doing so would require an investigation into the internal decision making of a court.
10 Attorney General C, author interview, May 5, 2014.
11 Attorney General D, author interview, May 9, 2014.
12 Attorney General A, author interview, April 7, 2014.
13 Attorney General B, author interview, April 25, 2014.
14 Counsel B, author interview, June 20, 2014.
15 Attorney General D, author interview, May 9, 2014.
16 For more on the principle of sub judice, see Sossin and Crystal (2013).
17 Attorney General D, author interview, May 9, 2014.
18 Ibid.
19 First Minister A, author interview, April 2, 2014.
20 Attorney General C, author interview, May 5, 2014.
21 Attorney General E, author interview, June 9, 2014.
22 Attorney General D, author interview, May 9, 2014.
23 Attorney General E, author interview, June 9, 2014.
24 Ibid.
25 Counsel A, author interview, April 3, 2014.
26 Attorney General B, author interview, April 25, 2014.
27 Counsel A, author interview, April 3, 2014.
28 Counsel B, author interview, June 20, 2014.
29 Attorney General B, author interview, April 25, 2014. In this example, Attorney General B's government was concerned that another government and several interest groups would challenge its legislative project.
30 Attorney General E, author interview, June 9, 2014.
31 Counsel B, author interview, June 20, 2014.
32 *Reference re Anti-Inflation Act,* [1976] 2 SCR 373.
33 *Anti-Inflation Act,* SC 1975, c 75.
34 *Reference re Marriage Commissioners Appointed under the Marriage Act, 1995, SS 1995, c M-4.1,* [2011] 327 DLR (4th) 669, 3 WWR 193.
35 Counsel A, author interview, April 3, 2014.
36 Attorney General A, author interview, 7 April 2014.
37 Attorney General D, author interview, May 9, 2014.
38 Attorney General B, author interview, April 25, 2014.
39 *Reference re Regulations in Relation to Chemicals,* [1943] SCR 1 [*Chemicals Reference*].
40 *War Measures Act,* 5 Geo V, 1914, c 2.
41 *Reference re Persons of Japanese Race,* [1946] SCR 248, [1947] AC 87.
42 *Reference re Wartime Leasehold Regulations,* [1950] SCR 124.
43 Counsel B, author interview, June 20, 2014.
44 Attorney General B, author interview, April 25, 2014.

45 Counsel B, author interview, June 20, 2014.
46 Attorney General E, author interview, June 9, 2014.
47 Attorney General D, author interview, May 9, 2014.
48 Attorney General E, author interview, June 9, 2014.
49 Attorney General C, author interview, May 5, 2014.
50 Attorney General D, author interview, May 9, 2014.
51 Counsel A, author interview, April 3, 2014.
52 Attorney General C, author interview, May 5, 2014.
53 Of course, the reverse could also be true. If governments are perceived to rely on the courts too often, the institutional legitimacy of the executive could be undermined over time. However, arguably, this is not as great a concern as the erosion of judicial independence because the executive has more opportunities to foster legitimacy compared to the courts. Indeed, the executive is elected, providing it valuable democratic legitimacy as relates to its use of the reference power. Moreover, the executive has the ability to respond to questions and concerns regarding its decisions in a direct manner either in Parliament or through the media. In contrast, beyond issuing a legal opinion, the courts have little means to foster institutional legitimacy in the eyes of other actors and the public.

Chapter 5: Why Not Refer Everything?

1 Cabinet conclusions, prepared by the clerk of the privy council, provide an overview of the topics discussed by Cabinet and a summary of the debates and decisions made during its meetings. This documentation often provides the title (but not name) of the minister who has presented an item for discussion, as well as a summary of the discussions, but it generally does not attribute specific arguments or statements to specific individuals. Although many aspects of Cabinet meetings are not subject to public disclosure, Library and Archives Canada provides access to all Cabinet conclusions from 1944, when they were first recorded, to 1976.
2 King's diaries are available to the public in Library and Archives Canada. King maintained a daily diary from 1893 to his death in 1950, providing over 30,000 pages of text.
3 The first case study, the *Padlock Act,* is examined in more detail than the second due to the greater availability of scholarly literature and archival materials respecting this Act; blasphemy in Canada has received relatively little scholarly analysis to date.
4 For example, Eugene Forsey, a leading academic at McGill University, was labelled a defender of communists for publicly condemning the *Padlock Act* as a threat to civil liberties. This label forced Forsey to write several letters defending his position, in which he clarified that he was not a communist sympathizer (see Hodgetts 2000).
5 *Switzman v Elbling,* [1957] 7 DLR 2d 337.
6 *Reference re Alberta Statutes, 1937,* [1938] SCR 100.

7 For example, among the several individuals and corporations to petition against aspects of the Social Credit legislation were the Canadian Life Insurance Officers Association, Dominion Mortgage and Investment Association, Investment Dealers' Association of Canada, Canadian Bankers Association, Edmonton Chamber of Commerce, and Boards of Trade of Toronto, Winnipeg, Calgary, Lethbridge, and Montreal (see Wilson 1975).

8 According to Mallory (1976) and Wilson (1975), the accepted grounds for disallowance are the following: provincial legislation clearly invades federal constitutional power or impedes a fundamental national interest; legislation is ultra vires, and no other remedy is available; or legislation is unreasonable, contrary to good government, and discriminatory, and no other remedy is available. That being said, at least formally, the disallowance power has no specific limitations.

9 Parliament is currently considering a bill that includes a provision to repeal section 296 of of the Criminal Code. This is Bill C-51, *An Act to Amend the Criminal Code and the Department of Justice Act and to Make Consequential Amendments to Another Act* (42nd Parliament, 1st Session).

10 Importantly, Patrick (2013, 5) notes that the definition of "blasphemy" is contested and that its meaning is often deeply reflective of context.

11 See *R v Sterry*, (1927) 5 Can Bar Rev.

12 The leading expert on Canadian blasphemy law, Jeremy Patrick (2013), has also been unable to uncover more information regarding the St. Laurent Cabinet's consideration of blasphemy.

13 There are of course reference cases where both sides of the dispute can claim some form of victory. Good examples are the *Patriation Reference* and, in some respects, the *Secession Reference*.

14 *Reference re Firearms Act (Can)*, [2000] 1 SCR 783 [*Firearms Reference*], Appendix A.

15 *Firearms Act*, SC 1995, c 39.

16 *Reference re Firearms Act (Can)*, [2000] 1 SCR 783 [*Firearms Reference*], para 61.

Chapter 6: Seeking the Court's Advice and the Delegation of Decision Making

1 Delegation in Canadian law and politics often refers to interdelegation, which is the delegation of constitutional jurisdiction between governments. One exception to this can be found in the work of Hirschl (2000, 2004), who uses Canada as a case within comparative analysis. That being said, Hausegger, Hennigar, and Riddell (2015) employ some of the delegation terminology and explanations in their discussion of why governments use the reference power, but they do not make explicit mention of this theoretical framework or corresponding literature. Similarly, Hennigar (2010) also refers to the concept of delegation in his study of concessions by the federal government in Charter litigation.

2 I must thank an excellent reviewer for reminding me of this point.

3 *Reference re Wartime Leasehold Regulations*, [1950] SCR 124 at para 3.

4 Attorney General D, author interview, May 9, 2014.

5 Provincial governments have been quite successful in securing the support of constituents through vocal opposition to the federal government, such as former Newfoundland and Labrador premier Danny Williams's provincially popular Anything But Conservatives campaign against the Conservative Party of Canada. This campaign not only put Williams on the national stage but also made him incredibly popular with provincial voters (see Marland and Kerby 2014).

6 Attorney General D, author interview, May 9, 2014.

7 Importantly, governments can also fund interest groups to challenge the policies of other governments or their own policies in court, thereby achieving some of the same strategic ends but in a manner that is less direct than initiating a reference case (see Pal 1993; and Brodie 2002).

8 Of course, the stalling tactics possible in the Canadian parliamentary system are much more limited when the governing party holds a majority in the legislature rather than a minority.

9 Using the term "friendly" to describe judicial review can be attributed to Whittington (2005, 2007).

10 *Reference re References,* [1910] 43 SCR 536 at 17.

11 Judicial independence is conceptually distinct from judicial impartiality. Judicial impartiality refers to neutrality and absence of bias in the attitude or state of mind of the adjudicator in relation to the issues and parties in a particular case, whereas judicial independence speaks both to a relation between the judiciary and other branches of government and to the autonomy of action by the members of the judiciary. See *Valente v R,* [1985] 2 SCR 673.

12 *Reference re Secession of Quebec,* [1998] 2 SCR 217 [*Secession Reference*], paras 10–15.

13 Ibid., para 15.

14 *Judicature Act,* RSPEI 1988, c J-2.1.

15 *Reference re Constitution Act 1867, ss 26, 27, and 28 (BC),* [1991] 78 DLR (4th) 245.

16 Attorney General D, author interview, May 9, 2014.

17 Marland (2014, 11) explains that there are several practical and institutional reasons why a provincial first minister can hold more power than the prime minister. He points to the fact that unicameral provincial legislatures are more often governed by a majority or supermajority government, and there is simply a lower level of public scrutiny and media attention respecting premiers compared to the federal government.

18 Importantly, the prime minister has the power to alter the mechanisms by which potential justices of the Supreme Court are selected and recommended to the governor general for appointment. More specifically, the prime minister can employ several possible measures and has variously done so: a judicial appointment advisory council, as used by Justin Trudeau in 2017; consultation with the minister of justice alone; informal consultation with Cabinet, provincial attorneys general, bar associations, and the chief justice of the Supreme Court; or parliamentary hearings,

including interviews of the nominated candidate. However, the formal power of the governor general to appoint justices on the advice of the prime minister is not subject to change without constitutional amendment. See *Reference re Supreme Court Act, ss 5 and 6*, [2014] 1 SCR 433 [*Nadon Reference*].

19 However, former presidents Jacques Chirac and Nicolas Sarkozy resigned their seats in the Constitutional Council, and President François Hollande refrained from joining the council entirely.

Conclusion

1 *Reference re Quebec Sales Tax*, [1994] 2 SCR 715 [*Quebec Sales Tax Reference*].

2 For an excellent example of the value of examining provincial appellate courts, see Greene et al. (1998). Hausegger, Riddell, and Hennigar (2013) make similar calls for more scholarship on provincial appellate courts.

References

Aberbach, Joel D., and Bert A. Rockman. 2002. "Conducting and Coding Elite Interviews." *PS: Political Science and Politics* 35 (4): 673–76.

"Advisory Opinions and the Influence of the Supreme Court over American Policymaking." 2011. *Harvard Law Review* 124: 2064–82.

Aranson, Peter H., Ernest Gellhorn, and Glen O. Robinson. 1982. "Theory of Legislative Delegation." *Columbia Law Review* 68 (1): 1–67.

Baier, Gerald. 2006. *Courts and Federalism: Judicial Doctrine in the United States, Australia, and Canada*. Vancouver: UBC Press.

Baker, Dennis R. 2010. *Not Quite Supreme: The Courts and Coordinate Constitutional Interpretation*. Montreal and Kingston: McGill-Queen's University Press.

Bakvis, Herman, and Stephen B. Wolinetz. 2005. "Canada: Executive Dominance and Presidentialization." In *The Presidentialization of Politics: A Comparative Study of Modern Democracies,* ed. Thomas Poguntke and Paul Webb, 199–220. Oxford: Oxford University Press.

Belleau, Marie-Claire, and Rebecca Johnson. 2008. "Judging Gender: Difference and Dissent at the Supreme Court of Canada." *International Journal of the Legal Profession* 15 (1–2): 57–71.

Betcherman, Lita-Rose. 2002. *Ernest Lapointe: Mackenzie King's Great Quebec Lieutenant*. Toronto: University of Toronto Press.

Bickel, Alexander M. 1962. *The Least Dangerous Branch: The Supreme Court at the Bar of Politics*. Indianapolis: Bobbs-Merrill.

Bourgault, Jacques. 2011. "Minority Government and Senior Government Officials: The Case of the Canadian Federal Government." *Commonwealth and Comparative Politics* 49 (4): 510–27.

Bowal, Peter, and Kelsey Horvat. 2011. "Three Forgotten Reasons to Mind Your Manners in Canada." *Law Now: Relating Law to Life in Canada*, November–December, 13–18.

Brandt, G.J. 1982. "Judicial Mediation of Political Disputes: The Patriation Reference." *University of Western Ontario Law Review* 20: 101–28.

Brodie, Ian. 2002. *Friends of the Court: The Privileging of Interest Group Litigants in Canada*. Albany: State University of New York Press.

Bzdera, André. 1993. "Comparative Analysis of Federal High Courts: A Political Theory of Judicial Review." *Canadian Journal of Political Science* 26 (1): 3–29.

Cairns, Alan C. 1971. "The Judicial Committee and Its Critics." *Canadian Journal of Political Science* 4 (3): 301–45.

Cairns, Alan C. 1977. "The Governments and Societies of Canadian Federalism." *Canadian Journal of Political Science* 10 (4): 695–725.

Cairns, Alan C. 1992. *Charter versus Federalism: The Dilemmas of Constitutional Reform*. Montreal and Kingston: McGill-Queen's University Press.

Cairns, Robert. 1992. "Natural Resources and Canadian Federalism: Decentralization, Recurring Conflict, and Resolution." *Publius: The Journal of Federalism* 22 (Winter): 55–70.

Cairns, Robert, Marsha Chandler, and William Moull. 1985. "The Resource Amendment (Section 92A) and the Political Economy of Canadian Federalism." *Osgoode Hall Law Journal* 23 (2): 253–74.

Cameron, David, and Richard Simeon. 2002. "Intergovernmental Relations in Canada: The Emergence of Collaborative Federalism." *Publius: The Journal of Federalism* 32 (2): 49–71.

Clément, Dominique. 2008. *Canada's Rights Revolution: Social Movements and Social Change, 1937–82*. Vancouver: UBC Press.

Clerk of the Privy Council. 1955. "Cabinet Conclusions, 1944–1976." Library and Archives Canada. April 6.

Cortner, Richard. 1968. "Strategies and Tactics of Litigants in Constitutional Cases." *Journal of Public Law* 17: 287–307.

Court of Appeal of Quebec. 2017. "Reference Concerning the Genetic Non-Discrimination Act." Press release, July 7. https://www.newswire.ca/news-releases/reference-to-the-court-of-appeal-of-quebec-concerning-the-genetic-non-discrimination-act-enacted-by-sections-1-to-7-of-the-act-to-prohibit-and-prevent-genetic-discrimination-633130953.html.

Crandall, Erin. 2010. "Intergovernmental Relations and the Supreme Court of Canada: The Changing Place of the Provinces in Judicial Selection Reform." Institute of Intergovernmental Relations, Queen's University.

Desserud, Don. 2009. "Whither 91.1? The Constitutionality of Bill C-19: An Act to Limit Senate Tenure." In *The Democratic Dilemma: Reforming the Canadian Senate*, ed. Jennifer Smith, 1–15. Montreal and Kingston: McGill-Queen's University Press.

Downs, Anthony. 1957. *An Economic Theory of Democracy*. New York: Harper.

Dufresne, Yannick, and Neil Nevitte. 2014. "Why Do Publics Support Minority Governments? Three Tests." *Parliamentary Affairs* 67 (4): 825–40.

Ely, John Hart. 1980. *Democracy and Distrust: A Theory of Judicial Review*. Cambridge, MA: Harvard University Press.

Epp, Charles. 1998. *The Rights Revolution: Lawyers, Activists, and Supreme Courts in Comparative Perspective*. Chicago: University of Chicago Press.

Epstein, Lee, and Jack Knight. 1998. *The Choices Justices Make*. Washington, DC: CQ Press.

Fine, Sean. 2014. "The Lawyer Who Challenged the Harper Government and Won." *Globe and Mail*, August 22. http://www.theglobeandmail.com/report-on-business/careers/careers-leadership/rocco-galati-is-always-fighting-for-long-shots/article20176185/?page=all.

Finkel, Jodi. 2008. *Judicial Reform as Political Insurance*. Notre Dame, IN: Notre Dame University Press.

Fiorina, Morris P. 1982. "Legislative Choice of Regulatory Forms: Legal Process or Administrative Process?" *Public Choice* 39 (1): 33–66.

Flanagan, Thomas. 2009. *Waiting for the Wave: The Reform Party and the Conservative Movement*. Montreal and Kingston: McGill-Queen's University Press.

Fletcher, Joseph F., and Paul Howe. 2000. "Public Opinion and the Courts." Ed. Peter H. Russell. *Choices: Institute for Research on Public Policy* 6 (3): 30–56.

Forsey, Eugene. 1976. "In Defence of Macdonald's Constitution." *Dalhousie Law Review* 3 (2): 529–39.

Fox, Justin, and Matthew C. Stephenson. 2011. "Judicial Review as a Response to Political Posturing." *American Political Science Review* 105 (2): 397–414.

Franks, C.E.S. 1987. *The Parliament of Canada*. Toronto: University of Toronto Press.

Ginsburg, Tom. 2003. *Judicial Review in New Democracies: Constitutional Courts in Asian Cases*. Cambridge, UK: Cambridge University Press.

Girard, Philip. 2015. "Law, Politics, and the Patriation Reference of 1981." In *Patriation and Its Consequences: Constitution Making in Canada*, ed. Lois Harder and Steve Patten, 115–36. Vancouver: UBC Press.

Goodyear-Grant, Elizabeth, J. Scott Matthews, and Janet Hiebert. 2013. "The Courts/Parliament Trade-Off: Canadian Attitudes on Judicial Influence in Public Policy." *Commonwealth and Comparative Politics* 51 (3): 377–97.

Graber, Mark A. 1993. "The Nonmajoritarian Difficulty: Legislative Deference to the Judiciary." *Studies in American Political Development* 7 (1): 35–73.

Greene, Ian, Carl Baar, Peter McCormick, George Szablowski, and Martin Thomas. 1998. *Final Appeal: Decision-Making in Canadian Courts of Appeal*. Toronto: J. Lorimer.

Hall, Peter A., and Rosemary C. Taylor. 1996. "Political Science and the Three New Institutionalisms." *Political Studies* 44 (5): 936–57.

Hart, John Frederic Vincent. 1991. "The Political and Legal Uses of Reference Cases by the Mackenzie King Government, 1935–1940." MA thesis, University of British Columbia.

Hausegger, Lori, Matthew Hennigar, and Troy Riddell. 2015. *Canadian Courts: Law, Politics, and Process*. 2nd ed. Don Mills, ON: Oxford University Press Canada.

Hausegger, Lori, and Troy Riddell. 2004. "The Changing Nature of Public Support for the Supreme Court of Canada." *Canadian Journal of Political Science* 37 (1): 23–50.

Hausegger, Lori, Troy Riddell, and Matthew Hennigar. 2013. "Does Patronage Matter? Connecting Influences on Judicial Appointments with Judicial Decision Making." *Canadian Journal of Political Science* 46 (3): 665–90.

Heard, Andrew. 2014. *Canadian Constitutional Conventions: The Marriage of Law and Politics*. 2nd ed. Oxford: Oxford University Press.

Hein, Gregory. 2001. "Interest Group Litigation and Canadian Democracy." In *Judicial Power and Canadian Democracy*, ed. Paul Howe and Peter H. Russell, 214–54. Montreal and Kingston: McGill-Queen's University Press.

Hennigar, Matthew. 2002. "Players and the Process: Charter Litigation and the Federal Government." *Windsor Yearbook of Access to Justice* 21: 91–109.

Hennigar, Matthew. 2007. "Why Does the Federal Government Appeal to the Supreme Court of Canada in Charter of Rights Cases? A Strategic Explanation." *Law and Society Review* 41 (1): 225–50.

Hennigar, Matthew. 2009. "Reference re Same-Sex Marriage: Making Sense of the Government's Litigation Strategy." In *Contested Constitutionalism: Reflections on the Canadian Charter of Rights and Freedoms*, ed. James B. Kelly and Christopher P. Manfredi, 209–30. Vancouver: UBC Press.

Hennigar, Matthew. 2010. "Exploring Complex Judicial-Executive Interaction: Federal Government Concessions in Charter of Rights Cases." *Canadian Journal of Political Science* 43 (4): 821–42.

Hiebert, Janet. 2002. *Charter Conflicts: What Is Parliament's Role?* Montreal and Kingston: McGill-Queen's University Press.

Hilbink, Lisa. 2009. "The Constituted Nature of Constituents' Interests: Historical and Ideational Factors in Judicial Empowerment." *Political Research Quarterly* 62 (4): 781–97.

Hildreth, Richard. 1991. "Managing Ocean Resources: Canada." *International Journal of Estuarine and Coastal Law* 6 (3): 199–228.

Hirschl, Ran. 2000. "The Political Origins of Judicial Empowerment through Constitutionalization: Lessons from Four Constitutional Revolutions." *Law and Social Inquiry* 25 (1): 91–149.

Hirschl, Ran. 2004. *Towards Juristocracy: The Origins and Consequences of the New Constitutionalism*. Cambridge, MA: Harvard University Press.

Hirschl, Ran. 2008. "The Judicialization of Mega-Politics and the Rise of Political Courts." *Annual Review of Political Science* 11 (1): 93–118.

Hodgetts, J.E. 2000. *The Sound of One Voice: Eugene Forsey and His Letters to the Press*. Toronto: University of Toronto Press.

Hogg, Peter W. 1992. "Formal Amendment of the Constitution of Canada." *Law and Contemporary Problems* 55 (1): 253–60.

Hogg, Peter W. 2006. "Canada: The Constitution and Same-Sex Marriage." *International Journal of Constitutional Law* 4 (4): 712–21.

Hogg, Peter W. 2012. *Constitutional Law of Canada*. Toronto: Carswell.

Holland, Kenneth M. 1990. "Judicial Activism and Judicial Independence: Implications of the Charter of Rights and Freedoms for the Reference Procedure and Judicial Service on Commissions of Inquiry." *Canadian Journal of Law and Society* 5: 95–110.

House of Commons Debates. 1890. 6th Parl., 4th Session, 4089 (Edward Blake).

House of Commons Debates. 1928. 16th Parl., 2nd Session, 364 (J.S. Woodsworth and E. Lapointe).

House of Commons Debates. 1937. 18th Parl., 2nd Session, 2290–94 (J.S. Woodsworth).

House of Commons Debates. 1938a. 18th Parl., 3rd Session, 114 (Vital Mallette).

House of Commons Debates. 1938b. 18th Parl., 3rd Session, 126–28 (E.J. Poole and A.A. Heaps).

Howitt, Peter, and Ronald Wintrobe. 1995. "The Political Economy of Inaction." *Journal of Public Economics* 56 (3): 329–53.

Huffman, James L., and MardiLyn Saathoff. 1990. "Advisory Opinions and Canadian Constitutional Development: The Supreme Court's Reference Jurisdiction." *Minnesota Law Review* 74: 1251–336.

Huscroft, Grant. 2004. "'Thank God We're Here': Judicial Exclusivity in Charter Interpretation and Its Consequences." *Supreme Court Law Review* 25 (2d): 241–67.

Huscroft, Grant. 2006. "Political Litigation and the Role of the Court." *Supreme Court Law Review* 34 (2d): 35–56.

Huscroft, Grant. 2007. "Constitutionalism from the Top Down." *Osgoode Hall Law Journal* 45 (1): 91–104.

Huscroft, Grant. 2010. "Politics and the Reference Power." Paper presented at the Canadian Political Science Association Annual Conference, Montreal, June 1.

Jay, Stewart. 1997. *Most Humble Servants: The Advisory Role of Early Judges*. New Haven, CT: Yale University Press.

Juda, Lawrence. 2003. "Changing National Approaches to Ocean Governance: The United States, Canada, and Australia." *Ocean Development and International Law* 34 (2): 161–87.

Kelly, James B. 1999. "The Charter of Rights and Freedoms and the Rebalancing of Liberal Constitutionalism in Canada, 1982–1997." *Osgoode Hall Law Journal* 37 (3): 625–95.

Kelly, James B., and Christopher P. Manfredi. 2009. "Should We Cheer? Contested Constitutionalism and the *Canadian Charter of Rights and Freedoms*." In *Contested Constitutionalism: Reflections on the Canadian Charter of Rights and Freedoms,* ed. Christopher P. Manfredi and James B. Kelly, 3–29. Vancouver: UBC Press.

King, W.L. Mackenzie. 1938a. "Diaries of William Lyon Mackenzie King, 1893–1950." Library and Archives Canada. July 5.

King, W.L. Mackenzie. 1938b. "Diaries of William Lyon Mackenzie King, 1893–1950." Library and Archives Canada. July 6.

Knopff, Rainer. 1981. "Legal Theory and the Patriation Debate." *Queen's Law Journal* 7: 41–65.

Knopff, Rainer, and F.L. Morton. 1992. *Charter Politics*. Scarborough, ON: Nelson Canada.

Kommers, Donald. 1994. "The Federal Constitutional Court in the German Political System." *Comparative Political Studies* 26 (4): 470–91.

L'Heureux-Dubé, Claire. 2000a. "The Dissenting Opinion: Voice of the Future?" *Osgoode Hall Law Journal* 38 (3): 495–517.

L'Heureux-Dubé, Claire. 2000b. "The Legacy of the Persons Case: Cultivating the Living Tree's Equality Leaves." *Saskatchewan Law Review* 63: 389–401.

Laskin, Bora. 1947. "Peace Order and Good Government Re-examined." *Canadian Bar Review* 25 (10): 1054–87.

LeBourdais, Isabel. 1966. *The Trial of Steven Truscott*. Toronto: McClelland and Stewart.

Lederman, W.R. 1966. "The Process of Constitutional Amendment in Canada." *McGill Law Journal* 12 (4): 371–83.

Lederman, W.R. 1985. "Democratic Parliaments, Independent Courts, and the Canadian Charter of Rights and Freedoms." *Queen's Law Journal* 11: 1–25.

Leslie, Peter M. 1988. "Bicommunalism and Canadian Constitutional Reform." *Publius: The Journal of Federalism* 18 (2): 115–29.

Lewis, J.P. 2013. "Elite Attitudes in the Centralization of Power in Canadian Political Executives: A Survey of Former Canadian Provincial and Federal Cabinet Ministers, 2000–2010." *Canadian Journal of Political Science* 46 (4): 799–819.

Lilleker, Darren G. 2003. "Interviewing the Political Elite: Navigating a Potential Minefield." *Politics* 23 (3): 207–14.

Lovell, George I. 2003. *Legislative Deferrals: Statutory Ambiguity, Judicial Power, and American Democracy*. Cambridge, UK: Cambridge University Press.

Lusztig, Michael. 1994. "Constitutional Paralysis: Why Canadian Constitutional Initiatives Are Doomed to Fail." *Canadian Journal of Political Science* 27 (4): 747–71.

MacCallum, Edward P. 2008. *Report of the Commission of Inquiry into the Wrongful Conviction of David Milgaard*. Government of Saskatchewan.

Macfarlane, Emmett. 2013. *Governing from the Bench: The Supreme Court of Canada and the Judicial Role*. Vancouver: UBC Press.

Makin, Kirk. 2013. "Supreme Court Needs More Women, Departing Judge Says." *Globe and Mail,* February 2. https://www.theglobeandmail.com/news/national/supreme-court-needs-more-women-departing-judge-says/article8149711/.

Mallet, Melanie. 2007. "A Primer on Treaty Making and Treaty Implementation in Canada." In *Constitutional Law of Canada*, vol. 1, 9th ed., ed. Joseph Eliot Magnet, 853–57. Edmonton: Juriliber Ltd.

Mallory, J.R. 1976. *Social Credit and the Federal Power in Canada*. Toronto: University of Toronto Press.

Mandel, Michael. 1994. *The Charter of Rights and the Legalization of Politics in Canada*. Rev. ed. Toronto: Thompson Educational Publishing.

Manfredi, Christopher P. 2001. *Judicial Power and the Charter: Canada and the Paradox of Liberal Constitutionalism*. 2nd ed. Don Mills, ON: Oxford University Press Canada.

Manfredi, Christopher P. 2004. *Feminist Activism in the Supreme Court: Legal Mobilization and the Women's Legal Education and Action Fund*. Vancouver: UBC Press.

Manfredi, Christopher P. 2007. "The Day the Dialogue Died: A Comment on *Sauvé v. Canada*." *Osgoode Hall Law Journal* 45 (1): 105–23.

Manfredi, Christopher P., and James B. Kelly. 1999. "Six Degrees of Dialogue: A Response to Hogg and Bushell." *Osgoode Hall Law Journal* 37 (3): 513–27.

Manfredi, Christopher P., and James B. Kelly. 2001. "Dialogue, Deference and Restraint: Judicial Independence and Trial Procedures." *Saskatchewan Law Review* 64: 323–46.

Manfredi, Christopher P., and James B. Kelly. 2004. "Misrepresenting the Supreme Court's Record? A Comment on Sujit Choudhry and Claire E. Hunter, 'Measuring Judicial Activism on the Supreme Court of Canada.'" *McGill Law Journal* 49: 741–64.

Manfredi, Christopher P., and Michael Lusztig. 1998. "Why Do Formal Amendments Fail? An Institutional Design Analysis." *World Politics* 50 (3): 377–400.

Manfredi, Christopher P., and Mark Rush. 2008. *Judging Democracy*. Peterborough, ON: Broadview.

Marland, Alex. 2014. "Introduction: Executive Authority and Public Policy in Newfoundland and Labrador." In *First among Unequals: The Premier, Politics, and Policy in Newfoundland and Labrador*, ed. Alex Marland and Matthew Kerby, 3–27. Montreal and Kingston: McGill-Queen's University Press.

Marland, Alex, and Matthew Kerby, eds. 2014. *First among Unequals: The Premier, Politics, and Policy in Newfoundland and Labrador*. Montreal and Kingston: McGill-Queen's University Press.

Martens, Allison M. 2007. "Reconsidering Judicial Supremacy: From the Counter-Majoritarian Difficulty to Constitutional Transformations." *Perspectives on Politics* 5 (3): 447–59.

Martin, E.A., and Jonathan Law, eds. 2012. *Oxford Dictionary of Law*. 7th ed. New York: Oxford University Press.

Mayhew, David R. 1974. *Congress: The Electoral Connection*. New Haven, CT: Yale University Press.

McConnell, W.H. 1968. "The Judicial Review of Prime Minister Bennett's New Deal." *Osgoode Hall Law Journal* 6 (1): 39–86.

McCormick, Peter. 2012. "Judging Selection: Appointing Canadian Judges." *Windsor Yearbook of Access to Justice* 30 (2): 39–58.

McCormick, Peter. 2016. "*Nom de Plume:* Who Writes the Supreme Court's 'By the Court' Judgments?" *Dalhousie Law Journal* 39 (1): 77–128.

McCormick, Peter, and Marc Zanoni. 2015. "The First by the Court Decisions: The Emergence of a Practice of the Supreme Court of Canada." *Manitoba Law Journal* 38 (1): 159–90.

McEvoy, John. 2005. "Refusing to Answer: The Supreme Court and the Reference Power Revisited." *University of New Brunswick Law Journal* 54: 29–42.

McLachlin, Beverly. 1990. "The Role of the Court in the Post-Charter Era: Policy-Maker or Adjudicator." *University of New Brunswick Law Journal* 39: 44–64.

McMurtry, R. Roy. 1982. "The Search for a Constitutional Accord – A Personal Memoir." *Queen's Law Journal* 8: 28–73.

Meekison, J. Peter, Hamish Telford, and Harvey Lazar. 2003. "The Institutions of Executive Federalism: Myths and Realities." In *Canada: The State of the Federation 2002: Reconsidering the Institutions of Canadian Federalism*, ed. J. Peter Meekison, Hamish Telford, and Harvey Lazar, 3–34. Montreal and Kingston: McGill-Queen's University Press.

Mendelsohn, Matthew. 2013. "A Viable Path to Senate Reform?" Mowat Centre, University of Toronto. https://mowatcentre.ca/a-viable-path-to-senate-reform/.

Merryman, John Henry, and Rogelio Pérez-Perdomo. 2007. *The Civil Law Tradition: An Introduction to the Legal Systems of Europe and Latin America*. 3rd ed. Stanford, CA: Stanford University Press.

Mills, Sean. 2005. "When Democratic Socialists Discovered Democracy: The League for Social Reconstruction Confronts the 'Quebec Problem.'" *Canadian Historical Review* 86 (1): 1–17.

Monahan, Patrick. J. 1984. "At Doctrine's Twilight: The Structure of Canadian Federalism." *University of Toronto Law Journal* 34: 47–99.

Monahan, Patrick. J. 1987. "Judicial Review and Democracy: A Theory of Judicial Review." *University of British Columbia Law Review* 21 (1): 87–164.

Moore, Michael. 1971. "The Spreading Chicken-and-Egg War." *Globe and Mail*, May 12, 7.

Morton, F.L., and Rainer Knopff. 2000. *The Charter Revolution and the Court Party*. Peterborough, ON: Broadview.

Muttart, Daved. 2007. *The Empirical Gap in Jurisprudence: A Comprehensive Study of the Supreme Court of Canada*. Toronto: University of Toronto Press.

Nasser, Shanifa. 2015. "In Wake of Charlie Hebdo Attacks, Secularist Groups to Seek End of Canada's Blasphemy Law." *National Post*, January 7. https://nationalpost.com/news/canada/in-wake-of-charlie-hebdo-attacks-secularist-groups-to-seek-end-to-canadas-blasphemy-law.

Neatby, H. Blair. 1976. *William Lyon Mackenzie King: The Prism of Unity, 1932–1939*. Vol. 3. Toronto: University of Toronto Press.

Office of the Attorney General. 2002. *Replacing the Privy Council: A New Supreme Court*. Government of New Zealand.

Olson, Susan. 1990. "Interest-Group Litigation in Federal District Court: Beyond the Political Disadvantage Theory." *Journal of Politics* 52 (3): 854–82.

Ontario Ministry of the Attorney General. 1983. "Letter to Australian High Commission." November 2.

Pal, Leslie A. 1993. *Interests of State: The Politics of Language, Multiculturalism, and Feminism in Canada*. Montreal and Kingston: McGill-Queen's University Press.

Patrick, Jeremy. 2008. "Not Dead, Just Sleeping: Canada's Prohibition on Blasphemous Libel as a Case Study in Obsolete Legislation." *UBC Law Review* 41 (2): 193–248.

Patrick, Jeremy. 2010. "Canadian Blasphemy Law in Context: Press, Legislative, and Public Reactions." *Annual Survey of International and Comparative Law* 16 (1): 129–63.

Patrick, Jeremy. 2013. "The Curious Persistence of Blasphemy: Canada and Beyond." PhD diss., Osgood Hall Law School, York University.

Persaud, Radhakrishnan. 1998. "The Role of Judicial Advisory Opinions in Canadian Constitutionalism and Federalism: The Senate, Patriation and Quebec Veto Reference Cases Considered." PhD diss., Queen's University.

Pierson, Paul. 2004. *Politics in Time: History, Institutions, and Social Analysis*. Princeton, NJ: Princeton University Press.

Pruysers, Scott. 2014. "Reconsidering Vertical Integration: An Examination of National Political Parties and Their Counterparts in Ontario." *Canadian Journal of Political Science* 47 (2): 237–58.

Puddister, Kate. 2016. "'The Most Radical Amendment of All': The Power to Secede and the *Secession Reference*." In *Constitutional Amendment in Canada*, ed. Emmett Macfarlane, 271–89. Toronto: University of Toronto Press.

Radmilovic, Vuk. 2010. "Strategic Legitimacy Cultivation at the Supreme Court of Canada: Quebec *Secession Reference* and Beyond." *Canadian Journal of Political Science* 43 (4): 843–69.

Radmilovic, Vuk. 2013. "Governmental Interventions and Judicial Decision Making: The Supreme Court of Canada in the Age of the Charter." *Canadian Journal of Political Science* 46 (2): 323–44.

Ray, Laura Krugman. 2000. "Road to *Bush v. Gore:* The History of the Supreme Court's Use of the Per Curiam Opinion." *Nebraska Law Review* 79: 517–75.

Riddell, Troy Q., and Ted Morton. 2004. "Government Use of Strategic Litigation: The Alberta Exported Gas Tax Reference." *American Review of Canadian Studies* 34 (3): 485–509.

Rogers, James, and Georg Vanberg. 2002. "Judicial Advisory Opinions and Legislative Outcomes in Comparative Perspective." *American Journal of Political Science* 46 (2): 379–97.

Ross, Rebecca. 2012. "Blasphemy and the Modern 'Secular' State." *Appeal* 17: 3–19.

Rubin, Gerald. 1960. "The Nature, Use and Effect of Reference Cases in Canadian Constitutional Law." *McGill Law Journal* 6 (3): 168–90.

Russell, Peter H. 1977. "The Anti-Inflation Case: The Anatomy of a Constitutional Decision." *Canadian Public Administration* 20 (4): 632–65.

Russell, Peter H. 1983. "Bold Statescraft, Questionable Jurisprudence." In *And No One Cheered: Federalism, Democracy and the Constitution Act*, ed. Keith Banting and Richard Simeon, 210–38. Toronto: Methuen.

Russell, Peter H. 1987. *The Judiciary in Canada: The Third Branch of Government*. Toronto: McGraw-Hill Ryerson.

Russell, Peter H. 2001. "Toward a General Theory of Judicial Independence." In *Judicial Independence in the Age of Democracy: Critical Perspectives from around the World*, ed. Peter H. Russell and David M. O'Brien, 1–24. Charlottesville: University Press of Virginia.

Russell, Peter H. 2004. *Constitutional Odyssey: Can Canadians Become a Sovereign People?* 3rd ed. Toronto: University of Toronto Press.

Russell, Peter H. 2008. *Two Cheers for Minority Government: The Evolution of Canadian Parliamentary Democracy*. Toronto: Emond Montgomery.

Russell, Peter H. 2009. "The Charter and Canadian Democracy." In *Contested Constitutionalism: Reflections on the Canadian Charter of Rights and Freedoms*, ed. James B. Kelly and Christopher P. Manfredi, 287–306. Vancouver: UBC Press.

Russell, Peter H. 2011. "The Patriation and Quebec Veto References: The Supreme Court Wrestles with the Political Part of the Constitution." *Supreme Court Law Review* 54 (2d): 69–76.

Russell, Peter H., F.L. Morton, and Rainer Knopff. 1989. *Federalism and the Charter: Leading Constitutional Decisions*. Ottawa: Carleton University Press.

Sadurski, Wojciech. 2005. *Rights before Courts: A Study of Constitutional Courts in Postcommunist States of Central and Eastern Europe*. Norwell, MA: Springer.

Salzberger, Eli M. 1993. "A Positive Analysis of the Doctrine of Separation of Powers, or: Why Do We Have an Independent Judiciary?" *International Review of Law and Economics* 13 (4): 349–79.

Salzberger, Eli M., and Stefan Voigt. 2002. "On the Delegation of Powers: With Special Emphasis on Central and Eastern Europe." *Constitutional Political Economy* 13 (1): 25–52.

Savoie, Donald J. 1999. *Governing from the Centre: The Concentration of Power in Canadian Politics*. Toronto: University of Toronto Press.

Savoie, Donald J. 2010. *Power: Where Is It?* Montreal and Kingston: McGill-Queen's University Press.

Scheppele, Kim Lane, and Jack L. Walker Jr. 1991. "The Litigation Strategies of Interest Groups." In *Mobilizing Interest Groups in America: Patrons, Professions and Social Movements*, ed. Jack L. Walker Jr., 157–83. Ann Arbor: University of Michigan Press.

Schertzer, Robert. 2016. *The Judicial Role in a Diverse Federation: Lessons from the Supreme Court of Canada*. Toronto: University of Toronto Press.

Scholtz, Christa. 2009. "The Influence of Judicial Uncertainty on Executive Support for Negotiation in Canadian Land Claims Policy." *Canadian Journal of Political Science* 42 (2): 417–42.

Seljak, David. 2000. "Resisting the 'No Man's Land' of Private Religion: The Catholic Church and Public Politics in Quebec." In *Rethinking Church, State and Modernity: Canada between Europe and the USA*, ed. David Lyon and Marguerite Van Die, 131–48. Toronto: University of Toronto Press.

Shapiro, Martin, and Alec Stone. 1994. "The New Constitutional Politics of Europe." *Comparative Political Studies* 26 (4): 397–420.

Smiley, Donald. 1962. "The Rowell-Sirois Report, Provincial Autonomy, and Post-War Canadian Federalism." *Canadian Journal of Economics and Political Science* 28 (1): 54–69.

Smith, Jennifer. 1983. "The Origins of Judicial Review in Canada." *Canadian Journal of Political Science* 16 (1): 115–34.

Snell, James G., and Frederick Vaughan. 1985. *The Supreme Court of Canada: History of the Institution*. Toronto: University of Toronto Press.

Songer, Donald R., Susan W. Johnson, C.L. Ostberg, and Matthew E. Wetstein. 2012. *Law, Ideology, and Collegiality: Judicial Behaviour in the Supreme Court of Canada*. Montreal and Kingston: McGill-Queen's University Press.

Sossin, Lorne. 2012. *Boundaries of Judicial Review: The Law of Justiciability in Canada*. 2nd ed. Scarborough, ON: Carswell.

Sossin, Lorne, and Valerie Crystal. 2013. "A Comment on 'No Comment': The *Sub Judice* Rule and the Accountability of Public Officials in the 21st Century." *Dalhousie Law Journal* 36 (2): 535–80.

Stephenson, Matthew C. 2003. "'When the Devil Turns ...': The Political Foundations of Independent Judicial Review." *Journal of Legal Studies* 32 (1): 59–89.

Stephenson, Matthew C. 2006. "Legislative Allocation of Delegated Power: Uncertainty, Risk, and the Choice between Agencies and Courts." *Harvard Law Review* 119 (4): 1035–70.

Stilborn, Jack. 1997. "National Standards and Social Programs: What the Federal Government Can Do." Research Branch, Library of Parliament.

Stone, Alec. 1992. *The Birth of Judicial Politics in France: The Constitutional Council in Comparative Perspective*. New York: Oxford University Press.

Stone Sweet, Alec. 2000. *Governing with Judges: Constitutional Politics in Europe*. New York: Oxford University Press.

Stone Sweet, Alec. 2003. "Why Europe Rejected American Judicial Review and Why It May Not Matter." *Michigan Law Review* 101 (August): 2744–80.

Strayer, Barry L. 1988. *The Canadian Constitution and the Courts: The Function and Scope of Judicial Review*. 3rd ed. Toronto: Butterworths.

Tate, C. Neal, and Torbjörn Vallinder, eds. 1995. *The Global Expansion of Judicial Power*. New York: New York University Press.

Taylor, John L. 1970. "Settlement of Disputes between Federal and State Concerning Offshore Petroleum Resources: Accommodation or Adjudication." *Harvard International Law Journal* 11: 358–99.

Thayer, James B. 1893. "The Origin and Scope of American Doctrine of Constitutional Law." *Harvard Law Review* 7 (3): 129–56.

Thomas, Paul E., and Graham White. 2015. "Evaluating Provincial and Territorial Legislatures." In *Provinces: Canadian Provincial Politics,* 3rd ed., ed. Christopher J.C. Dunn, 363–97. Toronto: University of Toronto Press.

Tridimas, George. 2009. "Constitutional Judicial Review and Political Insurance." *European Journal of Law and Economics* 29 (1): 81–101.

Tsebelis, George. 1990. *Nested Games: Rational Choice in Comparative Politics*. Berkeley: University of California Press.

Tushnet, Mark. 1996. "Policy Distortion and Democratic Debilitation: Comparative Illumination of the Countermajoritarian Difficulty." *Michigan Law Review* 94 (November): 245–301.

Tushnet, Mark. 1999. *Taking the Constitution Away from the Courts*. Princeton, NJ: Princeton University Press.

Vallinder, Torbjörn. 1995. "When the Courts Go Marching In." In *The Global Expansion of Judicial Power,* ed. C. Neal Tate and Torbjörn Vallinder, 13–26. New York: New York University Press.

Vanberg, Georg. 2005. *The Politics of Constitutional Review in Germany*. New York: Cambridge University Press.

Vanberg, Georg. 2015. "Constitutional Courts in Comparative Perspective: A Theoretical Assessment." *Annual Review of Political Science* 18 (1): 167–85.

Vaughan, Frederick. 1986. "Critics of the Judicial Committee of the Privy Council: The New Orthodoxy and an Alternative Explanation." *Canadian Journal of Political Science* 19 (3): 495–519.

Voigt, Stefan, and Eli M. Salzberger. 2002. "Choosing Not to Choose: When Politicians Choose to Delegate Powers." *Kyklos* 55: 289–310.

Waldron, Jeremy. 2006. "The Core of the Case against Judicial Review." *Yale Law Journal* 115: 1346–1406.

Watts, Ronald L. 1989. "Executive Federalism: A Comparative Analysis." Institute of Intergovernmental Relations, Queen's University.

Weaver, R. Kent. 1986. "The Politics of Blame Avoidance." *Journal of Public Policy* 6 (4): 371–98.

Wechsler, Herbert. 1959. "Toward Neutral Principles of Constitutional Law." *Harvard Law Review* 73 (1): 1–35.

Weiler, Paul. 1974. *In the Last Resort: A Critical Study of the Supreme Court of Canada*. Toronto: Carswell.

Wells, Paul. 2013. "The Supreme Court Senate Reference: It's Going Well." *Maclean's,* March 6. http://www2.macleans.ca/2013/03/06/the-supreme-court-senate-reference-its-going-well/.

White, Graham. 2012. "The 'Centre' of the Democratic Deficit: Power and Influence in Canadian Political Executives." In *Imperfect Democracies: The Democratic Deficit in Canada and the United States,* ed. Patti Tamara Lenard and Richard Simeon, 226–47. Vancouver: UBC Press.

Whittington, Keith E. 2005. "'Interpose Your Friendly Hand': Political Supports for the Exercise of Judicial Review by the United States Supreme Court." *American Political Science Review* 99 (4): 583–96.

Whittington, Keith E. 2007. *Political Foundations of Judicial Supremacy: The Presidency, the Supreme Court, and Constitutional Leadership in U.S. History*. Princeton, NJ: Princeton University Press.

Wilson, L. 1975. "Disallowance: The Threat to Western Canada." *Saskatchewan Law Review* 39: 156–82.

Zines, Leslie. 2010. "Advisory Opinions and Declaratory Judgments at the Suit of Governments." *Bond Law Review* 22 (3): 156–68.

Interviews

Attorney General A. April 7, 2014.

Attorney General B. April 25, 2014.

Attorney General C. May 5, 2014.

Attorney General D. May 9, 2014.

Attorney General E. June 9, 2014.

Counsel A. April 3, 2014.

Counsel B. June 20, 2014.

First Minister A. April 2, 2014.

Senior Department Official A. March 21, 2013.

Senior Department Solicitor A. February 26, 2013.

Statutes

Access to Information Act, RSC 1985, c A-1

Accurate News and Information Bill, SA 1937, c 9, Session III

An Act Respecting Freedom of Worship and Maintenance of Good Order, SQ 1953–54, 2–3 Eliz 11, c 15

An Act Respecting the Supreme and Exchequer Courts, SC 1891, c 25

An Act to Amend the Criminal Code (Blasphemous Libels), Bill C-5, 16th Parliament, 2nd Session, 1928

Act to Give Effect to the Requirement for Clarity as Set Out in the Opinion of the Supreme Court of Canada in the Quebec Secession Reference, SC 2000, c 26

An Act to Protect the Province against Communistic Propaganda, 1 Geo VI, 1937, c 11 [*Padlock Act*]

Agricultural Products Marketing Act, RSC 1970, c A-7

Anti-Inflation Act, SC 1975, c 75

Bank Employee Civil Rights Act, SA 1937, c 2, Session II

Bank Taxation Bill, SA 1937, c 1, Session III
Canadian Charter of Rights and Freedoms, Part I of the *Constitution Act, 1982*, being Schedule B to the *Canada Act 1982* (UK), 1982, c 11
Civil Marriage Act, SC 2005, c 33
Combines Investigation Act, RSC 1927, c 26
Constitution Act, 1867 (UK), 30 & 31 Vict, c 3, reprinted in RSC 1985, App II, No 5
Constitution Act, 1982, being Schedule B to the *Canada Act 1982* (UK), 1982, c 11
Constitution of India (1950), art 143(1)
Constitutional Questions Act, RSBC 1996, c 68
Credit Act, SA 1937, c 8, Session III
Credit of Alberta Regulation Act, SA 1937, c 1, Session II
Criminal Code of Canada, RSC 1985, c C-46
Dominion Trade and Industry Commission Act, 25–26 Geo V, 1935, c 59
Employment and Social Insurance Act, 25–26 Geo V, 1935, c 38
Electoral Boundaries Commission Act, SS 1986-87-88, c E-6.1
Farmers' Creditors Arrangement Act, 24–25 Geo V, 1934, c 53
Federal Courts Act, RSC 1985, c F-7
Firearms Act, SC 1995, c 39
Judicature Act Amendment Act, SA 1937, c 5, Session II
Judicature Act, RSPEI 1988, c J-2.1
Judicial Committee Act, 1833, 3 & 4 Wm IV, c 41 (UK)
Limitation of Hours of Work Act, 25–26 Geo V, 1935, c 63
Milk Industry Act, 1956 (BC), c 28
Minimum Wages Act, 25–26 Geo V, 1935, c 44
Mining and Mineral Rights Tax Act, 1975, 1975 (Nfld.), c 68
Natural Products Marketing Act, 24–25 Geo V, 1934, c 57
Order in Council PC 1993-1740, August 26, 1993.
Proposal for an Act Respecting Certain Aspects of Legal Capacity for Marriage for Civil Purposes. Order in Council PC 2003-1055, July 16, 2003.
Supreme Court Act, SC 1875, c 11
Supreme Court Act, RSC 1985, c S-26
Treaty of Peace between the Allied and Associated Powers and Germany [Treaty of Versailles]
US Const, art 3, s 2, cl 1, cl 2
War Measures Act, 5 Geo V, 1914, c 2
Weekly Rest in Industrial Undertakings Act, 25–26 Geo V, 1935, c 14

Cases Cited (Nondataset)

Aetna Life Insurance Co v Haworth et al, 300 US 227 (1937) (United States of America)
Arizonans for Official English v Arizona et al, 520 US 43 (1997) (United States of America)
Ashwander v Tennessee Valley Authority, 297 US 288 (1936) (United States of America)

Baker v Carr, 369 US 186 (1962) (United States of America)
Borowski v. Canada (AG) [1989] 1 SCR 342
Bush v Gore, 531 US 98 (2000) (United States of America)
EGALE Canada Inc v Canada (AG), [2003] BCCA 251 (BC Court of Appeal)
Egan v Canada, [1995] 2 SCR 513
Halpern v Canada (AG), [2003] OJ No 2268 (Ontario Court of Appeal)
Référence re Renvoi relatif à la réglementation pancanadienne des valuers mobiliéres, 2017 QCCA 756 (Quebec Court of Appeal)
R v Sterry, (1927) 5 Can Bar Rev
Re Judiciary and Navigation Act, [1921] 29 CRL 257 (Australia)
Re Truscott, (2007) ONCA 575, 225 CCC (3d) 321 (Ontario Court of Appeal)
Section 293 of the Criminal Code of Canada, [2011] BCJ No 2211 (QL), BCSC (British Columbia Supreme Court)
Switzman v Elbling, [1957] 7 DLR 2d 337
Valente v R, [1985] 2 SCR 673

Index

Note: (f) after a page number indicates a figure; (t) after a page number indicates a table.